MODERN
BRITISH
HISTORY ★ A
Garland
Series

Edited by
PETER STANSKY and
LESLIE HUME

THE EMANCIPATION
OF THE JEWS IN ENGLAND
1830–1860

Abraham Gilam

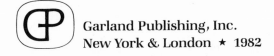

Garland Publishing, Inc.
New York & London ★ 1982

Library of Congress Cataloging in Publication Data

Gilam, Abraham, 1947–
    The emancipation of the Jews in England, 1830–1860.

    (Modern British history ; 7)
    Originally presented as the author's thesis (doctoral—
Washington University)
    Bibliography: p.
    Includes index.
    1. Jews—Great Britain.   2. Jews—Emancipation.
I. Title.   II. Series.
DS135.E5G53 1982   941'.004924   81-48359
ISBN 0-8240-5155-6

All volumes in this series are printed on acid-free,
250-year-life paper.
Printed in the United States of America

"You represent a community here in Britain, some 400,000 strong, which has shown what is necessary to demonstrate from time to time: how it is possible in a modern society to be part of the nation as a whole and yet to retain your own essential cultural and religious identity."

The Right Honorable
James Callaghan to the
Board of Deputies of
British Jews,
October, 1977

CONTENTS

Preface

The need for a comprehensive survey of the struggle
for Jewish emancipation in nineteenth century Britain is
obvious. Although the subject has attracted a great deal
of attention since the late nineteenth and early twentieth
centuries, there is not yet a single volume that analyzes
this historical episode in detail. The Anglo-Jewish
emancipation is an important event in the annals of a given
community and the subject merits a general work based on
various available sources, including manuscript material,
pamphlets, newspapers, periodicals, parliamentary papers
and personal memoirs.

During the hundred and twenty years that have passed
since the completion of Anglo-Jewish emancipation, a
number of works of great importance have been published
on the subject. H.S.Q. Henriques, The Jew and the English
Law (Oxford, 1908) is still a useful survey of the legal
disabilities affecting English Jewry during the pre-
emancipationist struggle. General works on Anglo-Jewish
history by Lucien Wolf, Albert Montefiore Hyamson and
Cecil Roth include descriptive chapters on the subject.
In more recent years, Judge Israel Finestein re-evaluated
Anglo-Jewish attitudes and opinions during the struggle
for emancipation in an important article he published in
1961. Ursula Henriques is one of the pioneers who embarked
on a serious research of the various pamphlets and primary
sources available on the subject. Her article in Past
and Present (1968) and her book Religious Toleration in
England, 1787-1833 (1961) are important contributions
to the study of Anglo-Jewish emancipation. Polly Pinsker
focused attention on the final stages of the struggle in
an article published in Jewish Social Studies in 1952
and a few years ago, Michael N.C. Salbstein made a pioneer-
ing attempt to integrate the sources and secondary work in
his doctoral dissertation at the University of London.
These works however do not sufficiently cover the
historiographical dilemmas created by the subject matter.
Major aspects have been reassessed in the present essay
and new insights have been incorporated in the body of
this dissertation, in view of an increased understanding
of complicated factors that have been illuminated by
recent research.

In addition to its importance as an autonomous subject,
the emancipation of the Jews in England has broad relevance
to European history. The struggle for Jewish freedom
during the years 1830-1860 was but a phase in the development of religious liberty in the country. The Jewish
endeavour to obtain civil and political rights followed
successful attempts by Protestant Dissenters (1828),
Roman Catholics (1829), Quakers, Moravians and Socinians
(1833, 1837 and 1838). The Jewish claim was laid on the

same grounds as its predecessors, so when the emancipation
was finally completed, all religious minorities residing
in the country could regard the Jewish achievement as
a further step toward the establishment of religious
freedom.

When comparing the Anglo-Jewish emancipation with
Continental emancipations, it is argued that in Britain,
civil rights were granted to Jews and other religious
minorities unconditionally. They were not asked to make
concessions at the expense of their religion, unlike the
requirements made in France, Germany or Italy. Even
though certain religious beliefs, such as prohibition
of marriages with non-Jews, were incompatible with the
expectations of modern citizenship, Jews were not told
to reform such tenets.

Similarly, Quakers were not forced to give up religious imperatives such as refusal to take oaths, to pay
for or fight in wars, though these principles could clash
with the modern notion of citizenship. During the process
of emancipation, Britain legitimized religious pluralism
by leaving the peculiarities of each sect untouched. Why
should English legislators grant such an unconditional
emancipation? The answer provided here is that religious
freedom was established in the country during a period
of compromise between conservative and liberal ideologies.
English statesmen, in particular Sir Robert Peel and
his followers, wanted to establish freedom of conscience
in the country while retaining the privileged position
of the Anglican Church. In order to retain church
establishment, British legislators had to recognize the
uniqueness of other creeds. They did not wish to separate
church and state, disestablish Anglicanism or secularize
public life. They did not confine religion to the sphere
of individual privacy. If England wanted to retain an
inequality before the law in favor of Anglicans, it had
no right asking other minorities to make concessions in
return for their own civil rights.

From a Jewish perspective, the equalization of Jews
in status with the rest of the population was accompanied
by weaker pressures, from their emancipators, to give up
some or all of their Jewishness. English Jews did not
face the ultimatum of renouncing ancestral heritage in
exchange for civil and political rights as their German,
French or Italian co-religionists had experienced during
their emancipation. Pressures to assimilate were social,
rather than legal or political. Victorian Jews have since
recognized their emancipation was more enlightened and
liberal than those on the Continent. In many respects,

iii

English Jews were fortunate that the question of their
emancipation was publicly agitated and debated relatively
late in the nineteenth century. The Anglo-Jewish
emancipation thus became an integral part of a wider drive
to establish religious freedom in the country. Jews also
benefited from the triumph of liberalism during the mid-
century. Their social acceptance was supported by rising
middle-class elements intensely involved in a campaign
for the institution of economic and religious liberty.
Because of the religious diversity of the population,
English nationalism tolerated pluralism instead of
assuming the xenophobic, intolerant and brutal attributes
that characterized German, French and Italian nationalisms.

Victorian Jewry became highly assimilated and gladly
gave up some of its particularistic Jewish loyalties
partly because the process of relaxing the ties with
Judaism had started long before the campaign for emancipation. During the eighteenth century, Anglo-Jewry was
rapidly losing its Jewish identity. Emancipation was a
highly desired goal from a Jewish point of view, for it
enabled willing Jews to integrate into British society
while retaining their Jewish attachments. Had
emancipation not been affected, it is questionable whether
a Jewish community would have survived at all. Emancipation was imperative for a community struggling for the
survival of its particular contents within a universal
framework. The emancipationist success in the United
Kingdom is, no doubt, one of the major historical
recollections that continue to shape the character,
quality and destiny of Anglo-Jewry.

This essay was originally presented as a doctoral
dissertation to the department of history of Washington
University. I am especially thankful to Dr. Richard W.
Davis, my thesis advisor, for his patience and interest
in the completion of this project. His criticism and
skepticism have helped in shaping the final form of this
work. I wish to pay tribute to Dr. Chimen Abramsky and
to Dr. Peter Stansky who have read the manuscript,
commented on its contents and encouraged its publication.
Dr. Richard Walter of Washington University deserves my
gratitude for allocating funds for the copy-editing and
typing of the manuscript. Last, but not least, are my
editor, Ms. Cheryl Deep, and my typist, Ms. Brooke
Petersen, whose care and attention were essential for the
completion of the revised version of this essay.

CHAPTER 1

THE SETTING OF THE STRUGGLE FOR JEWISH EMANCIPATION

Anglo-Jewish Anticipation of Political Emancipation

The deliberations over the pursuit of civic equality created a serious dilemma for Anglo-Jewry. As early as 1828-29 Jews witnessed the extension of political rights to Protestant Dissenters and Roman Catholics, despite the subborn opposition of reactionary elements of the polity and legislature. Even a notorious conservative like Wellington could no longer resist the mounting pressures of religious minorities to sweep away the anti-quated restrictions and disabilities imposed by archaic laws on religious convictions. After effecting Catholic emancipation, Wellington and Peel promised their followers this was the end of reform. But despite their public statements, the institution of religious freedom in Britain did not reach an end. In the 1830's, Quakers, Moravians and Socinians gradually earned civil and poli-tical rights. Reactionary Anglican circles had to watch and tolerate this progress despite feelings of resentment. Against this background, it is realistic to argue that the maintenance of the Jewish disabilities became an anachronism in Victorian England. Even before the struggle for Jewish emancipation had begun, enlightened and educated opinion held there was no justification for retaining a legal discrimination against one particular sect after other minorities had been equalized in status. No profound prophetic qualities were needed to predict that, sooner or later, Jews would obtain full citizenship in the United Kingdom.

British Jews, then, labored for their freedom in a relatively relaxed atmosphere, which some modern historians tend to confuse with indifference. Their leaders realized they were fighting prejudices and reactionary dispositions. In order to obtain what they wanted, Jews had to confront the privileged segments of the British establishment, the aristocracy and the clergy. Confident in the triumph of liberalism, none of the Jewish activists anticipated that opposition to emancipation would be so fierce. Jews hoped that in their case too, the Lords would capitulate and the Government would yield to public pressure to redress their grievance. They did not foresee a long and exhausting struggle that would drag on for thirty years.

British Jews did not prepare for an intense agitation nor join radical opposition or militant revolutionary groups to promote their cause. Unlike their co-religion-ists in Germany and Italy, who agitated the emancipationist

cause within the ranks of dissenting parties, Victorian
Jews lived fairly comfortably and wanted to secure the
status quo. The consensus inside Anglo-Jewry
was that the issue of emancipation must be dealt with
delicately because the community as a whole had much at
stake. The disabilities were no doubt a nuisance, but
they could be circumvented and never constituted a severe
hardship. Jews were not harassed or persecuted in Britain
during the ninteenth century. Most of them feared risking
the benefits of toleration in the country.

Economic historians agree that Anglo-Jewry prospered
during the mid-century. By the 1850's, middle class elements were predominant in the community and the eighteenth
century manifestations of pauperism gradually disappeared.
The historian V. D. Lipman describes the change effected
during that period as follows: "The outstanding change
in the economic structure of the community between 1815
and 1880 was that, at the beginning, the majority in numbers
were poor, or very poor -- just scraping a living or
supported by relief, and the middle class was a minority;
at the end of the period, the middle class comprised about
half the community, and the poor, though numerous, were
the minority." The 35,000 Jews living in Britain took
advantage of growing opportunities and improved their
position. Within a relatively short time, they branched
out into a number of occupations from which they had
previously been excluded.

The Jewish elite, comprised of wealthy families of
merchants and stock brokers long established in the country,
penetrated fields such as banking, insurance and even
heavy industry. David Salomons, for example, founded
the Westminster Bank; Moses Montefiore, the Provincial
Bank of Ireland, the Alliance Insurance Company (with
Nathan Mayer Rothschild) and the Imperial Continental
Gas Association. Isaac Lyon Goldsmid invested heavily
in the London docks and then in railways; David Jonassohn
and Ludwig Mond became the first two Jewish mine-owners.
In this way they interacted with the financial and
industrial elite of the country that was increasingly
gaining respectability and prestige in Victorian England.
They were also able to acquaint themselves with the
Noncomformist element, the backbone of the rising middle
classes, and collaborate with other dissenters from the
Church of England in promotion of such liberal issues as
religious and economic freedom.

Equally prosperous was the class of Jewish professionals, the most firm advocates of political emancipation.
The growth of this class depended on the removal of
obstacles to Jews wishing to enroll in the British
universities or to gain employment in the civil service.

Even at the bottom of the social scale a conspicuous improvement could be noticed: Jewish workers found employment in the clothing industry or entered crafts as carpenters, cabinet makers and printers. This development can be largely explained by the consistent efforts of communal institutions to fight poverty. Thus, attempts were successfully made by Jewish institutions such as Jews' Hospital, The Jews' Free School and later the Board of Guardians to apprentice boys in various trades.

The community as a whole benefited from the general economic prosperity and from the variety of opportunities in Victorian England. Relative affluence frequently creates conservative attitudes and the complacent mentality of Anglo-Jewry was no exception to the rule. Like their Nonconformist colleagues, the pillars of the Jewish community were led to caution and timidity rather than self-confidence by their affluence. Although anti-Semitism was a dormant force, it could still activate and trigger manifestations of hostility toward Jews. Some of the leaders may have inherited family traditions and recollections of the anti-Jewish outburst triggered by the passage of the Jewish Naturalization Act during the years 1753/54. From their point of view, keeping a low profile in public was advantageous. Naturally, members of the wealthy patriciate would feel ambivalent toward an active agitation of the emancipationist cause. They would suspect the endeavours would attract wide public attention to Jewish grievances. They would rather be exposed to disabilities than push Jewish concerns into the limelight.

It is impossible to understand the Victorian-Jewish mentality without keeping in mind that most of their leaders were not intellectuals. Perhaps due to the small size of the community, Anglo-Jewish intellectual life was never stimulating. Even assimilation into the non-Jewish world did not invoke the intellectual curiosity and cultural activity that could be seen at the same time in Continental Europe. The Anglo-Jewish patriciate was comprised of businessmen who were limited intellectually and whose assimilation contributed very little to the culture of the host country. It is a small wonder that such leadership did not unduly press general universalistic concerns and preferred comfort to freedom if the price seemed too high.

The conservatism absorbed by British Jews had some important implications for the internal cohesion of the community. The fierce controversies between Reform and Orthodox Judaism on the Continent during the period were muted in England. The two Reform congregations of Manchester and Bradford, founded by German Jewish

immigrants, and the branch of the London Reform Congregation led by the Goldsmids attracted an insignificant
fraction of Anglo-Jewry. The majority, however secularized,
remained loyal to the orthodox creed. Furthermore, the
English Reform movement was prominent for its moderation
and restraint. It was far more conservative than any
other Reform movement in the world, emphasizing some
doctrinal modifications, but mainly changes in decorum
and ritual.

Perhaps this relative restraint of the Reform
movement can be explained by the continuity and stability
of the orthodox tradition. Jews had resided in the United
Kingdom since the resettlement under Cromwell. Most of
the first settlers were persecuted Sephardim who brought
with them a highly developed aesthetic tradition admired
by non-Jews. Their ritual was exotic and captivating
and one could hardly remind them of the attacks made by
Jewish secularists against the Ashkenazi orthodoxy of
Eastern Europe. A visit to the Bevis Marks Synagogue,
the venerable Sephardi synagogue of London founded during
the seventeenth century, demonstrates the point. Even
today, all attendants wear top hats for services, the
ushers wear white gloves and a choir enhances the
melodious quality of the service. The preacher strongly
resembles a Protestant minister and the hall is lit with
candles rather than electricity. Elegance, decorum and
aesthetics are highly emphasized and attract the attention
of many Jewish and non-Jewish visitors alike. This was
a tradition not easily shattered, especially in view of
the high regard it gained from non-Jews, early manifested
by an 1809 visit of three royal dukes, Kent, Sussex and
Cambridge to Bevis Marks as guests of Abraham Goldsmid,
and more recently by the 1956 attendance of the Duke of
Edinburgh on the occasion of the 250th anniversary of the
opening of the synagogue.

The number of families long established in the country
was not large, but their presence created a sense of
continuity with a glorious past that was meaningful to
Victorian Jews in several ways. The feeling of pride in
the ancestral tradition made orthodoxy respectable. The
differences between Sephardim and Ashkenazim were blurred
as the nineteenth century proceeded. As Sonia Lipman
observes, marriages, partnerships and associations among
members of the two ethnic groups were common at least
from the late eighteenth and early nineteenth centuries.
Though the marriage of Moses Montefiore and Judith Cohen
in 1812 is conventionally considered an exception, the
marriage contracts of Bevis Marks show it was far from
unique. After 1795 mixed marriages became common,
including some of social importance, such as those between
Daniel Mocatta and Anne Goldsmid in 1801, David Lindo

and Mathilda Salomons in 1805, and Emanuel Lousada and
Jane Goldsmid in 1807. Relations between the two
communities were cordial as evidenced by Levi Barnet Cohen
bequeathing 25 pounds in his will to Bevis Marks.

Anglo-Jewry was in a rapid process of assimilation
into British society prior to the beginning of the drive
for emancipation. During the reigns of the four Georges,
the upper strata of the Jewish community was losing its
Jewish identity. The Jewish gentry was clean shaven,
elegantly dressed, English speaking and highly secularized.
The well-to-do attended the opera and the theatre, gossiped
and played cards in the City coffee houses, took the waters
at Bath and visited the sea shore at Brighton. They spent
their leisure time in lavish entertainments and grand
dinner parties. Some of the wealthy acquired estates in
the country and lost contact with Jewish congregations.
Jews neglected the Sabbath observance, scarcely attended
the synagogue and were lax in the performance of religious
duties.[1]

In this milieu, marriages out of the faith became
frequent and generally led to conversions. Most alarming
from a Jewish standpoint was that desertion from Judaism
was often designed to promote social ambitions. Samson
Gideon, the famous financier and loan contractor, had his
children baptized and brought up under the Christian
faith of his wife; and Isaac D'Israeli followed suit for
purely opportunistic reasons. Jessie Goldsmid, Benjamin's
widow, converted with her six sons, and the German-born
physician Dr. Meyer Loew Schomberg and his children also
abandoned the Jewish faith. Sir Francis Palgrave
(originally Cohen), barrister, constitutional historian,
antiquarian and first archivist of what is now the Public
Record Office, took a similar step. The famous tenor
John Abraham had his seven children baptized. Singing
teacher and composer John Barnett did the same. The English
Franks, descendants of Aaron Frank, the pillar of the Great
Synagogue, disappeared from the Jewish community toward
the end of the eighteenth century. Ricardo and Bernal
are names that can be added to this list.

This tendency was accompanied by a cultivation of
negative feelings toward Judaism, most conspicuously
represented by Isaac D'Israeli. In his article on the
Talmud, published in Curiosities of Literature, D'Israeli
denounced the idiosyncracy, extravagance and eccentricity
displayed through its pages. The Talmud should be read
as a curiosity of literature, he said, as a piece of folk-
lore or an anecdote, but never to be taken seriously as
an ethical code. The Talmud is an ancient codex pertaining
to a variety of aspects of the human condition but permeated
with the spirit of obstructionism. It is completely

estranged from the universalistic spirit of the
Scriptures and by adhering to its teachings, orthodox
Jews divorce their creed from enlightened morals. The
Talmud represented the ethic of the Pharisees, a mechanical
fulfillment of religious duties and an unreflective attitude toward faith. In D'Israeli's words, it was full of
"gross obscenities and immoral decisions."[2]

In the nineteenth century, the level of religious
observance among English Jews was low. A large proportion
failed to perform many important religious duties, including
the dietary laws and the keeping of the Sabbath, holidays
and fasts. Stephen Sharot notices the low attendance at
synagogue during the mid-century. According to the 1851
religious census, less than 3000 Jews attended synagogue
services on Sabbath morning, 29 March 1851.[3] This means
that only 9% of the 34,000 Jews living in England in 1851
attended the synagogue on Sabbath morning. The total
percentage of worshippers during the entire Sabbath, including Friday evening and Saturday afternoon services,
was lower than 16. This proportion was considerably lower
than the proportion of Christians who attended church the
next day; the index of attendance for the total population
was 40.5% on census Sunday. The data collected by Bernard
Susser indicates a breakdown in religious observance in
nineteenth century Devon.[4] By 1860, it was difficult
to obtain a quorum for weekly services in Plymouth and
even Sabbath attendance was sparse. Jews began to open
shops on the Sabbath and many of them neglected the
dietary laws while away from home. Marriages with non-
Jews became even more common as the nineteenth century
progressed.

Inasmuch as religious attachments declined, the mid-
Victorian era was marked by a new attitude toward
Jewishness. The eighteenth century pattern of a total
break with Judaism tended to disappear. Jews tried to
retain their ethnic tradition through the maintenance
of the rites of passage. Stephen Sharot observes that
in the nineteenth century most Jewish couples married
in the synagogue, most Jews sat Shiva after the death
of a parent and most Jewish boys of thirteen had a
Barmitzvah.[5] Despite the low attendance at the synagogue,
Jews filled them during the high Holy Days. Rates of
conversion declined dramatically. Bernard Susser notices
that in Devon and Cornwall conversions to Christianity
were almost unheard of after the 1830's.[6] Manifestations
of hatred and disdain of Judaism, such as those pronounced
by D'Israeli, vanished completely.

The struggle for emancipation was launched against
a background of relaxed attachments to the ancestral
traditions and an uncrystalized political consciousness.

Anglo-Jewry was fragmented along class, political and religious lines. The Jewish community was not well prepared for an intensive agitation: some of its members lacked motivation, desire and energy. Jewish instruction, adult education and the press (until the 1840s) were severely neglected. As a result, communication within Anglo-Jewry was poor and during the campaign for emancipation, wide segments were not offered a chance to participate in the agitation of the cause. The leadership felt complacent and satisfied with the security and comfort Jews enjoyed in Victorian Britain. Entirely sheltered in relative affluence, the Anglo-Jewish patriciate tended to ignore the imperatives of reality.

The Jewish Grievance

The disabilities imposed by law on British Jews attracted public attention from the 1820's. They were discussed and analyzed in numerous newspaper articles, periodicals and pamphlets and this sensitivity helped to clarify some of the ambiguities created by existing laws. Jewish historians agree that the English restrictions were of less consequence than those enforced against Jews in continental Europe. Frequently, the disabilities were ignored by the courts and rarely applied in actuality. If they were taken seriously, it was possible to circumvent the laws and to devise more desirable alternatives. Israel Finestein, for example, writes that "the civil disabilities [that] bore lightly upon the Jews for their social emancipation was extensive."[7] Cecil Roth comments in the same vein that "in England, they were so relatively unimportant that it was possible to discuss them interminably as it were on abstract grounds, and to postpone a conclusion to a preposterously late hour."[8] But this picture, drawn in comparative historical perspectives, can mislead the twentieth century observer. The evidence indicates that the legal privations had a direct impact on the well-being of British Jews. They had a considerable bearing on their daily life and consequently, the disabilities nourished strong feelings of resentment and bitterness. Jews often complained about specific grievances and hardships created by the operation of the restriction on their social, economic and political activities.

Legally, the most relevant question was whether the Jewish presence in the country was recognized at all. The Statutum de Judaismo of 1275, which imposed a variety of restrictions and excluded them from toleration in the country, was still unremoved. The statute left Jews to the mercy of the crown and was followed by their expulsion from the realm in 1290. So long as these two orders remained in the Statute Book, Jews were not legally tolerated in the country. It is true that the first statute was virtually repealed by 37 Henry III, c. 9, which removed all statutes concerning usury. But there was no direct piece of legislation to abolish the medieval legislation, so British Jews had no legal basis for their religious worship, education and charities until the nineteenth century. These matters were settled only in August 1846, when Parliament passed the Religious Opinion Relief Bill into law. For this reason Jews insisted on the removal of these medieval statutes,[9] as Francis Henry Goldsmid had done in his 1830 pamphlet.

The toleration of Jews in the country was also questioned by a dictum of Sir Edward Coke, still referred to in the nineteenth century, which labelled them 'infidels'

and 'enemy aliens'. As a result, Coke disqualified Jews
from giving evidence in the courts. Though this was
subsequently ignored and Jews were allowed to testify
in the courts, the dictum was still much quoted and used
as a precedent.

Another legal decision which similarly defined Jews
as aliens was made by Lord Eldon in 1816. By this decision,
Jews were denied the benefit of a grant from a private
trust known as the Bedford Charity, founded by Sir W.
Harpour during the reign of Queen Elizabeth I. The Bedford
Charity supported a school, paid for the apprenticeship
of a few children chosen by lottery, aided poor girls with
marriage portions and granted prizes to those who passed
their apprenticeship successfully. Two Jewish inhabitants
of Bedford, Michael Joseph and Joseph Lyon, had voted in
the election of the trustees of the charity and their
children were supported by its grants until 1816, when
the trustees denied them its benefits. Aided and supported
by a number of wealthy London Jews, including Isaac Lyon
Goldsmid, Lyon and Joseph sued the trustees in court.
After a defeat in a lower court, the two Jewish inhabitants
of Bedford appealed to the Lord Chancellor. Lord Eldon
was one of the most prominent and reactionary lawyers of
the time, especially known for his staunch opposition
to the establishment of religious freedom. He decreed
that the trustees of the Bedford Charity had a case and
that Jews should be excluded from benefits of the charity
on grounds of foreignness and non-citizenship. The decree
was finally removed in 1842, but its application till then
served as an example of how the lack of specification[10] of
Jewish toleration in England's law could be harmful.

The argument of non-toleration was similarly used to
justify a statute that forced Jewish parents to pay for
the upbringing of their children in a Protestant home,
if the children chose to convert (1 Anne, c. 30). This
Statute was removed in 1846 with all other direct discriminatory pieces of legislation due to religious opinion.
Though it was hardly used by the courts in the nineteenth
century, an anonymous Jewish pamphleteer, whose views
were radically anti-emancipationist, complained of its
existence.[11]

The conclusion that Jews were not legally tolerated
in the country was also reached by John Elijah Blunt,
barrister and master in chancery, who conducted an
investigation of his own into the civil disabilities of
the Jews.[12] Blunt particularly emphasized the implication
of the Toleration Act of 1689, which protected Protestant
Dissenters from penalties for refusing to attend services
in Anglican churches. Both Roman Catholics and Jews were
excluded from the scope of the Toleration Act, but the

former were relieved by an amendment, while the Jewish
position remained unaltered.

Before concluding the present branch of this treatise,
it should be noticed that as the law now stands,
the Jewish religion seems to some extent to be considered illegal. For it has been decided that a
legacy cannot be supported which is given to establish
a jeshuba [sic] for the instruction of Jews in their
religion, or to maintain a synagogue.[13]

The result of these ambiguities was that nobody actually
knew whether Jews could freely and legally practice their
religion in the country. When the Sephardi congregation
of London wanted to preach sermons in English during
services in 1829, legal counselors did not have an answer
for their Jewish clients. Some of the counselors suspected
that the translated sermons might offend pious Anglicans
by differing in doctrinal conceptions. The Sephardim
appealed to the civil and ecclesiastical lawyer Stephen
Lushington, a well known reformer, champion of Abolition
and advocate of religious reform. In response, Lushington
had to admit that the legal position of Judaism was very
anomalous and difficult and that statutes embodying 'anti-
quated principles of tolerance' had not been removed from
the Book, even if they were not consulted by the courts.[14]

Perhaps the most explicit discrimation against British
Jews was the prohibition on owning and buying land. Even
in this matter the law was not clear. An 1271 Ordinance
(54 & 55 Hen. III), found in the Bodleian Library in 1738,
forbade Jews to own land. But this Ordinance was contradicted by an Act of 1723 (10 Geo. I, c. 4) that recognized
Jewish ownership of landed property. In the nineteenth
century, the two pieces of legislation were not applied
consistently. Abraham Goldsmid, the prominent financier
in the city of London during the French Revolutionary Wars,
held his estate at Roehampton as a free born subject without
the intervention of trustees, and subsequently he sold
the estate to Chief Justice Lord Ellenborough with no
questions asked.[15] But when Moses Montefiore wanted to
purchase East Cliff estate in Ramsgate in 1830, he
encountered the limitation on buying land imposed by
54 & 55 Henry III. He could not buy the estate and was
forced to rent it for three years.[16]

Until a direct enactment settled the problem in
1833, it was disputed among lawyers. The majority opinion
was against Jews' right to landed property so long as the
1271 Ordinance had not been removed. The grievance was
demonstrated by Colonel Wilson in the House of Commons,
when he presented on 17 June 1830 a petition of non-Jews
favoring Jews' right to own land. The petitioner lamented

the 'uncertainty of legal opinions on the subject.' He described in detail the lack of precision in this matter, though he himself was convinced that Jews were legally permitted to own land.[17]   And the greatest farmer of turnpike tolls, Lewes Levy, who was worth 250,000 pounds when he died, declared in 1830 that the right of land ownership was seriously questioned in public and that this uncertainty damaged the interest of Jews like himself. Levy therefore petitioned Parliament, despite his own indifference to political emancipation, that "all doubts about this question may be prevented by declaratory law."[18]

In London, where the majority of Anglo-Jewry resided, Jews had to face two other kinds of restrictions. First, there was the exclusion from the freedom of the city and second was the selective admission to the Stock Exchange.

By excluding Jews from the freedom of the city, the Corporation forbade them to engage in retail trade within the boundaries of the Metropolis. In 1739, the Chief Justice Sir Robert Raymond ruled that Jews were unable to trade within city boundaries unless they had taken the oaths of allegiance, supremacy, uniformity and ab-juration on the New Testament.[19]   The injustice of this regulation was noticed by the Dissenting china manufacturer Apsley Pellatt, who raised the matter in the Common Council in 1830 and persuaded its member to repeal it.

Equally injurious was the 1697 limitation on the number of Jews allowed to operate on the Stock Exchange. Out of a total of one hundred and twenty-four, only twelve Jews were permitted to become stock brokers. Considering that London Jewry was excluded from the professions, teaching and academic careers, agriculture and civil service, being a stock broker was a much desired occupation and the competition among Jews over each available broker's medal was frantic. Jews had to pay as much as 1500 pounds for such a medal, and an additional sum of 500 pounds for its transfer to a relative or a partner. When Moses Montefiore passed his medal gratis to his brother Horatio upon his retirement from business, it was worth 1625 pounds.[20] For middle class Anglo-Jewry, such a restriction was a barrier to economic advancement. A pro-Jewish advocate, P. Anchini, was scandalized in 1828 by the illiberality of the City, and appeals such as his led the Common Council to abandon this regulation during the same year.

> Good God! and are such degrading transactions suffered
> to exist in a Christian country, nay, in the land
> of liberty? Is it among a people governed by one of
> the wisest constitutions in the whole world that
> the traffic of privileges is authorized? Is it among
> Protestants that the infamous simony of the court
> of the Vatican is practised?[21]

Other disabilities affected the position of Jews all over the country, not only in London. The admission of Jews to the legal profession was hindered by the Inns of Court. Each of the Inns had its own customs, but in most cases a subscription to the oaths was required prior to admission to the bar. Francis Henry Goldsmid explained that "the observance or non-observance of these statutes must depend on custom or on the will of those by whom the oaths are to be administered."[22]

Lincoln Inn, for example, insisted on the sacramental test before calling anybody to the bar. The situations became difficult for Jews in 1828 because they were deprived of the indemnity formerly applied to this test. I.L. Goldsmid suddenly realized that his son, who was unable to subscribe to the new declaration on conscientious grounds, would not be allowed to practice. Fearing for his son's career, he appealed to Wellington and urged him to make a concession at least in this matter, but the Prime Minister did not concede to the request.[23]

Entry into medicine was not restricted by any disability, but Jewish physicians could hardly distinguish themselves in this field since honors were usually bestowed on graduates of Oxford and Cambridge. Nonconformists were discouraged from attending the two universities by the application of the statutory oaths and the religious tests, including subscription to the Thirty-Nine Articles. At Oxford University these tests were required prior to matriculation and at Cambridge as a condition to admission to academic degrees. Lower degrees were opened to all non-Anglicans in Cambridge in 1854 and in Oxford two years later. In this way restrictions were created for practicing Jews pursuing medical careers. The legal writer Basil Montague indeed notices that for most Jews medical careers were limited even though formal disabilities did not apply to this field.[24]

The Jewish existence in the United Kingdom was made difficult by a number of discriminatory acts. They were prevented from attending many of the public schools either by compulsory prayers or by regulations in the school charters. Their religious worship depended on an obscure order in council of Charles II of the year 1674. This had actually left open the question whether they were allowed to maintain their synagogues. Anglo-Jewry had to endow its own hospital and poor relief, although Jews had to pay for the provision of the Poor Law, which discriminated against members of the Jewish faith. It was with bitterness that an anonymous pamphleteer testified in 1834 that "the poor's rates and the various other parish assessments are levied without distinction to Jew or Gentile, to bond or free, but the inmate of the workhouse is exclusively confined to one class."[25]

    Among active emancipationists a consensus prevailed
that the legal disabilities had significant consequences
for many English Jews. From their testimonies it appears
that the restrictions not only produced a general sense
of injustice, but their perpetuation distressed the Jewish
community in more than one way. The orientalist Arthur
Lumley David, for example, complained that the disabilities
"deprived the Jews of various means of acquiring sub-
sistence."[26] Similarly, Robert Grant pointed out that the
issue at stake was more than an abstract injustice. He
reminded the Commons during the presentation of the first
Jewish relief bill that the operation of the law caused
the exclusion of Jews from professional and educational
opportunities.[27] Bernard Van Oven argued in the same vein
that Jews were barred from the advantages of citizenship
but not relieved from the burdens:

> They are incapacitated from the advantages and rights
> which others enjoy. Thus, whilst they are compelled
> to serve on juries, to act as Constables and Head-
> boroughs, any step in the honourable profession of
> law is strictly denied to them; they cannot take
> place at the Bar; they dare not aspire to the Bench;
> from these as well as from all other offices of
> dignity or value they are effectually shut out, either
> by the nature of the oaths proposed or by the mode
> of administering them; but neither of these means
> avails them to escape from the minor offices, the
> drudgeries which all would be glad to avoid; in
> those cases, when their services are desirable, the
> oaths are so altered, both in substance and in the
> mode of administering them, as to be accordant with
> their religious principles.[28]

    In response to opposition to Jewish emancipation
and to arguments that Jews lacked in mental cultivation
and abounded in pauperism, Van Oven wondered how Jews
could develop themselves when they were excluded from all
educational opportunities. How could they distinguish
themselves in the professions, arts and sciences when
they were prevented from entering them? How could one
accuse them of avarice when they were left little choice
but business, money-lending or pawnbroking? Van Oven
expressed the feeling of "bitterness with which they feel
the injustice done to them", which most emancipationists
acutely sensed.

    Van Oven, who was a physician by profession, was an
outspoken representative of a motivated class of Jewish
professionals involved in the campaign for emancipation.
Included in this group were Francis Henry Goldsmid, Arthur
Lumley David and the Polish-born Hebrew professor Hyman
Hurwitz. Other advocates were the lawyer and professor

of political economy, Jacob Waley; the prominent jurist George Jessel; and the mathematician James Joseph Sylvester, who was second wrangler at Cambridge in 1837, but as a Jew, was unwilling to subscribe to the Thirty-Nine Articles and consequently could not obtain a degree or a fellowship.[29]

It is significant that one of Goldsmid's first motions in Parliament, after his 1859 election by the constituency of Reading, provided for the abolition of unnecessary oaths pertaining to admission to various professions.[30] The role played by professionals in this campaign was delineated by the Jewish Chronicle after the appointment of the first Jewish judge, John Simon:

> We have had the experience that the power of wealth is insufficient in such a cause. It is due also to those who, by embarking in the arduous and difficult, no less than distinguished profession of law, have opened a new field of honour to their brethren in this country; that they should receive the acknow-ledgement of the services which they render, for, whilst engaged apparently in a purely personal enterprise, they are in fact and reality fighting lustily the battle of freedom for their people.[31]

In 1830 Jews were not included in the franchise. The 7 & 8 Will. III, c. 27 enacted that no person should be allowed to vote in parliamentary elections unless he had first taken the oaths. The returning officer at the poll was empowered to administer the oaths of allegiance and supremacy at the request of any candidate for election. Generally the law was disregarded, but had a candidate wished, he could have legally deprived Jewish electors of the vote. The law was amended in 1835 by an enactment that abolished the requirement of taking these oaths for electoral purposes.[32]

After 1828 Jews were unable to fill municipal offices because the declaration substituted for the sacramental test, implemented by the Corporation Act of 1661 and the Test Act of 1673, removed that occasion for indemnification. By redressing the grievance of Nonconformists, the Government enacted a declaration that included the words 'on the true faith of a Christian', which the conscientious Jew would not spell out.

Jews were excluded from Parliament and national offices because they would not subscribe to the oath of abjuration that ended with the disqualifying words. The words 'on the true faith of a Christian' had first appear-ed in the oath of allegiance (1605), which had to be taken upon entry into municipal and national offices. Subsequently,

an act of Charles II made admission to Parliament
conditional on the same oath. The words were removed
from the oath in 1688, but they reappeared in the oath
of abjuration of the Pretender (13 Will. III) and in some
other oaths and declarations. Since then, the
abjuration had to be sworn upon admission to corporate and
national offices and upon entry into Parliament.[33]

Some of the activists thought the degradation implied
by the operation of the disabilities was more harmful than
the actual restrictions imposed on Jews. The disqualification for public service meant Jews were not considered
trustworthy by their countrymen. Jews felt dishonored and
insulted by the legal discrimination. David Salomons
expressed a prevalent sentiment when he said "that the
disabilities of which British Jews complain entail on them
positive injury, is an undoubted fact. These disabilities
also lower them in the scale of society and degrade them
in the eyes of their fellow subjects."[34]

This view was shared by a wide circle of Jewish
emancipationists. An anonymous pamphleteer claimed that the
disabilities created the derogatory image Jews had in the
public eye. He reminded the reader of the popular anti-
Jewish prejudices manifested in expressions such as 'don't
Jew me' and in the stereotyped depiction of Jews in the
drama.[35]

Isaac Lyon Goldsmid felt that the shame experienced
from the disabilities was more injurious than the actual
privations. When in 1845 he led a deputation of the Reform
congregation to the Prime Minister, Sir Robert Peel,
Goldsmid claimed that he and his co-religionists "desired
to be placed on an equality in point of civil privileges
with other persons dissenting from the established church
not so much on account of the hardship of being excluded
from particular stations of trust or honour, as on account
of the far greater hardship of having a degrading stigma
fastened upon us by the laws of our country."[35]

It is true that in comparison with other European
states, England was more tolerant and humane. Although
not benefiting from full citizenship granted to French,
Belgian, Dutch or Danish Jews, they could circumvent many
of the difficulties. A good portion of Anglo-Jewry
prospered. It is also true that most of the disabilities
were not enacted directly against Jews and were imposed
on other religious minorities as well. But after the
1830's, the Jews remained the only unemancipated religious
community in the country. The Government and Parliament
were reluctant to mend the law and redress the Jewish
grievance. The disabilities were considered an anachronism
in the nineteenth centruy, yet the Jewish cause had to be

agitated for more than thirty years until the disabilities were removed from the Statute Book.

Non-Jewish sympathizers stressed the injustice and
aggravation caused to the Jews. William Hazlitt, for example,
compared the restrictions with the oppression of Jews in
Papal Rome. Despite the difference in degree, the spirit
behind the Roman persecution and the British discrimination
was the same.[36] In the House of Commons, Ralph Bernal
Osborne, himself of Jewish origins, classified the
prejudice against Jews as identical to the hatred that
led to their banishment from the kingdom in 1290. The
civil disabilities, he explained, were as humiliating as
the yellow badge Jews were coerced to wear in the Dark
Ages.[37]

It is difficult for the modern observer to remain
untouched by the acute offense sensed by Victorian Jews.
Goldsmid's passionate protests, Salomons's restrained
criticism and Jewish Chronicle's bitterness are testimonies of the emotional response to the struggle for
emancipation. They fought for the obliteration of the
terms "disabilities", "privations", and "restrictions" from
the civilized vocabulary. That such terms are no longer
used in a political and legal context is to the credit
of the emancipationist endeavor.

Sources Of Support And Opposition

The struggle for Jewish emancipation cannot be understood without reference to the religious minorities that lent their support. Jewish emancipation was not an isolated event but a phase in a historical evolution toward the establishment of religious freedom. The origins of this evolution can be traced to seventeenth century England, yet the idea of religious pluralism was crystallized only in the nineteenth century.

The highlights of the campaign for religious liberty were the 1828 removal of the Test and Corporations Act and the 1829 Catholic Relief Act. In the 1830's, religious liberty was extended to Quakers, Moravians and Socinians. Next came the Jews' turn and those who had been discriminated against in the past were asked to espouse the Jewish cause. In this way, the Jewish grievance was not allowed to remain a narrow sectarian issue. Its agitation assumed a national dimension and involved a wide circle of non-Jewish sympathizers whose contributions and participation was vital throughout the years of the Jewish campaign.

From the beginning, Jewish emancipation was endorsed by the Protestant Dissenting Deputies. The Deputies looked sympathetically on the Jewish attempt to link their cause with the repeal of the Test and Corporation Acts, but this initiative failed because of government opposition. Fearing to risk Peel's backing, the Dissenting Deputies yielded and accepted the declaration that substituted for the repealed sacramental test. The new declaration left the Jews in an inferior position, for they could neither take it nor benefit from the annual Indemnity Act that had previously protected them from the operation of the sacramental test. Despite their capitulation, the Dissenting Deputies promised to back future Jewish endeavors.

The Nonconformist attitude was displayed in a variety [38] of petitions to Parliament in favor of Jewish emancipation. It was also reflected in appeals from individuals and congregations and in votes for pro-emancipationist candidates at elections. Occasionally, individuals or isolated congregations dissented from the majority opinion and joined the opposition to Jewish emancipation. The most noteworthy illustration is the hostility of two London aldermen, Brown and Wood, who in December, 1835 prevented David Salomons from taking his seat in the Aldermanic court after his election of the Aldgate Ward. But this in no way represents the feelings of the majority. Dissenters believed in the importance of religious liberty and they were ready to fight with other religious minorities[39] for the removal of such encroachments as church rates.

The intensity of Noncomformist support in the Jewish
cause is witnessed in a pamphlet by an Anglican vicar,
Henry Mackenzie of Great Yarmouth. The pamphlet addressed
those who defended Jewish emancipation; they did not attend
his parish church and their position on the question was
different from his own. Mackenzie identified the supporters
as follows: "Perhaps my dissenting friends (of whom I
trust I have many) will permit me also to say a few words
in kindness, which apply more to them than to members of
the national church."[40] The vicar warned of the possible
injury to the Protestant cause and contended that Jewish
emancipation would only strengthen "the encroaching power
of Papal Rome." The pamphlet illustrates how wide and
popular was Nonconformist sympathy with Jewish freedom.

Two dissenting denominations are noteworthy for
their efforts on behalf of the Jewish interest, Unitarians
and Quakers. Unitarian support of Jewish civil rights
began in the eighteenth century and was urged by an
outstanding leader of the movement, Dr. Joseph Priestly.
David Ricardo, a Unitarian convert from Judaism, revealed
his interest in the promotion of the cause in a letter
to I. L. Goldsmid.[41] William Hazlitt, an ardent advocate,
was the son of a Unitarian minister. The Member for
Preston, John Wood, based his advocacy on the fact that
"it is well known in the House that I am a Unitarian
Dissenter, and a more obnoxious title can scarcely exist
in the apprehension of our folter heads, indeed, I believe
they look on the Jews with at least equal favour."[42] A
number of Unitarian congregations passed resolutions
defending the Jewish endeavour and the organ of Unitarian
opinion, the Monthly Repository, generally encouraged
the Jewish activists.[43]

A main reason for the strong Unitarian feeling on this
subject was the insecurity they themselves had experienced.
Having been equalized in status with other Nonconformists
as late as 1813, the Unitarian legal position in the
country was still precarious. Naturally, they were more
sensitive to emancipationist efforts than other religious
sects.

Another major source of support was the Society of
Friends. Among Quaker politicians, the most prominent
collaborator was John Bright. He attacked the Whigs in
the House of Commons for their lack of enthusiasm and
commitment. He also demanded extreme measures for the
attainment of the goal, namely the creation of new peers
sympathetic to the cause. Elizabeth Fry, the famous
prison reformer and philanthropist, expressed her positive
attitude in an 1833 letter to I. L. Goldsmid in which
she informed him of the expressions of sympathy on the
part of Joseph Pease, the first Quaker admitted to the

House of Commons.[44]   Pease advised Lionel de Rothschild
in the matter of swearing on the Old Testament in 1850.
Having experienced the same problems before, his advice
was of considerable value to the Jewish emancipationists.

In a recent study of Anglo-Jewish emancipation,
Michael Salbstein describes the close interaction of the
two communities,[45] reinforced by the frequent occurrence
of business partnerships between Quakers and Jews.   For
example, the Quaker architect Joseph Avis designed the
Bevis Marks Synagogue in 1700-1701 and afterwards
returned the fees for his work to the Sephardi congregation.
During the subscription for the establishment of the
Jews' Hospital in Mile End, a number of Quakers donated
considerable sums of money to the Jewish charity, among
them William Allen, the philanthropist, scientist and
head of a banking house.   In business circles, other
instances of collaboration could be noticed: In 1824,
Nathan Mayer Rothschild, Samuel Gurney, Moses Montefiore
and Alexander Baring founded the Alliance (British and
Foreign Fire and Life) Insurance Company.   The auditor
of the new company was Thomas Fowell Buxton, member of
a prominent Quaker family.

The feeling of rejection by the Anglican mainstream
unified Nonconformists regardless of their religious
persuasion.   The more radical and unacceptable a dissenting sect, the more likely it would be involved in
emancipationist struggles.   Thus, the minority groups
that felt most discriminated against, tended to
associate with Jews and to favor their cause.

The evidence does not reflect how various denominations reacted to the Jewish endeavour, but some
testimonies suggest that one dissenting group was
especially hostile to Jewish emancipation.   This was the
Methodist minority.   Even their representative in
Parliament, the railways investor Joshua Westhead, felt
forced to apologize to many of his Methodist constituents
when he voted in favor of the Jews in 1848.   Westhead
freely admitted that his view on the matter contrasted
with those of many of his co-religionists.   He himself
"found no easy task to overcome the prejudices which he
previously held on this issue."[46]   Because of the populist,
emotional and anti-intellectual quality of Methodism,
its members were susceptible to popular prejudices and
beliefs.   Anti-Jewish sentiments were strongly entrenched
in radical circles and were openly propagated by such
activists as William Cobbett.   Having appealed to these
elements, Methodists were inclined to accept various
popular stereotypes and conceptions.   In all likelihood,
the derogatory Jewish image and the negative attitude
toward Jewish progress were rooted in the Methodist

attachment to lower class radicalism. It is important
to remember that opposition to Jewish emancipation
originated not only in the right wing, but also in the
left. One of the reasons Jewish cooperation with Chartist
circles could not be attained was the intense anti-Semitic
expression in this milieu. Feargus O'Connor, for example,
frequently attacked the Jews in his <u>Northern Star</u>. The
radical Cobbett, a direct inspiration for many Chartists,
denounced British Jews and branded them as a petty
bourgeois element. His hatred of Jews was based on his
antagonism with urbanism, industrialization and capitalism,
with which Jews were identified in certain radical circles.

     The Jewish relationship with the Roman Catholic
minority was problematic and complicated. The English
Catholics strongly identified with the Jewish desire, but
clashes between the two communities over Catholic
persecutions of Jews overseas poisoned the atmosphere
and hindered the collaboration. In the early years of
the struggle for emancipation, it seemed the Catholics
would also endorse the Jewish claim wholeheartedly. In
1829 Daniel O'Connell wrote a friendly letter to I. L.
Goldsmid and urged him to fight for the cause fervently
and relentlessly. O'Connell advised the Jews not to
refrain from forceful measures because militance was
imperative in this case. "You must, I repeat, force
your question on the Parliament. You ought not to
confide in English liberality. It is a plant not genial
to the British soil. It must be forced. It requires
a hot-bed. The English were always persecutors."[47]

     In the House of Commons, the Member for Cork, Vincent
Scully, declared that he represented the largest Catholic
constituency in the Empire, including four bishops, some
hundreds of clergymen and half a million inhabitants,
all of whom strongly supported Jewish relief. And the
Member for Dublin, John Reynolds, claimed in 1851 that the
thirty-seven Catholic M.P.'s always championed Jewish
emancipation. Every argument now used against the Jews,
he said, had been previously employed against Catholic
emancipation.[48]

     But conflicting interests made tensions between the
two minorities unavoidable. The Catholics wanted an
abolition of the oath designed for them by the legislation
of 1829 and including offensive passages in which they
had to affirm non-recognition of the ecclesiastical
supremacy of the pope in the kingdom. Obviously, they
looked forward to attempts to abolish the oaths, so they
could swear as Protestants did.

     In 1857 Palmerston introduced an Oaths Bill to amal-
gamate the current oaths, excluding the Roman Catholic,

and instituting a single formula acceptable to all
religious sects. During the debate in the House over
the bill, a number of Catholic M.P.'s strongly disapproved. They felt its passage into law would leave
them in a disadvantageous position as they would remain
the only ones to pronounce oaths that reflected
unfavorably on their religion. Their demand to include
the Catholic oath in the scope of the new bill was
unacceptable to the governement. They knew well that
a previous similar attempt made in 1854 by Lord John
Russell had failed even in the House of Commons, where
majorities for religious liberty were usually secured.
The Catholic politicians must have known there was no chance
for the success of their motion, yet they insisted on
having their way at the expense of the Jewish interest.
By amending the proposed bill in their favor, the Catholics
would have secured its defeat without gaining anything.
Furthermore, their inclusion in the scope of the new bill
would not have gained any tangible result for them, beyond
a theoretical solution to an abstract problem; whereas
for the Jews, the bill might have settled the problem
of parliamentary representation.

The Jewish Chronicle, probably reflecting a wide
opinion, was outraged by the initiative that could achieve
nothing for the Roman Catholics but would definitely
undermine the Jewish cause:

> The conduct of the Roman Catholic party in the
> matter strongly reminds us of the unnatural mother
> in Solomon's judgement.   'It shall be neither mine
> nor thine, but cut it asunder', she exclaimed.
> True, its grievance is well founded; true, it is
> desirable that the Premier should have found it
> practicable to accede to its wish. But on what
> ground could an antagonism be justified which
> should oppose the redress to another man's wrong
> because justice is refused to his own? [49]

The newspaper reminded the Catholic politicians that during
the struggle for their own emancipation, I. L. Goldsmid
agreed to withdraw Jewish claims because they could injure
their cause. The affair finally ended with a Roman Catholic
concession. When Palmerston's Oaths Bill reached the Upper
House, the Catholic peers voted for it. But damage had
nonetheless been done to the Jewish cause.

Tensions increased as a result of Catholic persecutions
of Jewish minorities overseas. Anglo-Jewry reacted strongly
to the oppression of helpless Jewish communities and did
not hesitate to denounce the papal establishment for its
part in such activities. The 1840 blood accusation against
Damascus Jewry unified the Anglo-Jewish population and

stirred massive protests. English Jews resented the
restrictions imposed on Roman Jewry by the Papacy as a
reaction to the 1848 revolution and it was petrified by
the abduction of the infant Edgar Mortara from his
parents' home to be raised as a Roman Catholic. The Jewish
view on these issues was generally represented by Sir
Moses Montefiore, whose relentless efforts to intervene
on behalf of the oppressed gained general recognition.

Many modern Jewish historians are ambivalent toward
Montefiore. He is often depicted as a weak character
manipulated by his strong-minded friend, Louis Loewe.
Montefiore is harshly criticized for his illiberal disposition and paternalistic attitude toward communal
affairs. In many respects, Montefiore epitomizes the
limitations of the Anglo-Jewish patriciate, the social
milieu into which he had been born. His reluctance to
pursue the emancipationist drive is also damaging.
Montefiore opposed a militant campaign and feared that
emancipation would accelerate the process of assimilation.
However, Montefiore ought to be credited for his courage
and dedication to the Jewish diaspora. More than any
other Jew, he exemplified a genuine desire to retain a
Jewish identity throughout his integration into non-Jewish
society. Despite his orthodox observance and traditional
leanings, he was socially accepted in Victorian Britain.
To European Jews he exhibited a new assimilationist
pattern of adjustment to modernity with a simultaneous
adherence to the ancestral heritage.

Montefiore's resentment of the Catholic persecutions
was shared by Anglo-Jewry at large. His example stirred
other Jews to action. For example, they appealed to
Cardinal Wiseman about the Mortara Affair but their
protest did not lead to any result.[50] The Jewish Chronicle
admonished a group of Catholic clergymen who responded
to such petitions with total indifference. A modern
observer of Jewish-Catholic relations during that phase,
Joseph Altholz, admits that the English Catholic response
to the Mortara Affair was an 'ominous silence'.[51] English
Catholics refused to criticize their Pontiff and sympathized with the Papal attempt to baptize the child and bring
him up as a good Catholic.[52] The growing estrangement,
however, did not lead to a Catholic withdrawal of support
from the Jewish cause. Of necessity, the Catholics saw
the Jewish cause as similar to their own, chose to support
it for their own reasons, and were prefectly capable of
segregating their prejudices from political expediency.
Altholz concludes that

> The Catholics recognized that the grounds on which
> the Jews claimed emancipation were identical with
> those on which they had themselves obtained it, and

their own security depended upon the maintenance of those principles. Their practical attitude toward the Jews was thus determined neither by theology nor by anti-Semitism, but by political considerations proceeding from their own position as a Catholic minority in a Protestant nation.

The major source of opposition to Jewish freedom had always been the church of England. For extreme partisans of the church, the maintenance of its establishment and involvement in secular affairs were highly important. They wanted religion to dominate public life through the exercise of church rates, religious tests, church property and legislation. The emancipation of Jews could be harmful to their interest as had the relief of Protestant Dissenters and Roman Catholics. Thus, the bishops were the prime movers against various relief bills reaching the House of Lords.

In their endeavors to defeat Jewish emancipation, the bishops were aided by a group of lay sympathizers representing the fervid, narrow, Protestant militance which was dying out after mid-century, but was still active and influential on occasion. Anti-Jewish statements were often accompanied by anti-Catholic abuses and by aggressive reactionary outbursts. Most notable in this group was Sir Robert Inglis, an ultra-conservative who had beaten Peel at the Oxford University parliamentary election of 1829. He was known for his staunch resistance to the removal of Catholic, Jewish and Nonconformist disabilities, so his hostility to Jewish freedom was based on a general distrust of religious liberty. Charles Newdegate, M. P. for North Warwickshire, was the most notorious anti-Catholic speaker in Parliament. He was a Conservative with Protectionist leanings who spent the better part of his life in Parliamentary service. Another staunch opponent was Colonel Charles Sibthorp, and ultra-Tory and ultra-Protestant who served in Parliament as M. P. for Lincoln. Sibthorp was often ridiculed for his bluntness, eccentricity and old-fashioned prejudices. This sort of opposition to Jewish emancipation was largely founded upon reactionary dispositions and right wing conservatism.

But Anglican opposition to Jewish relief also originated in liberal sources whose exponent was Thomas Arnold, the popular headmaster of Rugby famous for the revolutionary educational reforms he had introduced. As a Broad Churchman and Liberal clergyman Arnold sympathized with Catholic relief and church reforms. He labored to reinvigorate Anglicanism and in the 1840s his influence was generally recognized. Arnold's objections to Jewish freedom was based on his religious views. He wanted to establish a national Christian church that would embrace all believers in the supremacy of the crown. Christianity was the common denominator that unified the entire Western civilization, a mechanism of integration that tied atomistic individuals into an organic unity. Arnold was prepared to go as far as including Roman Catholics in the pale of his national church, provided they would eventually modify certain theological doctrines. Jews, however, were categorized as 'infidels and heretics'. They were strangers and had no right of citizenship. In an 1836 letter to W. W. Hull, Arnold expressed himself quite lucidly:

> I want to take my stand on my favourite principle, that the world is made up of Christians and non-Christians; with all the former we should be one, with none of the latter. I would pray that dis-tinctions be kept up between Christians and non-Christians. Then I think that the Jews have no claim whatever to political right. If I thought of Roman Catholicism as you do, I would petition for the repeal of the Union tomorrow, because I think Ireland ought to have its own church established in it; and if I thought that Church anti-Christian, I should object to living in political union with a people belonging to it. But the Jews are strangers in England, and have no claim to legislate for it than a lodger has to share with the landlord in the management of his house.[53]

Arnold's view had a tremendous influence on the Evangelical party; in particular, he influenced its leader, Anthony Ashley Cooper, the seventh Earl of Shaftesbury (1801-1885). Jews played a crucial role in Shaftesbury's millenial visions. Their restoration to Palestine and their subsequent conversion to Christianity should have heralded the Second Coming. Therefore Shaftesbury tried to promote their conversion as he was deeply involved in projects to re-settle Jews in the Holy Land. For this purpose he drafted a proposal to his father-in-law, Lord Palmerston.[54] He also patronized efforts to convert Jews by presiding over the London Society for Promoting Christianity Among Jews. The Society became the headquarters of Evangelical opposition to Jewish emancipation and its meetings at Exeter Hall were notorious for their anti-Jewish and anti-Catholic expressions.

Although Shaftesbury claimed he had regarded the Jews with 'reverence', he tolerated their abuse during the proceedings of the London Society. He may not have shared anti-Semitic prejudices, but he certainly did not protest against its intensive circulation at Exeter Hall. With regard to Jewish emancipation, Shaftesbury was

unyielding. He never masked his negative feelings about
the subject and delineated the non-profession of
Christianity as a disqualification for citizenship. Time
and again he repeated the idea that non-Christians ought
not to become legislators for a Christian nation, and he
espoused Arnold's view that the Christian faith was the
major component of modern nationality. So strong was
Shaftesbury's opposition that in 1855 he rejected
Palmerston's invitation to join the cabinet as Chancellor
of the Duchy of Lancaster, fearing he might clash with the
Liberal supporters of Jewish emancipation.[55]

The peculiar relationship of Shaftesbury to Jews and
Judaism reflects a mixture of love and hatred. His
attitude toward Jewish emancipation was ambivalent and
contradictory, as can be expected from a perplexed and
an emotionally unbalanced personality. Perhaps his
compulsiveness and hypersensitivity drove him to
fanaticism, which was so well displayed with regard to
the Jews. Despite his sympathy with the suffering of
persecuted Jews overseas, Shaftesbury denied English Jews
civil rights on dogmatic grounds. His Philo-Semitism
and humanitarianism stood in sharp contrast to the intense
opposition to emancipation and the toleration of abuses
in the London Society.

Within the Anglican church there were a few supporters
of the Jewish cause. Some of them were liberals, who
genuinely espoused the cause of religious liberty. Most
outstanding among them was the Archbishop of Dublin,
Richard Whately, the leader of the liberal wing of the
church. Whately was one of the earliest sympathizers
with the Jewish drive and his 1833 speech in the House of
Lords took its place as an important part of the emancipationist propaganda. The speech was reprinted as a
pamphlet and republished in the Jewish Chronicle. Whately
was qualifed to advocate the cause because of his staunch
opposition to the maintenance of the oaths. His aversion
to oaths sworn on secular occasions was so intense that
he petitioned the Queen for relief from the duty of swearing
in the Knights of Saint Patrick. In his view, liberality
was an imperative of Christian thought. He explained
in a letter addressed to the Bishop of Norwich that freedom
of conscience was a major element of his own belief:

> ... I took a different view on the question (as you
> will have seen) from many others on both sides. I
> may perhaps have even damaged the immediate cause
> of Baron Rothschild, by advocating a principle (to
> the great dismay of one at least of the supporters
> of the bill), which would leave Parliament as open
> to a Mohametan or a Pagan as to a Jew, and by
> waiving altogether the question whether a Jew is

a fitting person to seat in Parliament; but I must
maintain my own principle, which is that a law giving
to Christians generally as such, or to Christians
of any particular church, a monopoly of any civil
rights, is to make Christ's kingdom, so far, a
kingdom of this world and is a violation of the rule
of 'rendering to Caesar the things that are Caesar's'.
I cannot doubt that the apostles were suspected of
designing that whenever their party should become
strong enough, their followers should by law enforced
by secular power compel all men to profess
Christianity, or at least, exclude others from office,
and I cannot doubt that they always intended to be
understood and were understood as denying any such
design.[56]

Expressions of support of Jewish relief were often
coupled with pleas for church reform. The termination
of the Anglican monopoly over power and wealth was considered
an imperative for the purification of the Anglican
establishment. An anonymous clergyman supported the
separation of church and state, so the former could confine
itself to spiritual affairs.[57]   In 1847, Gladstone followed
the same path. He saw no inconsistency between the High
Church observance and the liberal policy of removing
religious disabilities. On the contrary, separation of
church and state, short of disestablishment, would be
advantageous to both sides: the state could satisfy all
citizens regardless of their religious affiliation, while
the church would not have to relax its standards in order
to work with Parliament.[58]

Other unexpected, and perhaps undesirable, support
was lent to the Jewish campaign by Christian pietists who
hoped to promote Jewish conversion to Christianity through
assimilation. Due to the growing missionary efforts during
the nineteenth century, attention was paid to Judaism and
Jews were given a more sympathetic hearing than they have
ever had in the past. The major conversionist organ was
the London Society for Promoting Christianity Among Jews
which, as we have already seen, was fundamentally hostile
to the Jewish struggle. Its members stressed that
emancipation ought to be rewarded to the Jews provided
they converted first.

The London Society, however, gave birth to a group
that became known as the Philo-Judean Society, which was
dissatisfied with the traditional conversionist philosophy.
The Philo-Judeans regarded conversionist efforts as an
intervention in providence and they tried to treat the
Jews more liberally. They hoped their endeavors would
lead the Jews to look upon Christians kindly and thus,
they would be led "into the pale of the Christian church."

The Philo-Judean Society, founded in 1826, protested
vigorously against the persecutions of Jews in Eastern
Europe by organizing meetings and lobbying in Parliament.
In 1827 the Society petitioned Parliament to remove the
disabilities and these petitions were the first phase of
an organized agitation of the Jewish cause. A year later
the Philo-Judean Apsley Pellatt raised the question of
Jewish exclusion from the City's freedom in the Common
Council.

The new attitude is reflected in the arguments of
the Rev. John Oxlee in favor of Jewish emancipation.
Oxlee was a famous divine, an autodidact and a scholar
of Jewish law. In his studies of the Talmud, he tried
to prove that the teachings of Christianity are embedded
in oral law, so the Jews ought to develop an awareness
of the Christian character of their belief and to openly
espouse the Christian faith. Oxlee resented the conversionist effort, which he considered futile. The Jewish
religion continued to exist because of divine will, and
there was an explicit theological justification for the
Jewish survival. The Jewish mission to Christianity was
to exemplify their loyalty to the Scriptures. By living
among Christians and influencing them, Jews could reinforce
the adherence to the Old Testament, their national
aspirations would serve "the restitution of the original
platform of church government, as established in Jerusalem."
For these reasons he supported the full emancipation of
British Jews, hoping their integration into the Christian
environment would lead to their conversion.[59]

Aspirations such as Oxlee's were the sources of a
modern Philo-Semitic impetus that was felt in Victorian
England. Pro-Jewish sentiments were occasionally manifested in other European countries too, but nowhere were
they as influential and conspicuous as in Britain. These
sentiments had some consequences for the Jewish struggle
and in more than one way they helped to buttress the cause.

The strongest Philo-Semitic motivation was exemplified by Augustus Frederick, Duke of Sussex, the sixth son
of George III and Queen Victoria's favorite uncle who
was estranged from the court for many years due to his
liberal disposition. Augustus Frederick gave a warm support
to all progressive policies of his time, including the
abolition of slave trade, Catholic relief, the removal
of the civil disabilities of Dissenters and Jews, the
abolition of the Corn Laws and Parliamentary reform. His
interest in the advancement of art and science was well
known and he always patronized schemes of benevolence.

Sussex was an intellectual. His Kensington Palace
library   comprised   50,000 volumes, among them 1000

editions of the Bible. He was deeply interested in Hebraic
scholarship and possessed an enormous collection of Hebrew
manuscripts. Although a pious Anglican, the royal duke
patronized the Jewish community and sponsored its various
charities. His philanthropy, benevolence and friendli-
ness toward Anglo-Jewry were eulogized by the Voice of
Jacob after his death in 1843:

> Conscious of the too well founded mistrust felt by
> Jews concerning the interference of so many would
> be 'friends of Israel', he more than once dispelled
> apprehension by the open and faithful assurance,
> 'I am not for conversion'. The portrayal of the
> kindly feelings cherished by this distinguished
> man for the Jewish community, the friendly relations
> in which he placed himself towards them, and the
> beneficial influence which he exercised in their
> behalf, call for a special memoir.[60]

The Duke of Sussex pleaded the Jewish cause in the
House of Lords during the years 1830-34; in later years,
he was often incapacitated by his ailments and on occasion
could not meet the Jewish activists in his house due to
the severity of his condition. His involvement in the
campaign was intense, however, and the Jews recognized
his commitment to their cause. Frequently they toasted
his health at their meetings. The Duke's advocacy did
not of course pass unnoticed by the enemies of Jewish
emancipation. According to the Peelite Morning Chronicle,
"it will be remembered that just a fortnight ago, the
weekly organ of the Tories represented one of the King's
brothers as an infidel and an enemy to Christianity,
merely because his Royal Highness rejoiced in the abatement
of the illiberal prejudices against the Jews."[61]   The
Duke took a bold stand on the issue, notwithstanding the
hostility of his brothers, George IV and William IV.
The point was well stated by the Voice of Jacob:

> The illustrious prince gave the impulse; he imparted
> the warmth that could not fail to produce a veri-
> fying power, which once promoted in a genial soil,
> brought forth a rich and abundant harvest. Although
> he was opposed to the government and estranged from
> the court, his popularity with the middle classes
> was great and his influence over them unabounded ...
> Strong in the kind and steady friendship of the Duke
> of Sussex, animated by his presence, guided by his
> counsel, and assisted by his influence with the
> middle classes, the Jews were at length enabled to
> surmount the most onerous and humiliating restrictions
> by which they were fettered in the City of London.[62]

The Duke of Sussex was a prominent champion of religious freedom. He was fully committed to the emancipation of other minorities too but the Jews, more than anybody else, felt deprived by his death. They honored his name by calling the Jews' and General Literary and Scientific Institute 'Sussex Hall', hoping it would promote the activities the Duke patronized while alive.

Another expression of support of emancipation based on pro-Jewish sentiments was illustrated by the participaton of John Cam Hobhouse. Born to a Dissenting mother, he was sent at an early age to a Unitarian school in Bristol. As a young man Hobhouse associated with Byron and became a sympathizer with Napoleon. He was affiliated with radical circles and in 1829 he entered Parliament as representative for Westminster. In 1831 he succeeded his father as the second Lord Broughton and a year later he was appointed Secretary of War. Hobhouse served in the two cabinets of Lord Melbourne and later in Russell's ministry as President of the Board of Control.

His socio-political views moderated as the years advanced, but he remained lively, friendly and generous. Hobhouse identified strongly with oppressed nations, especially with Poles and Greeks. Loyal to the romanticist legacy of Byron, he labored on their behalf in various public committees. Such sentiments may explain his strong feelings about Jewish freedom. Hobhouse was moved by the suffering of Jews and supported their liberation wholeheartedly. He first raised his voice on behalf of the Jewish cause in 1820, upon the arrival of German Jewish survivors of pogroms and riots. Hobhouse gave notice in the House of Commons of his intention to introduce a measure for the removal of the disabilities and for facilitating the naturalization of persecuted Jews in England. The Jews were indifferent to this initiative and the public did not respond warmly, so Hobhouse never brought the promised bill.

No less enthusiastic was Colonel George Gawler, an English Christian who propagated the idea of Jewish settlement in the land of Israel. Gawler took part in the battle of Waterloo as a senior commander and was the first governor of the newly established colony of South Australia (1838-1841). On his return to England he took up the cause of agricultural settlement of Palestine by Jews and circulated his ideas till his death. Gawler sought to provide a solution both to the permanent unrest in the Middle East and to the Jewish problem in Europe. He proposed that the re-settlement of Palestine be executed by the British. To that purpose, he accompanied Sir Moses Montefiore on his third trip to the Holy Land (1849) and apparently was the one who persuaded Montefiore to develop the country.

Gawler believed the destiny of Jews was linked with the future of the British Empire. Britain was entrusted with the responsibility of restoring the Jews to their homeland and thus promote the Second Coming. In the colonization of Palestine under British auspices, he found a moral justification of British imperialism. Judaism was the foundation of the Protestant faith and its defense, an imperative for English expansionism. The prosperity of the Jews was essential to Protestantism because the Jews were "a loyal, well-behaved and deeply interesting race, upon which the everlasting consent of the God and Father acknowledged by Protestant Christianity rests."[63] In this way he related his Fundamentalist belief to his imperialistic aspirations.

Gawler's reason for supporting emancipation was that "Conservative in politics as I am, I am truly rejoiced to see the progress of civil emancipation for your brethren in England and throughout Europe for the reason because I think they highly deserve it at the hands of the civilized world, and for another, that I believed every step towards emancipation is a movement towards Palestine." In an 1848 letter to Jacob Franlin he promised to participate in a mass meeting at Sussex Hall, but he warned against an exclusive Jewish adherence to a single political party. He himself was a Tory and wished to persuade his party that the true interests of Conservatism lay with the destiny of the Jews.[64]

The Jewish cause, not surprisingly, gained great support from middle class elements. This social stratum was especially sensitive to religious grievances because of the high proportion of Nonconformists in its ranks. During the mid-century, middle class elements fought for the extension of religious and economic liberty and they sympathized with any claim in this direction. The evidence supports this generalization.

Dr. Bernard Van Oven emphasized in one of his pamphlets that objections to Jewish freedom were largely founded on class prejudices:

It is easy to understand that when such a monopoly of power was once established (no matter how, whether by the fears or the wishes of the majority), that it would be the decided interest of the privileged class to perpetuate it, to obtain for themselves the honours and emoluments of high sections, to keep all other classes of the community in a kind of vassalage, to employ them in the minor and mere nominal offices of the state, but inflexibly to oppose their advancement to places of trust and dignity.[65]

Van Oven felt that the overwhelming opposition to Jewish freedom originated in the privileged orders, the aristocracy and clergy. The hostile Member for Argyll-shire, Walter Campbell, agreed with Van Oven that the major obstacle was the Lords' attempt "to subvert the power of the middle classes" and their refusal "to make the brute force of a numerical majority supreme."[66]

The petitions to Parliament also reflect a genuine middle class interest in the advancement of Jewish emancipation. There is little expression of support on the part of working men, though workers too had no easy access to the legislature. It is true that the petitions cannot reflect aristocratic attitudes toward emancipation, for the nobility had no need to petition Parliament. The landed estate dominated the House of Lords and was highly influential in the House of Commons, so it had other outlets. Parliamentary divisions and speeches, however, indicate clearly that the staunchest opposition came from the gentry. The reactionary country gentlemen and the conservative magnates disliked changes in the religious status quo. They defeated the various relief bills in the Upper House, where the Whig aristocracy, which also represented middle class interests, was in the minority.

To illustrate the point, only a few of the numerous available petitions will be mentioned: In 1829 Joseph Hume presented a petition from the inhabitants of Callan in the Kilkney, saying that the petitioners "in their desire to promote the prosperity of their country, stated that they had reason to believe that a great deal of capital would flow into it and promote the industry, if the existing restrictions against the Jews were removed."[67] A year later, William Huskisson read a petition from "bankers, merchants and other inhabitants of Liverpool", praying the House to remove the Jewish disabilities. The petition was signed by 2000 people, including the mayor and "every banker and almost every merchant of weight in the town."[68]

On 14 March 1833 the Marquis of Westminster presented a petition from 1500 persons living in London, "almost all of whom were of the highest respectability, though belonging to almost every profession and class of men in society, merchants, shopkeepers, lawyers and clergy-men."[69] And in 1851, the banker and M. P. for Northampton, Raikes Currie, described to the House a meeting of Londoners to draw up a petition to Parliament in support of Baron Rothschild. Currie said the meeting was peaceful and respectable, attended primarily by "men of greatest eminence and high standing in the commerical world, by such men as Mr. John Dillon and Mr. Samuel Morley."[70]

This was the social background against which the struggle for Jewish emancipation was carried on. The issue transcended narrow sectarian goals and was related to a wider scope of social changes. The emancipationist drive generated sympathy in wide circles that identified with the liberationist aspirations of British Jews. The Jewish agitation took place in a society that witnessed an intensive campaign for the liberation of slaves, that heard the voice of John Stuart Mill raised in behalf of the emancipation of women. During the same period, Marx talked about human emancipation and toward the end of the century, Ibsen dramatized the agonies of self-emancipation from the conventions of society. Emancipation was a slogan in liberal milieus and a synonym for progress and enlightenment. It signified a universal hope for redemption that had nourished more than one generation.

Notes

[1]See T. M. Endelman, <u>Jewish</u> <u>Modernity</u> <u>in</u> <u>Georgian</u> <u>England</u>. <u>Acculturation</u> <u>And</u> <u>Integration</u> <u>In</u> <u>A</u> <u>Liberal</u> <u>Setting</u> Ph.D. Dissertation, Harvard University, 1976.

[2]Isaac D'Israeli, "The Talmud", in <u>Curiosities</u> <u>Of</u> <u>Literature</u> (New York, 1877), Vol. I, 177-185; See also his <u>Genius</u> <u>Of</u> <u>Judaism</u> (London, 1833) and <u>Vaurien</u>: <u>Or</u> <u>Sketches</u> <u>Of</u> <u>The</u> <u>Times</u> (London, 1797), ch. XXVIII.

[3]Stephen Sharot, "Secularization, Judaism and Anglo-Jewry", <u>A</u> <u>Sociological</u> <u>Yearbook</u> <u>of</u> <u>Religion</u> <u>In</u> <u>Britain</u> 4 (1971), 121-140.

[4]Bernard Susser, "Social Acclimatization of Jews in Eighteenth and Nineteenth Century Devon", <u>Industry</u> <u>And</u> <u>Society</u> <u>In</u> <u>The</u> <u>North</u> <u>West</u> ed. Robert Burt (Exeter, 1970), 51-69.

[5]Sharot, pp. 121-130.

[6]Susser, pp. 67-68.

[7]Israel Finestein, <u>A</u> <u>Short</u> <u>History</u> <u>Of</u> <u>Anglo-Jewry</u> (London, 1957), p. 79.

[8]Cecil Roth, <u>Essays</u> <u>And</u> <u>Portraits</u> <u>In</u> <u>Anglo-Jewish</u> <u>History</u> (Philadelphia, 1962), p. 17.

[9]F. H. Goldsmid, <u>Remarks</u> <u>On</u> <u>The</u> <u>Civil</u> <u>Disabilities</u> <u>Of</u> <u>British</u> <u>Jews</u> (London, 1830).

[10]<u>Voice</u> <u>Of</u> <u>Jacob</u>, 10 May 1842.

[11]<u>Statement</u> <u>Of</u> <u>The</u> <u>Civil</u> <u>Disabilities</u> <u>And</u> <u>Privations</u> <u>Affecting</u> <u>The</u> <u>Jews</u> <u>In</u> <u>England</u> (1828).

[12]J. E. Blunt, <u>A</u> <u>History</u> <u>Of</u> <u>The</u> <u>Establishment</u> <u>And</u> <u>Residence</u> <u>Of</u> <u>Jews</u> <u>In</u> <u>England</u> <u>With</u> <u>An</u> <u>Inquiry</u> <u>Into</u> <u>Their</u> <u>Civil</u> <u>Disabilities</u> (London, 1830), pp. 113-114.

[13]Blunt, p. 118.

[14]Endelman, pp. 51-76.

[15]Apsley Pellatt, <u>Brief</u> <u>Memoir</u> <u>Of</u> <u>The</u> <u>Jews</u> <u>In</u> <u>Relation</u> <u>To</u> <u>Their</u> <u>Civil</u> <u>And</u> <u>Religious</u> <u>Disabilities</u> (London, 1829), pp. 21-22.

[16]Lucien Wolf, <u>Sir</u> <u>Moses</u> <u>Montefiore</u>, <u>A</u> <u>Centenary</u> <u>Biography</u> (London, 1884).

[17] Hansard, New Series, Vol. 25, p. 347.

[18] See petition in Journals of House of Commons, Vol. 85, p. 347.

[19] H. S. Q. Henriques, The Jew And The English Law (1908), pp. 198-200.

[20] Diaries of Sir Moses and Lady Montefiore, ed. Louis Loewe (London, 1890), Vol. I, p. 87.

[21] P. Anchini, A Few Remarks On The Expediency And Justice of Emancipating The Jews, Addressed to The Duke of Wellington (London, 1829), p. 13.

[22] F. H. Goldsmid, p. 24.

[23] I. L. Goldsmid to Wellington, 9 May 1828, in Lionel Abrahams, "Sir I. L. Goldsmid And The Admission Of The Jews Of England To Parliament", Transactions Of The Jewish Historical Society Of England (Trans. J.H.S.E.), Vol. IV, pp. 143-154.

[24] Basil Montague, A Letter To Henry Warburton, Esq. M. P. Upon The Emancipation Of The Jews (London, 1833), p. 18; also, The Jews: Their Present State And Prospects (c. 1838).

[25] The British Jew To His Fellow Countrymen (London, 1833), p. 55.

[26] A. L. David, Letter On The Emancipation Of The Jews (London, 1833), p. 55.

[27] Hansard, third series, Vol. 23, p. 1292.

[28] Bernard Van Oven, An Appeal To The British Nation, pp. 9-11.

[29] On the participation of these individuals in the campaign see Jewish Chronicle, 8 August 1845.

[30] Sessional Papers, 30 March 1860.

[31] Jewish Chronicle, 4 July 1856.

[32] H. S. Q. Henriques, p. 198.

[33] On the history of the oaths see: David Salomons, A Short Statement On Behalf Of His Majesty's Subjects Professing The Jewish Religion (London, 1835); D. S. Alteration Of The Oaths Considered In A Letter To The Earl Of Derby (London, 1835); D. S. Notes On The History Of The Oaths of Allegiance, Supremacy & Abjuration (London, 1857).

[34] David Salomons, A Short Statement, p. 7.

[35] The British Jew To His Fellow Countrymen, pp. 28-29.

[36] William Hazlitt, "Emancipation Of The Jews", Tatler No. 176, 28 March 1831.

[37] Hansard, third series, Vol. 125, pp. 89-91.

[38] Bernard Lord Manning, The Protestant Dissenting Deputies (Cambridge, 1952), pp. 211-212.

[39] See Morning Chronicle, 10 December 1835.

[40] Henry Mackenzie, A Letter To The Parishioners Of Great Yarmouth By Their Minister (Yarmouth, 1847), p. 10.

[41] David Ricardo to I. L. Goldsmid in Abrahams, pp. 130-131.

[42] John Wood to I. L. Goldsmid, 6 February 1829, Letter Book of I. L. Goldsmid, Watson Library, University College, ff. 31.

[43] John Bowring to I. L. Goldsmid in Abrahams, p. 160.

[44] Abrahams, p. 164.

[45] N. M. C. Salbstein, The Emancipation Of The Jews In Britain, With Particular Reference To The Debates Concerning The Admission Of The Jews To Parliament, 1828-1860 Ph. D. Diss. London University, 1974, p. 64.

[46] Hansard, third series, Vol. 98, pp. 620-621.

[47] Daniel O'Connell to I. L. Goldsmid in Abrahams, pp. 151-152.

[48] Hansard, third series, Vol. 117, pp. 1100-1101.

[49] Jewish Chronicle, 8 June 1857.

[50] Jewish Chronicle, 7 February 1851.

[51] Joseph Altholz, "A Note On The English Catholic Reaction To The Mortara Affair", Jewish Social Studies XXVII (1961), 111-118.

[52] Altholz, p. 112.

[53] A. P. Stanley, The Life And Correspondence Of Thomas Arnold, D. D. (London, 1877), Vol. I, p. 28; see also, Thomas Arnold to Richard Whately, 10 May 1836, Whately Papers, Lambeth Palace, MS 2164, f. 30.

[54] On Shaftesbury's position see Georgina Battiscombe, Shaftesbury, The Great Reformer, 1801-1885 (Boston, 1975); Edwin Hodder, The Life And Work Of The Seventh Earl Of Shaftesbury 3 Vols. (Cassell, 1887); Barbara Tuchman, Bible And Sword (New York, 1956), pp. 175-207.

[55] Battiscombe, pp. 243-246.

[56] E. J. Whately, Life And Correspondence of Richard Whately, D. D. Late Archbishop of Dublin (London, 1886), Vol. II, pp. 149-151.

[57] A Clergyman's Apology For Favouring The Removal Of The Jewish Disabilities (London, 1847).

[58] P. T. Marsh, The Victorian Church In Decline, Archbishop Tait And The Church Of England (Pittsburgh, 1969) p. 98.

[59] Rev. John Oxlee, Three Letters Humbly Submitted To The Consideration Of His Grace The Most Reverend The Lord Archbishop Of Canterbury, Primate Of All England And Metropolitan On The Inexpediency And Futility Of Any Attempt To Convert The Jews To The Christian Faith In The Way And Manner Hitherto Practised (1842).

[60] Voice of Jacob, 5 May 1843. See also Mollie Gillen, Royal Duke, Augustus Frederick, Duke of Sussex, 1773-1843 (London, 1976); Roger Fulford, The Royal Dukes (1933).

[61] Morning Chronicle, 19 October 1835.

[62] Voice of Jacob, 26 May 1843.

[63] Colonel George Gawler, The Emancipation Of The Jews Indispensible For The Maintenance Of The Protestant Profession Of The Empire And In Other Respects Most Entitled To The Support Of The British Nation (1847).

[64] Correspondence of Colonel George Gawler and Jacob A. Franklin, Mocatta Miscellaneous Papers. In particular his letter from N. Service Club, 26 June 1848, and from Pankhurst, Isle of Wight, 21 March 1848.

[65] Van Oven, pp. 3-4.

[66] W. F. Campbell, A Short Statement Of The Grounds Which Justify The House of Lords In Repeating Their Decision Last Year Upon The Jewish Question (1849), p. 17.

[67] Hansard, third series, Vol. 81, p. 445.

[68] Ibid. Vol. 24, p. 376.

[69] Ibid. Vol. 26, p. 775.

[70] Ibid. Vol. 118, p. 1365.

Chapter 2

ANGLO-JEWISH ATTITUDES TOWARD POLITICAL EMANCIPATION

The anticipation of political emancipation provoked
a serious debate inside the Anglo-Jewish community and
sharpened the divisions between its various factions.
The desirability of obtaining civil rights and the means
of pursuing this end occasioned violent polemics. Emancipation was related to internal Jewish problems, so
attitudes toward the struggle were largely determined
by the perception of one's Jewishness. Civil and political
emancipation compelled Anglo-Jewry to define its identity:
Was participation in public life compatible with Jewish
loyalties? Would integration lead to excessive acculturation or perhaps even to the repudiation of Judaism?
Did the public and the legislators seriously expect (as
was sometimes suggested) a relaxation of devotion to the
ancestral faith in exchange for civil rights?

Less fundamental debates arose over the ways and
means of campaigning for Jewish freedom. Should the
Jewish community agitate vigorously through mass meetings,
assemblies, and perhaps even through an organized society
that would promote the cause outside Parliament? Should
British Jews identify with one of the political parties
or would it be more prudent to separate the Jewish claim
from party politics? Should the Jews accept piecemeal
concessions that would gradually redress their grievance
or should they stand firmly for achieving all their demands
at once? These were complicated questions confronting an
ethnic group whose leaders had limited political experience.
All these questions frustrated Anglo-Jewry and challenged
its traditional pattern of social organization. The
struggle for emancipation was a long and tedious effort,
accompanied by setbacks and rebuffs. The difficulties,
disappointments and complications spurred a solidarity and
cohesion that were formerly missing. The emancipationist
endeavour was the critical phase in fostering Anglo-Jewish
identity and is still a landmark in the unique tradition
of this particular community.

As accurately described in the Voice of Jacob, the
Jewish community was split into three main factions whose
basic attitudes toward political emancipation differed
fundamentally. First there was a group of ultra-orthodox
Jews who bitterly opposed the struggle. They believed
complete equalization of Jews in status and rank with
Christians was an interference with the will of Providence
and an attempt, for secular ends, to acculturate in a
foreign environment at the expense of primary loyalties
to Judaism. As the Voice of Jacob put it, this faction

was composed of those who,

> ... dreaded a diversion of the Jewish mind from the
> religious interests of the Jews, as a people, through
> the seductions offered by the opening of new avenues
> to personal ambition, the ardent pursuit of which,
> they maintain, is calculated to estrange the indivi-
> dual from certain higher duties that devolve upon
> him with all Jews. These hold that there are public
> offices which a pious Jew cannot conscientiously
> discharge with efficiency.[1]

The opposite position to this ultra-orthodox stance
was taken by those who desired complete Jewish assimilation
into the non-Jewish environment. By definition, members
of this group retained looser affiliations with Judaism;
if they chose to remain Jewish, it was conditional on
reforms which would purge the ritual of all references
that threatened their identification as Englishmen. The
Voice of Jacob characterized this group as having no
doubts about fighting an army which enlisted Jews in its
ranks. They would fight fellow Jews if the latter were
enemy nationals. Quite logically, the assimilationists
saw no reason they should not be eligible for full
citizenship and insisted on the rejection of any concessions short of complete equality.

The majority of Anglo-Jewry, however, followed a
moderate leadership which, although affiliated with
orthodox congregations, was far from being slavishly pious.
The majority group wished to retain its loyalties to the
Jewish heritage, but at the same time wanted all or some
civil rights. The tactics employed by this party were
gradualist and pragmatic. Its members believed in pressing
the government to redress various grievances as the
occasion arose. They believed that, in the end, they
could get rid of the disabilities by demonstrating their
injustice and unpopularity. Even party radicals like
David Salomons, did not reject piecemeal solutions. There
were, however, within this moderate majority of Anglo-
Jewry subdivisions of religious observance, party affiliations and a variety of social attitudes. This chapter
will examine the position of the three factions in depth.

A letter to the editor of Voice of Jacob by an
anonymous correspondent neatly illustrates the orthodox
view. The writer identified himself as a Tory since "he
could not imagine the possibility of a Tory government's
disposition to intermeddle with the synagogue."[2] He
might support the admission of Jews to corporate offices,
but nothing more. In his opinion, the admission of Jews
to Parliament or to the army would necessarily clash with
commitments to their faith. He was particularly worried

about Sabbath observance. This opposition to Jewish emancipation was based on the fear of excessive assimilation and the consequent abandonment of Judaism. The writer pointed out the extent of secularization of emancipated French and Dutch Jews and the neglect of religious observance even by the lower classes in these countries. The employment of purely anti-assimilationist grounds for the rejection of political emancipation is perhaps the most striking mark of identity of the ultra-orthodox party.

The impact of this opposition was, for the most part, insignificant in the course of the campaign, despite attempts to use it by adversaries of the Jewish cause, most notably Sir Robert Inglis and Bishop Samuel Wilberforce. Jewish resistance to emancipation for these reasons became noticeable during David Salomons's campaign to again be alderman for Aldgate Ward in 1835. Salomons was not the only Liberal candidate on that occasion, but he managed to attract most of the Jewish votes. Surprisingly enough, the other Liberal candidate, John Humphrey (1794-1863), merchant and M.P. for Southwark between 1832-1852, enjoyed strong support from Morris Emanuel, a wealthy Jewish silversmith. Emanuel accused Salomons of having neglected to contribute to various local Jewish charities, though the two synagogues in the area supporting Salomons's candidacy, produced evidence to the contrary. Typically, the charge against the leading Jewish emancipationist was relaxation of Judaism. The Observer, which reported the news on November 15, 1835, remarked that "some of the strictest members of the Jewish persuasion are said to have felt much displeased at the popularity which the sheriff has acquired among the great mass of the citizens of London and consider the principal movement in his favour to be actually pointed to the conversion of the whole Jewish population of the country to Christianity."

A number of Jewish historians have identified the Hebrew tutor at Cambridge University, Joseph Crool (d. 1829)[3] as an influential spokesman of the ultra-orthodox party. True, Crool denounced Jewish efforts to remove the disabilities on purely religious grounds. He regarded such endeavors as a direct interference with Divine Will and as a violation of Israel's sacred mission in the diaspora. Crool viewed emancipation as an attempt to assimilate and obliterate Jewish religious tenets.[4] With this belief, he addressed the staunchest enemy of Jewish emancipation in the House of Commons, Inglis, and communicated to him his radical opinions. The Jewish emancipationists paid little attention to this propaganda. The only close response Crool received explains fairly well why he was not taken seriously: In Rev. F. R. Hall's opinion, Crool was neither well-read nor well-informed about Judaism.

"He was abounded in prejudices," Hall said and doubted his belief in the divinity of Christ. "He was not a man of good sense", the Rector of Fulbourn concluded his judgement of Crool.[5]

Crool was known for his absurd adherence to superstitious fables, such as the story of the Angel Gabriel who appeared to the Fathers and Prophets of the Jews. Perplexed, quarrelsome, negligent of his appearance and usually stained with ink, Crool became an object of ridicule in the Cambridge colleges. The Westminster Review rebuked the University for keeping him to abuse his distress for their own purposes.[6] The review suggested that Crool was pressed to write Inglis by the masters of Cambridge University to publicly demonstrate orthodox discontentment with the emancipationist endeavor. Crool's letter to Rev. I. W. Whittaker, dated from March 24, 1828, strengthens this impression. The Hungarian-born tutor complained to Whittaker of his financial difficulties and the hardship of earning a living as a tutor.[7] His major problem was never getting a chance to deliver lectures at the university, although entitled by custom to twenty lectures a year. It seems Crool's patrons did not regard him highly. Thus, Joseph Crool cannot be considered exemplary of orthodox opposition to emancipation. Ultra-orthodox Jews could not believe in the divinity of Christ or get involved in the academic life of an Anglican University. His fantastic views on the subject were not indicative of this milieu, even though effectively so used by the anti-emancipationist propaganda.

The most zealous emancipationists were members of the secessionist Reform Congregation of London, of which the Goldsmids played the most prominent role. Their belief in the necessity of religious reform was triggered by their assimilationist philosophy. As Robert Liberles recently showed, there was a direct relationship between theological convictions and the political ideology of the radical emancipationists who were alarmed by the anomaly of the Jewish existence in Europe. Despite the general enlightenment and liberality sweeping Europe, the Jew remained an alienated, secluded and unacceptable character. To normalize the Jewish condition, they sought to formulate a compromise that would accommodate both ancient Judaism and modern universalism. They did not seek complete repudiation of the Jewish creed, but rather its modification in the interest of modernity. In this respect, English reformers conformed to the theoretical framework devised by their Continental counterparts.

The English Reform movement differed from traditional Judaism in agreeing to abridge the prayers, repudiate the Talmudic doctrines, dispense with one of the two days

of holidays celebrated consecutively, question the use
of phylacteries, and refuse to commemorate the
destruction of the Temple.[8] The British reformers
focused their attack on traditional Judaism by rejecting
the divinity of the oral law, which for them, was a source
of obstructionism and regression in Judaism. Though more
positive toward the Bible, an anonymous pamphleteer could
state explicitly: "It should be our earliest task to
examine the oral law and earnestly and attentively compare
it with the Bible, and in both volumes seek for proof of
the alleged divinity of the origin."[9] But ordinarily,
the Bible was not a target for their reforming zeal, in
contrast with the Biblical criticism developed by German
Jewry. Possibly, the popularity of the Scriptures among
English Protestants mellowed the reservations which might
have arisen under different circumstances. The point
must be clearly made, in conclusion, that the differences
between the English Reform and orthodox creeds concerned
profound theological matters; they were not limited to
ritual alone.

The radical assimilationists were ready to pay a
price for their emancipation by making concessions at the
expense of their Jewishness. The best illustration of
this aspect can be seen in their dealings with Sir Robert
Peel in 1845. Before finally espousing the removal of
municipal disabilities affecting Jewish subjects, the
Prime Minister received two deputations which claimed
to represent the Jewish cause. The first was headed by
Moses Montefiore on behalf of the Deputies, representing
the emancipationist party that remained loyal to
traditional Judaism. The second delegation, including
Isaac Lyon Goldsmid, Aaron Asher Goldsmid, Moses Mocatta,
Benjamin Elkin and J. G. Henriques, spoke for the Reform
party. The delegates informed the Premier that unlike
their orthodox co-religionists, they would not be satisfied with a partial relief measure and would continue to
agitate relentlessly until they achieved full civic equality,
including parliamentary representation. Goldsmid told
Peel that the Jews had proven their desire for and worthi-
ness of emancipation by reforming their ritual. Indeed
he gave the impression that emancipation ought to be a
reward for religious accommodation. Jewish opinion was
generally scandalized by these statements, which were
advanced by Goldsmid as the convictions of Jewry as a
whole.

Consequently, frictions developed between the two
parties. After the Reform congregation broke from the
orthodox majority in the 1840s, Moses Montefiore refused
to allow Rev. David Marks, minister of the Burton Street
Synagogue, to solemnize marriages. F. H. Goldsmid protested vigorously and even appealed to the Attorney General,

but the latter justified the exclusion of the
secessionists from the performance of this rite. In
1842, in response to the adoption of a revised prayer
book, the chief Ashkenazi Rabbi, Solomon Hirschell, and
Haham Meldola, minister of the Portuguese Synagogue,
united to excommunicate the new secessionist congregation.
Furthermore, the new synagogue was excluded in 1853 from
representation on the Board of Deputies and from the
educational grants allocated to the Jewish community in
1852. According to the 'Model Deed' arrangement, only
schools controlled by the chief rabbi were eligible for
grants from the parliamentary endowments, an arrangement
that was subsequently revoked in response to strong protests inside the community.

The conflict was so severe that in 1845 I. L. Goldsmid
laid the issue of marriage registration before the Prime
Minister. But Peel politely rejected the suggestion
that he should intervene in a matter strictly internal
to Anglo-Jewry.[10] Goldsmid was not satisfied and
threatened to raise the grievance in Parliament. The
leadership of the orthodox establishment grew alarmed
because this might publicly question their control over
marriages, burials, poor relief, education and religious
worship. The Voice of Jacob, the orthodox mouthpiece
against Reform Judaism, complained that "the interposing
deputation to Sir Robert Peel, composed of members from
that congregation, was avowedly to have the effect of
forcing our internal differences upon the attention of
the Imperial Parliament."[11] The orthodox illiberality
in this matter was a source of tremendous dissatisfaction
inside Anglo-Jewry, sharpening dissension inside the
orthodox party. One is surprised how devoted British
Jews were to the Anglican ideas of establishment and
exclusion of nonconformity from basic rights. Needless
to say, these internal frictions only weakened the cause
of emancipation and they presented Anglo-Jewry in an illiberal light.

The ideology of this party and its basic attitudes
toward emancipation were recorded in the writings of
three leading reformists: Francis Henry Goldsmid, Bernard
Van Oven and Henry Faudel. Goldsmid admitted that Jews
were less cultivated in their lifestyle than non-Jewish
countrymen. This regression sprung from the operation
of disabilities which denied them opportunities for self-
improvement. Since man was a product of his environment,
the Jewish deficiency was a reflection of the limitations
imposed by society. Although he employed arguments popular
with the sympathizers, Goldsmid's tone was apologetic.
"The latter part of the accusation against the Jews,
which charges them with deficiency in mental cultivation,
is of a more serious nature. Yet, of this also I must,

I fear, admit the partial truth; whilst I at the same
time maintain that this also is the result, as well of
disabling laws as of the prejudices, which have
constantly prevailed against men of that religion."[12]

For Goldsmid, Jewishness had to be reconciled with
British nationality. He illustrated the Jewish contribution to culture, commerce and industry of the countries
where Jews enjoyed full citizenship. He argued the Jew
was always ready to place his country's interest above
narrowly conceived ends of his own.[13] The Reform
ideology was optimal from his point of view, because it
both preserved Judaism and reinforced patriotism: "We
have acted with the purpose of presenting in our devotional
guide the whole of the Jewish dogma; receiving, as we did,
without any reserve, the thirteen articles of faith,
considered by Maimonides the summary of what has, since
the establishment of our religion, been believed by the
faithful Israelite."[14]

Goldsmid, however, emphasized that religion was no
longer the primary commitment of modern man. English
Jews, like everybody else residing in the country, were
first and foremost human beings. They had a number of
affiliations: professional, national, cultural, social
as well as religious. Jewishness was a component of one's
personal identity, but not the predominant aspect of his
existence. This was the common denominator in Goldsmid's,
Van Oven's and Faudel's philosophy.

One of the most intelligent agitators of the Jewish
cause was Bernard Van Oven, who similarly based his advocacy on secularist-liberal grounds. Van Oven stressed
the irrelevance of religious opinions to civil rights
and the consequent anomaly caused by the old statutes.
He also rejected the notion that Christianity could validly
constitute a moral qualification for admission to political
life. The existence of the disabilities was a violation
of basic constitutional principles and the assertion of
full civil rights was "an act conformable to the principles
of social justice."[15] Therefore Jews ought to agitate
firmly and consistently. They ought not to compromise
with concessions or pursue the path of conciliation, but
demand resolutely their due. He was highly critical of
the relative mildness manifested by the community with
regard to the struggle for emancipation.

The friends of order, they have always opposed any
agitation even for the obtaining of their rights;
and have, as it seems to me, conducted themselves in
this matter, at least, too peaceably, for the history
of the last quarter of a century clearly shows that
patience under political wrongs will not lead to their

redress, but that for such evils to be remedied, they must be clearly exposed and loudly and perseveringly denounced."[16]

Van Oven's advocacy lacked the apologetic tone frequently recorded in Goldsmid's writings. Van Oven was proud of his Jewish identity, boasted of his brethren's talents and praised their philanthropy. He boldly shattered a number of anti-Jewish myths. For example, he attacked the press for misleading the public by depicting Jews as wealthy. The number of rich Jews in comparison with non-Jews was small, and within Anglo-Jewry most individuals belonged either to the middle strata or to the working classes. The press also helped to propagate the notion of a Jewish tendency to criminality. When a non-Jew committed a felony, his religious persuasion was never mentioned in newspaper reports, but when a Jew was brought to trial for the same offense, the press commented pointedly on his faith.

A third spokesman for this party was Henry Faudel, member of a wealthy and prominent Jewish family of stock brokers, who differed from the two previous activists and from most reformists. Faudel endorsed the answers given by Continental rabbis to Napoleon's interrogations of 1806 and 1807. According to Faudel, the opinions of the Sanhedrin "may fairly be taken as a standard of the Jewish view" and "every English Jew holds similar opinions." He justified the renunciation of some Jewish tenets in exchange for civil rights and repudiated all national aspirations of the Jewish people. As far as he was concerned, his feelings about Jewishness were identical to those of English Catholics or Protestant Dissenters about their religion.

For Henry Faudel, the difference between Judaism and Christianity was only semantic. He adopted the deistic view by stressing morality above ritual. Jews shared with their countrymen a fundamental corpus of belief and a firm commitment to humanitarian, universalistic and ethical concerns. These were far more important than the remainder of institutional religion. "The Jew will subscribe freely and willingly to the principles laid down by the founder of Christianity, because they are the bases of his religion. There is nothing in the practice of Christians to which the Jew can object; there is nothing in the precepts of Jews to which a Christian can object."[17]

Faudel's attitude toward Jewish institutions and life was especially critical. He felt humiliated by the large proportion of pauperism among Jews and held the leadership responsible because it neglected poor relief. He scorned the community's internal distinctions, the

snobbery of the nouveau riches and the authoritarian
disposition of the pillars of the community. Jews were
to a great extent responsible for the derogatory image
from which they suffered. The solution was self-help and
self-improvement: education, welfare, charity and growing
assimilation. He also urged Jews to fight bigotry through
communication with the non-Jewish environment: "I will
readily admit that it is only the prejudices of the
ignorant and vulgar which draw the distinctions between
yourself and the Christian; enlighten him therefore where
requisite; associate as much as possible with him; let
your press address him, prove by your acts, your words
and dealings the falseness of the assertions against you
and his sneer loses all its sting from its inapplicability."[18]

All three activists cited above believed in the need
to prepare for Jewish emancipation. They maintained that
emancipation should be internal, not only external, effected
through reformation of manners, elimination of pauperism
and ignorance, spread of education and greater contact
with the non-Jewish environment. They stressed the
desirability of Jewish accommodation to the nationality,
culture and lifestyle of their homeland. In a sense,
the three devised conditions of their own for the
establishment of Jewish freedom. They wanted to see a
new character evolving as a consequence of liberation
and a new spirit prevailing in the entire community.
Emancipation would effect a profound change in Jewish life
and mentality. It could not end with the modification
of material conditions. These activists designed a
religious reform and articulated an ideology that stressed
a total reformation, providing an aspiration that was
uniquely reformist; no other party ever defined it so
clearly and acutely.

The new human model for the reformists was the
Victorian gentleman, an image offering a middle class
ideal that would enable them to acquire social prestige.
Because this notion was so vague, anybody acting like a
gentleman could be considered one. Manners, conduct,
speech, education and etiquette formed a gentlemanly
persona and Victorian Jews could easily conform to such
requirements. The lifestyle, formalities and conventions
of upper class Englishmen were very appealing and,
naturally, the desire to adopt them was strong. Unlike
Continental societies, Victorian England played down racial
or ethnic distinctions, so by imitating the right forms,
Jews could make themselves more acceptable in their environment. This was the substitute they found for the
unattractive Ghetto mentality that had become anachronistic
as integration into British society advanced throughout
the century. All emancipationists, particularly reformists,

felt the need to promote the Anglicization of English
Jews and preached it consistently.

The reformist ideology was widely circulated through
the highly influential Jewish Chronicle. Founded in 1841
and a power in the Jewish world since 1844, the newspaper
felt committed to the advancement of liberal and progressive ideas. Like the Reform Party, it was strongly
dissatisfied with the Anglo-Jewish establishment and
launched fierce attacks on the paternalism of the elite.
The Jewish Chronicle And Workingman's Friend represented
the Jewish proletariat by giving full expression to their
grievances. On a number of occasions, the newspaper
denounced "Jewish warehousemen, shopkeepers, bankers and
masters" who refused to employ or apprentice Jewish workers,
supposedly because the latter would abstain from labor
on the Sabbath.[19] It also reprimanded the governing bodies
of the community for their reluctance to increase welfare
and poor relief, which the Deputies considered of individual philanthropic concern. Above all, the organ spoke
boldly against discrimination based on religious observance
in matters of employment:

> It cannot be conceived as possible that every stead-
> fastness of faith which so peculiarly distinguishes
> our working classes and which so especially entitled
> them to our warmest respect and admiration, sustained
> as it is with so much difficulty and amid so many
> privations, should be turned as a weapon of destruc-
> tion against them, to debar them from obtaining the
> only reward their honest industry requires, the means
> of support for themselves and their families.[20]

The Jewish Chronicle was one of the most ardent
emancipationist voices heard inside the community. It
advocated a relentless, even militant, campaign for the
removal of the civil disabilities. The newspaper had no
reservations in this matter: it was ready to stir public
opinion, to agitate the question across the country, to
demonstrate and protest until the goal had been achieved.
Joseph Mitchell, one of the proprietors, organized the
1840s mass agitation in support of Rothschild's admission
to Parliament. He was a leader of "The Jewish Association
For The Removal Of Civil And Religious Disabilities", a
working class organization that labored for the cause
during the critical phase in 1847-48.

Abraham Benisch, editor and driving spirit of the
Chronicle, was one of the most zealous emancipationists
in London. Born in Bohemia in 1811, Benisch attended
Vienna University, where in the late 1830s he was the mover
in forming a society for the restoration of Jews to
independence in Palestine. He came to England in 1841

and continued his proto-Zionist efforts, which were
exceptional at the time. In 1842 he became editor of
Voice of Jacob; later he founded the Hebrew Observer
and in 1854 became editor of Jewish Chronicle And
Hebrew Observer, after the two newspapers amalgamated.
During his editorship, Benisch exercised an enormous
influence on Jewish opinion and his position was compared
to John Delane's. Benisch expected English Jews to labor
relentlessly for the cause and once even expressed the
wish that they would identify with the political party
that sponsored emancipation:

> By way of introduction we will state that although
> in politics these columns, exclusively devoted to
> the religious, moral, intellectual and social
> interests of the Jewish community, are neutral, we
> belong from conviction to the Liberal party; and
> we must trust that our pages have and will at all
> times reflect these sentiments.[21]

Benisch's political radicalism was evidently a product
of the Central European reality he lived in for a long
time, but in England it could not captivate the imagination
of most emancipationists. The expectations he expressed
were often at variance with their idea of the struggle
for emancipation. The Jewish Chronicle frequently
recorded accusations of indifference, apathy and lack of
interest in emancipation, which most activists would have
probably viewed as unjustified.

The newspaper promoted religious reform and manifested hostility toward the narrow-mindedness and
exclusiveness of the unreformed creed. "Away with all
the burdensome lumber that bids defiance to understanding
and sets reason at naught; away with all the false precepts
which pretending to make man serve his creator better,
make him serve his fellow creatures worse."[22] According
to this perspective, the Jewish heritage ought to be
accommodated to liberality, modernity, progress and
enlightenment through a thorough reform.

As for the problematic issue of Zion, the newspaper
maintained that all aspirations for restoration to the
Biblical homeland were purely anachronistic. The idea
was manifested explicitly throughout the era of
emancipation, despite Benisch's peculiar position on the
subject. An 1860 article, for example, stated that
restoration to Zion was a vague dream for an indefinite
future because it depended on too many political circumstances over which Jews had no control.[23] The nationality
of Jews was English, their commitments primarily to Britain
and their attachment to the country of their domicile:
"English blood circulates through our veins; we have been

born and bred in a land where the plant of liberty has
ever flourished as in its native soil; we have imbibed
that noble pride which is inseparable from free born
Englishmen."[24] Despite the readiness to cultivate the
cultural aspects of Jewishness, the Chronicle generally
shared the conviction that no deviations were acceptable
with regard to their national identity.

The majority of Anglo-Jewry adopted the attitude of
a conservative leadership affiliated with orthodox
congregations and attached to the Board of Deputies.
This party sought to obtain civil rights without giving up
its Jewish identity; the conservative element rejected
all concessions; the more liberal element was willing to make
some adjustment to a secular way of life. All members
of this party acted through the traditional communal institutions, all strongly identified as Jews and all
cherished the communal autonomy. Within this party one
can distinguish three factions: the orthodox group led
by Montefiore and Louis Cohen, the liberal-conservative
headed by Rothschild, and the radical-activists who followed Salomons.

Moses Montefiore was the most prominent leader of
the orthodox group. At that time he lived as a retired
country-gentleman, sharing his time with the East Cliff
Estate in Ramsgate and his Park Lane residence in London.
In the early stages of the struggle, Montefiore was keen
for the cause but when faced with difficulties and strong
opposition in Parliament, he apparently modified his
views. As President of the Board from 1835, Montefiore
was reluctant and unenthusiastic. He objected to organized public agitation and minimized the Deputies'
involvement in the campaign. His diaries show the fear
that integration and secularization might clash with the
tenets of religion. As an orthodox Jew, he felt the strains
in his own political life. When approached in 1837 by
William Thornborrow with an appeal to offer his candidacy for the shrievalty of London and Middlesex, Montefiore
refused. Only after being pressed with the argument that
his election would be meaningful to the progress of
emancipation, did he yield, and then with stipulations
that he would not attend church services and at all city
feasts he would be allowed his own meat and dishes.[25]

After his election to sheriff, Montefiore was
congratulated by friends but was far from comfortable in
his new office. The sheriffs' inauguration dinner, for
instance, fell on the commencement of the Jewish new year,
and he realized he would have to walk to the Guildhall
instead of going in his carriage.[26] On July 6, 1837,
he dined at the Old Bailey with the mayor, sheriffs and
other distinguished persons. Montefiore ate on dishes

sent from his home and noticed "that everybody was most
attentive to him", which he appreciated, but still felt
uncomfortable.[27] He also revealed his tension in an
interesting letter addressed to his confidant, Louis
Loewe. Montefiore wrote about his conversation with the
Assize Judges, Lord Denman and Baron Alderson, on the subject
of Sabbath observance and the sheriff's duty to attend
services in church. The two judges proved liberally inclined,
so Montefiore was always excused on such occasions. However, one notices the embarrassment the conventional and
conforming Montefiore felt, even though he had "thus had
the happiness to perform my duty to God by the strict
observance of the Sabbath, and with not only the consent
but the approbation of the judges."[28] His devotion to
orthodoxy was great, so he could easily ignore criticism
and reservation. "Let them call me a bigot if they like;
it is immaterial to me what others do or think in this
respect."[29]

Montefiore's efforts on behalf of emancipation were
proportionate to his desire for it. He wanted a peaceful
agitation that would focus on specific grievances and lead
to a gradual settlement. Solutions to specific problems
ought to be found behind closed doors, through negotiations
with politicians at dinner parties and receptions. His
aversion to popular organization was compatible with his
paternalistic attitude toward public affairs. As far
as he was concerned, emancipation was not the crucial
matter on the agenda. Far more pressing were the opression
of Jewish minorities overseas and the development of
religious life inside the community.

The same attitude was manifested by the two chief
rabbis of the period. Solomon Hirschell, who served in
this office for forty years until his death in 1842, was
a highly conservative figure. He wore a fur hat and his
beard was untrimmed. He had no formal education, rarely
did he preach in public and he spoke English only when
necessary. His literary production was virtually nothing.
He preached in Yiddish and strongly opposed even mild
reforms. In 1836 Goldsmid asked Hirschell to endorse
a pamphlet on emancipation, but he said that even though
he would not take a hostile position, he feared that those
who entered public life would be forced to "transgress
the commandments". Hirshcell's successor, Nathan Marcus
Adler, came from Hanover and was far more adjusted to
modernity. He preached in English, dressed in the fashion
of the time and was involved in public life. His tenure
of office marked a new era in the history of the rabbinate,
for he provided a persona modeled after the Protestant
ministry. But Adler's innovative ventures were limited
to the sphere of decorum. Otherwise, he leaned heavily
toward conservatism and was uncompromising with regard

to religious reforms. He refused to repeal the excommunication of the Burton Street Congregation. On
emancipation, he was ambivalent. He signed a number of
petitions and wrote a letter to the _Times_ repudiating the
allegation that he was indifferent to the removal of the
disabilities,[30] but in general, he was largely uninvolved
in the campaign and rather cool toward organized Jewish
endeavors.

The orthodox element was strongly represented on
the Board of Deputies by Louis Cohen (1799-1882). For
two generations Cohen was a commanding figure in the
Anglo-Jewish community and shared prominently in its
management of affairs. He was a colleague and generally
active supporter of Montefiore. On the Board of Deputies
he exercised great influence and was the main authority
on its existing constitution. Cohen became a member of
the stock exchange in 1819 and served on committees for
fifteen years. The firm of Louis Cohen & Sons was founded
by him. He had a special liking for the science of Botany
and was a fellow of the Royal Botanical Society.

Cohen believed the Deputies should refrain from
taking part in the campaign, concentrating instead on the
traditional functions they had always fulfilled. He
represented the kind of Anglo-Jewish orthodoxy that dominated the governing institutions. Both he and his wife,
Floretta Keyser, the first Anglo-Jewish female Hebrew
instructor, easily integrated into a secular world. Their
religious observance was no barrier to their social
acceptance and assimilation; their portraits in the London
Jewish Museum reveal a couple indistinguishable from other
wealthy English people of the period. Louis Cohen looks
clean shaven and his wife wore no wig, but was elegantly
dressed in the current fashion. The Montefiores, the
Cohens and other orthodox Anglo-Jewish families of the
same milieu associated with non-Jews, enjoyed the pleasures
of this world and seemed perfectly at home in their class
and time. Their orthodoxy was no problem during the process
of assimilation.

Then why were they reserved about the removal of the
disabilities? Two reasons may explain the caution, restraint
and ambivalence entertained in this circle. First, many
were sympathetic to Conservatism and refused to associate
with Liberalism for the sake of emancipation. Secondly,
they wished to avoid excessive public attention because
of the harm it might produce. Experience had taught them
to avoid the limelight.

A large number of English Jews inclined toward Toryism.
Louis Cohen was a Tory, and Montefiore, although discreet
about his political views, is reported to have voted in

elections for Conservative candidates.[31] Montefiore was
a conservative by conviction, believing in an hierarchical
order and authoritarian government. He was created baronet
upon his own request, after the recommendation of Peel
in 1846. In 1833, when informed that Henry Brougham had
spoken illiberally of Jews in Parliament during a debate
on the Jewish question, he instantly exclaimed 'so much
for Whig friends'. Other conservative Jews also believed
that from their point of view, the Tory ideology was
advantageous or at least, that full Jewish identification
with one political party was imprudent.

The Voice of Jacob warned the Jewish electors that
too exclusive a support of Liberalism could undermine their
position in the country: "It would be an extreme case,
in which we would wish to see our brethren meddling with
party politics, as Jews; for it is much more honourable
to them to continue acting upon their respective convictions of what would best promote the interests of their
native country, on the broad view, than unite for any object
merely sectional." On the same occasion the October 27,
1843 newspaper issue stressed that the Tory ideology was especial
appealing to Jews because it sustained 'established authority'. On March 28, 1845, the newspaper again stated that
"considering the conservative characteristics of Judaism,
it is not strange to find so many of its professors
conscientiously impelled to support the government, even
when their own civil and political interests have been
obviously identified with those of the Liberal party."
British Jews owed a particular gratitude to Sir Robert
Peel, who lent his strongest support to their protests
and demonstrations during the Damascus persecution of 1840.
Although impressed by the sympathy shown by Palmerston
and other Liberals, the Jews found that the moving spirit
behind the public response to their call was a Tory
leader.[32]

Indicative of the orthodox position was the letter
of 'A Liberal-Conservative' correspondent of the Hebrew
Observer, Edward Falk of Southampton. The writer described
how the Tory councilman of his town, Mr. Stebbing, passed
a resolution to petition Parliament to emancipate English
Jews. The 1853 petition was signed by 75% of the total
population of 40,000, including clergymen, parish clerks,
sextons and other officials of the established church.
Jews like Falk, who supported Stebbing, welcomed the motion.

One object of addressing you is to remove the charge
of lukewarm feeling in the community at large, and
the second to put aside the stigma endeavoured by
certain parties to attach to the Liberal-Conservative
Jews of this town in voting for candidates who were
opposed to the measure and to show that Conservatism
is not in opposition to the same; Mr. Stebbing, the

gentleman who proposed the resolution at the Town
Council, is a staunch Conservative.[33]

Yet the writer admitted that many Orthodox Jews who voted
for Stebbing were far from enthusiastic about emancipation
because they suspected it would accelerate assimilation
and damage the practice of the Jewish religion.

The second motive that may explain the ambivalence
of conservative Jews about emancipation was the fear of
increased public attention to the Jewish minority. After
all, the Dissenting Deputies who represented a far more
powerful and numerous minority acted cautiously during
the struggle for their own civil rights for the same
reason. Anti-Jewish sentiments still pervaded wide circles
and there were good reasons to keep a low profile. In
Parliament, the reactionary wing of the Tory party expressed
stereotyped, usually derogatory, views on Jews and Judaism.
Their speeches produced feedback in the country. Jews
were often depicted as Christ-killers, usurers and exploit-
ers. William Cobbett specialized in this genre and his
Political Register surpassed all other publications in
insulting the Jews. "My dislike for the Jews is that which
our forefathers had of them; I dislike them as insolent
ruffians, who mock at the religion and morality of Christians;
I dislike them as people that never work and form a body
of wretches who live by trick; I dislike them as usurers
and the great agents of these systems of usury by which
so many nations have so severely suffered, and this nation
above all others."[34] An anonymous pamphleteer admitted
in 1848: "Thank God, I have no prejudices, but I do hate
the Jews."[35] That serious anti-Jewish feelings could be
aroused by the debates over emancipation was clearly
suggested in 1829. According to the Times, the Bishop
of Norwich, on going through his diocese to confirm, was
insulted in public several places for having espoused
Jewish emancipation. At Ipswich the church walls were
covered with placards stating that "the next day being
Saturday, his Lordship could confirm the Jews, and the
day following the Christians."

No less unpleasant were the sneers and bigoted remarks
of pro-emancipationist liberals. Lord Glenelg, for example,
said in Parliament in 1852, that the Irish people were
responsible for a debt of seven and a half million pounds,
including 'interest, at a rather Jewish rate'. The Jewish
Chronicle was infuriated by this remark[36] made by a
sympathetic and liberal-minded person. The Times, one
of the most ardent supporters especially during the editorship of John Delane from 1841 to 1877, nevertheless published
comments offensive to English Jews. Its editorial of
January 30, 1830, for instance, portrayed them as apathetic
to their own emancipation and hinted that if a financial
gain were at stake, Jews would have acted far more

enthusiastically. In December, 1852, the <u>Times</u> attacked
Disraeli's budget with derogatory references to his ancestral
religion. The <u>Chronicle</u> immediately responded in an
article titled "The Times and Its Abuse Of The Jews",
stating that the matter had nothing to do with Disraeli's
Jewish origins.[37] Advocates of emancipation like <u>Punch</u>
could present most derogatory and stereotyped Jewish images
that were sources of embarrassment to Anglo-Jewry. "The
firm advocate in Parliament of the claim of the Jews", the
anonymous writer of <u>The British Jew To His Fellow Country-
men</u> (1833) complained, could abuse them in public or sneer
at them in private; "yet we see this very individual, this
noble minded man still in some measure, within the power
of the tyrant prejudice and demonstrating the same in one
of the noblest, wisest, ablest orations ever uttered within
the walls of Parliament or of any other assembly, in which
he introduces 'Jew jobbing of seats in the House of Commons'".
The emancipationists were perplexed by the contradiction
between the enlightened endorsement of emancipation on
universalistic grounds and the personal bigotries of the
same advocates.

Such were the reservations maintained by the right
wing of the Jewish establishment, but the center and left
had no such scruples. Here religious opinions were less
rigid and exacting and emancipation was espoused wholeheartedly. The moderate conservative party included
people like the Rothschilds, Henry Keeling and Rabbi Morris
J. Raphall.

Rothschild assumed the leadership in 1847, following
his success at the polls. Inside Anglo-Jewry he was
identified as a moderate who favored a limited degree of
religious reforms, liberalization of communal government
and conciliation with the Reform secession. But Rothschild
would not strive to promote such causes and generally backed
rabbinic authority, even when it was autocratic. Thus,
he was attacked on a number of occasions for keeping silent
during the violation of liberal principles. A letter to
the editor of the <u>Chronicle</u> signed by N. Solomon of London
summarized the dissatisfactions with the Jewish Baron. The
writer chided Rothschild for acquiescence in the orthodox
refusal to bury the Barbados-born merchant and religious
reformer Benjamin Elkin (1783-1848). Elkin had a burial
plot in the cemetery of the Great Synagogue, but was denied
burial there because of his excessive leanings toward
Reform. Solomon also accused Rothschild of silently
ignoring the excommunication of the Burton Street Congregation,
an act which seemed at odds with the Baron's liberal convictions. Finally, Rothschild was blamed for the rank
and file apathy pervading the campaign, for he resolutely
disregarded all organizational attempts to promote the
cause. "Before I conclude, I take the liberty to ask the

Jewish Association how they relished being deserted by the
magnate whom they fondly hoped would have honoured their
last public meeting in presiding over its deliberations."[38]

The main charge against Rothschild was the neglect
of potential middle and lower class Jewish support of
emancipation. On April 6, 1847, the Chronicle lamented the
exclusion of the masses from the campaign, mainly because
of the leaders' 'spirit of exclusiveness, which seems
to rely upon the few instead of the many.' On May 21, 1858,
the newspaper complained that "Baron Rothschild clearly
disregarded the whole Jewish body in this question. He
considered it partly personal and partly that of the
Liberals." The editorial stated that when the Deputies
tried to organize agitation for the promotion of the cause
during the year 1857, their services were turned down.
After the 1857 election, the newspaper felt obliged to
reproach Rothschild for the complete neglect of his Jewish
constituents. "As the baron had failed to show the Jewish
electors that special regard which is generally evinced
by candidates to any numerous body whose support it is
desired to gain, as he evinced no public meeting of Jews
for the purpose of addressing them ... We were sorely
afraid lest slighted self love (shall we say self esteem?)
should vent itself by hanging back at the critical moment."

Rothschild's aloofness was ascribed to snobbery and
lack of respect for his inferiors. Perhaps he entertained
such sentiments, but the distance he kept was also founded
on a conscious and carefully considered strategy. Lionel
de Rothschild did not want the public to identify him as
the Parliamentary representative of the Jewish community.
He did not want organized Jewish support or a distinct
Jewish pressure group. Rather he chose to appeal to the
whole Liberal interest of the City, indeed of the country.
A separate Jewish association would not only be unnecessary
but a positive disadvantage and not only for Rothschild.
Jewish emancipation was and must be seen as a Liberal cause,
and the Jews would do wisely to promote it by affiliating
with the Liberal Party. A Jewish elector of the City
cogently expressed what Rothschild and his followers had
in mind in a letter to the Chronicle (January 4, 1850).
No Jew should expect any benefit from Rothschild's admission
to Parliament, he argued, because the Baron did not represent a Jewish constituency. That Jews would particularly
gain from Rothschild's presence in Parliament was a
consequence, but he could not commit himself to any distinct
Jewish interest. English Jews should regard the Baron only
"as their champion and in his person strive for the
establishment of their rights as Englishmen, rights hitherto
unjustly withheld."[39]

The idea was put even more strongly by an anonymous correspondent of Voice of Jacob who, on July 30, 1847, expressed vehement opposition to the agitation organized by the working class "Jewish Association For The Removal Of Civil And Religious Disabilities". The activities of this body, he complained, were 'inopportune in time' because the Liberals had already declared their support of Rothschild and hence, transformed the question from a narrow sectarian issue into a national concern. The Jewish Association might "clash with the powers already in operation and hence it might provoke opposition from quarters which have hitherto looked on positively, only because the cause was Liberal and not Jewish." The anonymous elector concluded with the comment: "I cannot refrain from expressing the hope that this society, if it will be not still born, will soon die of inaction, indeed, such an anticipation is by no means unreasonable when it is born in mind that Baron Rothschild, when addressing an almost exclusively Jewish public at Sussex Hall, passed over its existence in profound silence." Another letter to the same newspaper, printed on October 22, 1847 and signed by Amicus Judaeorum, similarly tried to dissuade Jews from 'injudiciously agitating' the question before the debates in Parliament had started, because a separate protest might alienate the Liberals.

Rothschild's policy was to insist on his right of admission to the House of Commons. He did not try to force himself or attract attention by stormy scenes during Parliamentary sessions. He waited patiently until others concurred with his claim. Rothschild disapproved of the course taken by Salomons in 1851 and he expressed his criticism in public.[40] Even though he exposed himself to radical attacks inside the Jewish community, he gained sympathy both from Liberals and the wide public. As for his attitude to Jewish agitation, one can only state that he reflected the narrowness and limitation of nineteenth century liberalism.[41]

Whereas Hirschell and Adler chose to remain uninvolved in the struggle for emancipation, a number of clergymen felt differently. Aaron Levy Green (1821-1883), in 1851 second reader of the Great Synagogue and later preacher of the Old Portland Street Synagogue, publicly defied one of the staunchest foes of Jewish emancipation, the Rev. George Croly, in an eloquent pamphlet.[42] The most respected religious authority backing the cause was Morris J. Raphall (1798-1868), rabbi, author and publisher. Raphall once acted as secretary to Solomon Hirschell and there did translations from Maimonides, Albo and Herz Wessely. In 1841 he was appointed minister of the Birmingham Synagogue and master of its school. He continued in these capacities for eight years and then sailed

to New York in 1849 where he served as rabbi and preacher
of Bnei Yeshurun congregation until 1866.

Raphall believed emancipation was essential for the
Jew to exist in the modern world. He urged his co-
religionists to do everything they possibly could in
pursuit of the cause.

> As society is now constituted, it is impossible that
> exceptional laws should be applied to any class of
> men, singling the Jews out, rating them below the
> rest of their fellow citizens, and denying them a
> participation in rights enjoyed by all around them.
> It is impossible that such a state of things should
> exist without, in some (considerable) degree, impairing
> the harmony of the social systems. [43]

Raphall wanted active agitation, including an organized
Jewish interest group that would labor outside Parliament.

Emancipation, for him, did not necessitate any sac-
rifice of Jewishness. On the contrary, assimilation to
Christian society required better Jewish acquaintance with
their own culture and the ability to demonstrate its
achievement in the non-Jewish environment. Emancipation
had an internal value - the strengthening of commitments
to a Jewish way of living - which could be achieved through
education, diffusion of knowledge and the development of
the cultural aspects of the Jewish heritage. Once emancipated, Raphall predicted, Jews would be expected to speak
up for their own tradition so they should prepare at once
by studying the literature, rabbinic sources and observances
of Judaism. "Even now, when the proclamation of emancipation has become law in some countries, and is about to
come in many more, even now the Talmud is still the rule
of conduct to most Jews, who revere it as the pilot under
whose auspices they not only weathered the storm, but
hope once more to enter the heaven which the God of their
fathers deigned to promise should again be open to receive
them."[44]   In other words, there was no reason assimilation
should lead to the abandonment of rabbinic Judaism. No
one had asked English Jews to give up their religion, and
if they knew how to present it properly, they could easily
make it acceptable to the Christian world. Raphall's
experience with the Hebrew Review And Magazine Of Rabbinic
Literature suggested he was right. There was a strong
general interest in this attempt to popularize Jewish
knowledge, as indicated by the number of subscriptions
from non-Jews.

The left wing of the Jewish mainstream was represented
by David Salomons, whose attitudes were generally close
to the Reform Party, though he never broke completely

with Jewish orthodoxy and for the most part collaborated
with the Deputies. Yet Salomons left no doubt he wanted
a militant campaign and active agitation on behalf of
emancipation. In 1835 he wrote in a pamphlet: "Conscious
of the injustice of their cause, the Jews of England can
never cease pressing it on the legislature, until they
are placed on a parity with those of their fellow citizens,
whose tenets also differ from the doctrines of the
Established Church."[45] At a certain point he expressed
his willingness to collaborate with the Jewish Association,
so the Jewish Chronicle could consider him the most
suitable candidate to lead the popular agitation of the
cause.[46] But Salomons, too, remained skeptical about
Jewish organized efforts and preferred to fight as a
Liberal. In 1844, the Voice of Jacob noticed Salomons'
desire to separate the Jewish issue from his own election
as alderman for the Portsoken Ward. "So little has
Mr. Salomons desired to make the election a religious matter,
that the original deputation inviting Mr. S. to stand,
scarcely contained two Jews." Nonetheless, he received
massive support from 'the poorest and least educated
classes of the Jews' in the ward. In his campaigns Salomons
chose to stress the general grievance of discrimination
because of religious opinions, applicable to all nonconformists.

While on the Board of Deputies, Salomons tried to
reconcile the differences between the mainstream and the
Reform party. He disapproved of the illiberal majority
positions on the exclusion of the Burton Street Congregation
from the Board, the right of solemnizing marriages and
the parliamentary grants allocated for religious education.
In 1853, in consequence of Montefiore's unfair vote for
the exclusion of Reform delegates from representation in
the Board, he resigned his membership as the Deputy of
the New Synagogue. As an ardent emancipationist and
staunch Liberal, Salomons could not acquiesce in banishment based on religious beliefs.

Salomons' attitude toward his Jewishness was problematic. Basically he was a secularist and Jewishness
was only a religious affiliation. He was involved in
communal affairs, a leading patron of the Westminster
Jews' Free School and an active member of the New
Synagogue. But he had other loyalties as well and
sometimes they came first. Salomons would occasionally
attend the synagogue, celebrate the holidays and adhere
to the rites of passage. But he drew a sharp distinction
between attendance and orthodox observance. In 1857 he
strongly objected to the maintenance of rabbinic divorces,
which the House of Lords was ready to legalize for Jewish
subjects. In 1850 he fully identified with a Jewish drive
to retain control over burial grounds against the explicit

new avenues to Anglicization. Its hero, David Salomons,
"was an excellent representative of the English gentleman"
of whom the Jewish community "might feel proud". Aristocratic, elegant, reserved, well-mannered and patriotic,
Cohen was the epitome of an Anglo-Jewish assimilationist.
English culture, lifestyle and manners were highly
appealing; they were the sources of Britain's greatness
and the causes of her superiority. The merit of
Anglicizing, he pointed out in his 1853 The Lords And
The Jews, was that one could retain his Judaism untouched.
It did not necessitate the repudiation of Jewishness as
long as the Jew proved his eagerness to acculturate.
Cohen publicly demonstrated his Jewish affiliations:
for fifteen years he served as President of the Board of
Deputies (1881-1895), he patronized Jews' College and
was deeply attentive to Jewish education.

One important question about Anglo-Jewry remains.
What was the attitude of the majority toward emancipation?
Did they share the ambivalence and apathy of the
conservative elite? A number of Jewish historians, most
notably Judge Israel Finestein, are impressed by
contemporary evidence that most Jews were indifferent to
their own emancipation.[48] This attitude was undoubtedly
embraced by a portion of the community, but a considerable
part, if not the majority, of Jewry was anxious to advance
emancipation and agitated the cause whenever the occasion
arose.

If the popular Jewish activity is often obscured,
it must be remembered that the leading emancipationists
deliberately discouraged the masses from participating
in the struggle. Neither did non-Jewish advocates ask
for popular demonstrations. Among the numerous letters
addressed to I. L. Goldsmid by Christian sympathizers,
only a few, such as the Marquis of Westminster's and
M. L. Mozley's, urged the organization of a movement
for promoting civil rights. Lord Holland and Robert
Grant resisted such endeavors. The rank and file of
Anglo-Jewry was advised by its best friends to remain
cautious and restrained as Jews and demonstrate their
sentiments through existing political institutions, such
as the Liberal Party and the municipal town councils.
The response proved highly satisfactory.

One should also keep in mind the difficulaties of
recruiting broad support during the early years of the
campaign before the Anglo-Jewish press or Sussex Hall
existed. Furthermore, the prevalence of conformity to
current social values among middle class Jews prevented
the majority from agitating the cause as fiercely as
Continental Jewries might have done. Expressions of radical
protest were toned down in Victorian middle class circles

and the Jews naturally absorbed the prevalent negative attitude toward radical dissension.[49]

The earliest report about popular activity on behalf of emancipation dates from the year 1828 and arose from an advertisement by the secretary of the Parliamentary Agent For The Relief Of The Jews In England, Samuel Levy Keyzer. The secretary called upon other persons interested in Jewish freedom to convene in the London Tavern to discuss the issue. No other information pertaining to this organization is accessible, with the exception of a letter published in the Observer of August 18, 1828. Keyzer urged sympathizers to assemble "for the purpose of preparing a petition to both Houses of Parliament, and of adopting such other measures as may appear conducive to obtaining an object so honourable to this community as the removal of legal disabilities under which the Jews now labour."

In the early 1830s, the campaign drew limited public interest and even Parliamentary debates were not well attended. The conservative opposition, however, took advantage of this situation to diffuse rumors that most Jews were either hostile or indifferent to emancipation. In response to these allegations, the leading emancipationists sent a letter to Robert Grant, in which they stated:

> We understand that an attempt has lately been made
> to diffuse a report that only two or three indi-
> viduals among the Jews take a warm interest in the
> removal of the disabilities affecting them and that
> the community in general and even the most
> influential of the persons who compose it regard
> the subject with indifference. After the presenta-
> tion within the last few weeks of a petition signed
> by a thousand of Jewish inhabitants of London in
> which they stated their extreme anxiety to see that
> measure carried into effect, and also of similar
> petitions from almost every part of the country where
> Jews reside, it may well be considered superfluous
> labour to deny the truth of the report to which we
> have referred.[50]

The claim made in this letter can be easily substan-
tiated by independent evidence of numerous petitions from
Jews all over the country. As Baron Rothschild correctly
observed in 1857 in response to similar allegations, it
was evident that favorable petitions throughout the struggle
came from those parts of the country where Jews lived,
whereas those against "emanated from all parts of the
country which, from lack of intercourse with Hebrews, could
not possess any practical knowledge of them."[51] Apparently,

this argument convinced Lord Holland to speak with Lord
Grey and other members of the Whig cabinet for the purpose
of "removing the false and injurious impression of your
brethren being insensible or unthankful to those who exert
themselves in promoting their just claims."[52]

In June, 1841, in preparation for Parliamentary
elections, a crowded meeting of the electors of the Portsoken Ward was held and the Morning Chronicle of June 23rd
observed that among the participants was a large number
of Jews. The meeting concluded with a resolution promising
support to the four Liberal candidates for the representation of the City. Mayer Rothschild, whose entrance
was loudly cheered, was unanimously called to the chair
and he opened the evening with an address that was
received warmly. In March, 1844 the Portsmouth town council
petitioned Parliament to remove the Jewish disabilities.
The moving spirit behind the initiative was the Jewish
Tory councilman Emanuel Emanuel.[53]

Meanwhile, David Salomons offered his candidacy for
the Aldermanic seat of Portsoken Ward and he won the
election because of the massive Jewish support. Montefiore
and Anthony de Rothschild were present at the poll to
solicit support on his behalf.[54] After the election,
Jewish workingmen subscribed twenty pounds to a testimonial in his honor. They held a meeting at the Mart
Coffee House to collect the money and there decided to
continue the collection at a mass meeting at the Three
Nuns Tavern in Aldgate.[55] The Jewish Chronicle was proud
that the initiative came from workingmen.[56] During this
meeting, J. L. Miers, a worker, proposed to form clubs
promoting emancipation like the Roman Catholics had formed
during the 1820s. A Mr. Jones, also a laborer, seconded
the proposal and held it to be "disgraceful that the Jews
should be the only body in the country labouring under the
badge of civil disqualification. Catholics, dissenters
and every other Christian sect had succeeded in throwing
off their shackles, and why should not the Jews succeed?"
And after Salomons' rejection from the Court of Aldermen,
his supporters petitioned the mayor against the exclusion;
eight out of the thirteen signatures on the petition can
be identified as Jewish.[57]

Toward the end of 1844, David Barnett, a Jewish
alderman of Birmingham, urged his town council to appeal
to Westminster in favor of English Jews.[58] In July, 1847,
a large meeting of electors of the Aldgate, Portsoken,
Billingsgate and Tower Hamlets Wards assembled at Sussex
Hall to encourage the Liberal candidates, two of whom,
Lionel de Rothschild and Sir George Larpent, addressed
the meeting.[59] In these four wards, there was a heavy
concentration of lower and middle class Jews. In Birmingham,

the Jewish electors defeated one of their staunchest
adversaries, Richard Spooner. The latter had divided with
the Tory reactionaries in Parliament and now asked the
Jewish population for support. A heated debate developed
during the election meeting in which Spooner addressed
the Jews, but it was decided unanimously to vote against
him.[60] In Portsmouth, a Jewish activist arranged Jewish
support for advocates of the cause, Mr. Baring and Sir
George Staunton.[61]

The most remarkable proletarian participation was
through the Jewish Association For The Removal Of
Civil And Religious Disabilties, active during the years
1847-48 and generally assembling at the Fishmonger's Arms,
St. James Place, Aldgate. During the days of its activity,
the Association held a number of meetings and drafted
petitions to Parliament. Founded through the initiative
of Joseph Mitchell of the <u>Jewish Chronicle</u>, it had 120
members in its prime. The Association maintained that the
Jewish agitation of the cause ought to be popular,
aggressive and democratic. In one of its assemblies in
1847, a member called S. Goldsmid said that "it had been
hinted to him that the Jews ought not to agitate the
public mind in any public question at the present time;
he, however, dissented from that opinion and considered
the present as the only time to urge their fellow citizens
to accord them civil and religious liberties. We must
agitate the question so long, till our object is obtained."
In January, 1848 the Association showed its popularity as
the masses flocked to a public demonstration under its
auspices in Sussex Hall.

> Although it had been announced that the chair would
> be taken at eight o'clock, the theatre of the
> institution, the gallery and the platform were crowded
> by the anxious visitors an hour before the time
> appointed; and the greater anxiety prevailed in the
> vicinity of the Jews' and General Literary and
> Scientific Institution. There could not have been
> less than 900 people present and hundreds had to
> go away who could not gain admittance into the
> crowded hall.[62]

Most leading emancipationists attended the meeting and
were warmly greeted, but unfortunately, they failed to
take advantage of the energy, good will and readiness to
promote the cause. Because of their conspicuous indifference, the Association lost its popularity and eventually
disbanded.

During the same years, Rothschild was aided by a number
of individual supporters who acted on their own. In April,
1848, a Jewish optician from Norwich, A. Keyzor, published

a pamphlet on Jewish emancipation.[63] Another individual
effort made at the time was Harry Harris'. The jeweler
from Truro constantly reminded public figures and Jewish
emancipationists of the need to move the question in
Parliament. Harris wrote Lord Falmouth, Lord John Russell
and Sir Robert Peel. Lionel de Rothschild thanked him
for a 1847 letter and complimented Harris for 'the zeal
and public spirit displayed by his exertions', while
Montefiore sent lengthy replies to his queries.[64] The
struggle for emancipation proved an educational experience
for active citizenship.

In May, 1852, a meeting at Sussex Hall of Jewish
electors from Tower Hamlets addressed George Thompson
and A. S. Ayrton and gave them the opportunity to face the
Jewish electors and non-electors of the ward. The
assembly was 'most numerously and respectably attended'
and the two candidates, both radical rivals of Russell,
found an enthusiastic reception in that hall.[65] During
the election meetings at Liverpool and Portsmouth in the
same year, Jewish participation was significant.[66] A
conference of Jewish electors of Norwich resolved to withdraw support from the Marquis of Douro, Wellington's son,
who had previously promised to vote for emancipation in
Parliament, but once elected divided against it.[67] In
the Norwich town council, a Jewish alderman moved that a
petition should be signed and forwarded to Westminster for
the removal of the Jewish disabilities.[68]

Not until the 1857 election was the majority of
Liberals finally persuaded of the true importance of the
Jewish vote. Russell's election by the London constituency, despite the lukewarm support of the party, proved
that Jewish emancipation could influence general political
issues. Prior to the election, the Jewish Chronicle
doubted whether Jews would come to the polls since the
election fell on the Sabbath.[69] But metropolitan Jewry
arrived in time and the result of its vote was dramatic:

> From all sides accounts reach us of the unparalleled
> enthusiasm exhibited by the mass of Jews in voting
> for Baron Rothschild. They rushed to the polling
> booths, they almost dragged their Christian
> acquaintances to the poll, persuading them to vote
> for their favourite candidates. Nor was there less
> gratitude for past services evinced to Lord John
> Russell. The noble lord, an eyewitness tells us,
> was on Saturday last just on the point of entering
> a cab, when a Jew, evidently of the working classes,
> rushed forward, gently laying hold of the object of
> his enthusiasm, exclaimed excitedly: 'Are you indeed
> Lord John Russell?', 'Yes, I am', was the reply.
> 'Then good luck to you and God bless you', was the

exclamation of the admirer. Lord John smilingly
entered the cab and drove off.[70]

London was not the only place in the country where
Jewish enthusiasm on behalf of emancipation was vividly
shown that year. In Liverpool, Jewish support secured
a Liberal victory,[71] although the city was at the time a
Tory stronghold. In Middlesex, Jews helped to defeat
the anti-emancipationist Lord Winchelsea.[72] Similar
Jewish opinion was manifested in Plymouth, where Jews
sympathized with the pro-emancipationists Mr. Collier
and Mr. White.[73] After the election Collier said:
"May I be allowed to state that the conduct of the members
of the Hebrew persuasion has been most consistent and
worthy (loud applause). They have unanimously and without
a single exception, I believe, voted for Mr. White and
me (all but one). Well, we let him pass (laughter).
I say that the members of the Hebrew persuasion have acted
most worthily and I trust, as do all true Liberals, that
their just rights will soon be conceded to them."

Even after the Liberal victory of 1857, Jewish
interest in the cause was expressed through an identification with the Party or the town councils. In May, 1857,
a Jewish resident of Penzance, a Mr. Joseph, presented
a petition in the town council and asked that it be placed
in the town hall for the collection of signatures. A
similar effort was made in Sheffield, where the moving
spirit was B. Samuel. On May 4, 1857, a public meeting
in the town hall of Tavistock considered petitioning
Parliament on behalf of the Jews. One of the major
speakers, Rev. J. Taplin, told the audience he had
contemplated acting when a plea from a Jewish gentleman,
Lewis Hyman of Plymouth, confirmed his resolution. A
portion of the expenses of the Tavistock meeting was defrayed
by Jacob Nathan, the president of the Plymouth Jewish
congregation. W. W. Alexander made a similar contribution
in Bristol.

The election of Jewish town councillors was also a
way to get involved in the struggle for civil rights.
On October 18, 1857, David Barnett once more offered his
candidacy for a seat on the Birmingham town council.
His reason for desiring to be continued was, by his own
statement, the belief that he could induce the town council
to back emancipation.[74] During the same year, Birmingham
returned another Jewish councillor, Simon King Marks.
In Hereford, Abraham Meyer was elected for the third
time for the Ledkury Ward and in Rochester, J. B. Levy
was also re-elected. "It is hardly necessary to say that
all the Jewish councillors are Liberals", the Chronicle
remarked casually.[75]

Even after obtaining full civil rights, many British
Jews continued to demonstrate their political awareness.
In May, 1859, Jewish loyalties were tested once again.
The occasion was the general election of which the results
in that constituency were reported in a letter from Bristol:
"The great struggle here being over, the Hebrews of this
city have recorded by their votes their grateful acknow-
ledgements to the Liberal cause by voting 26 to 5; while
at Cheltenham, where the polling took place on the Sabbath,
the majority for the Liberal candidate was mainly indebted
to the Jews."[76] The results of the election in Bedford
were identical.

In view of the evidence, it seems difficult to argue
that British Jews were indifferent to their own emancipation. They may not have acted as a distinct Jewish body,
but they acted vigorously in their own way. Many of them
responded willingly to the call to lend their support by
voting either for sympathetic Liberal candidates in national
elections or for Jewish candidates in municipal elections.
The Liberal Party provided a suitable means of participation
in political life and quite logically became the most
popular channel for the expression of Jewish political
awareness.

Notes

[1] *Voice of Jacob*, January 31, 1845.

[2] *Voice of Jacob*, February 28, 1845.

[3] Israel Finestein, "Anglo-Jewish Opinion During The Era Of Emancipation", *Trans. J. H. S. E.* XX (1962), 113-143.

[4] Joseph Crool, *Restoration Of Israel* (1812); "The Fifth Empire", in *A Discourse by Thirty-Six Men* (1829); *The Last Generation* (1829).

[5] *Jewish Chronicle*, July 30, 1848.

[6] *Westminster Review* 19 (1833), p. 110.

[7] Joseph Crool to Rev. I. W. Whittaker, March 24, 1828, *Jewish Museum Papers*.

[8] See Quizinus, *Cursory Glance At The Present State Of The Jewish People* (Edinburgh, 1844), probably written by Ashenheim of Edinburgh. See also Robert Liberles, "The Origins Of The Jewish Reform Movement In England", *Association Of Jewish Studies Review* 1 (1976), 121-150.

[9] *Jewish Emancipation By An Israelite* (1845). The strong negative attitude to the Oral Law was manifested by Benjamin Elkin, *Is The Oral Law Of Divine Origin And Therefore Binding On The Jews? The Question Debated By A Member Of The Community.* (1842).

[10] Reform Congregation of Burton Street to Peel, February, 1845, *Peel Papers*, B. L. ADD MSS 40560, f. 130. Peel was solicited by 'British Jews' to support or introduce a measure which would empower the Registrar General to furnish marriage registration books to any person representing more than fifty Jewish householders. I. L. Goldsmid to Peel, February 18, 1845 *Peel Papers*, B. L. ADD MSS 40560, f. 128.

[11] *Voice of Jacob*, April 8, 1845.

[12] F. H. Goldsmid, *Remarks On The Civil Disabilities Of British Jews*, p. 29.

[13] F. H. Goldsmid, A Few Words Respecting The Enfranchisement Of British Jews To The New Parliament (1833), pp. 5, 10-11.

[14] F. H. Goldsmid, The Appeal To The Congregation Of The West London Synagogue Of British Jews To Their Israelites Throughout The United Kingdom (1846), pp. 7-8.

[15] Bernard Van Oven, An Appeal To The British Nation On Behalf Of The Jews, p. 16.

[16] Bernard Van Oven, Ought Baron Rothschild To Sit In Parliament?, p. 18; See also his introduction to Debates In The House Of Lords On The Motion For The Second Reading Of The Removal Of The Civil Disabilities Of The Jews (1834); and his letter to the Times, February 3, 1830, titled "Emancipation of the Jews".

[17] Henry Faudel, A Few Words On The Jewish Disabilities Addressed To Sir Robert Harry Inglis, Bart. M. P. (1848), p. 20.

[18] Henry Faudel, Suggestions For The Jews For Improvement In Reference To Their Charities, Education And Government By A Jew (1844), p. 13.

[19] Jewish Chronicle, December 21, 1849.

[20] Jewish Chronicle, November 14, 1851.

[21] Quoted by John M. Shaftesley, "Dr. Abraham Benisch As Newspaper Editor", Trans. J. H. S. E. 21 (1968), 214-231 from Jewish Chronicle, November 20, 1860.

[22] "The Necessity of Internal Reform", Jewish Chronicle, April 11, 1848.

[23] Jewish Chronicle, February 17, 1860.

[24] Jewish Chronicle, September 27, 1848. See also "The Nationality Of The Jews", in the issue of August 4, 1848.

[25] Diaries Of Sir Moses And Lady Montefiore, Vol. I, p. 107.

[26] Diaries, p. 108.

[27] *Diaries*, p. 110.

[28] Moses Montefiore to Louis Loewe, <u>Collection Of Letters Between 1845 and 1847</u>, in possession of Mr. Raphael Loewe.

[29] *Diaries*, pp. 108-9.

[30] <u>Hebrew Observer</u>, April 15, 1853.

[31] D. C. Sebag-Montefiore, Esq. believes that Montefiore would have chosen to remain neutral in party politics because of his desire to secure permanent British support in his colonization projects. The evidence available, however, indicates that he leaned to Toryism, though he preferred to conceal his political affiliation from the public.

[32] Peel to Montefiore, June 27, 1840, <u>Letter Book Of Board Of Deputies</u>, ff. 193-4. In response to a resolution of the Deputies thanking Peel for his efforts, he replied: "I am highly gratified by the assurances contained in that resolution. From my deep conviction of the gross & cruel injustice which has been inflicted upon the Jews in the East, I shall continue to watch with great interest the proceedings that may be adopted for the purpose of eliciting the whole truth, and procuring such redress as the circumstances of the case may admit of, and if any interference on my part shall have contributed in the slightest degree to promote the course of justice and humanity in this respect, I shall derive the utmost satisfaction from the reflection."

[33] <u>Hebrew Observer</u>, March 11, 1853 & March 18, 1853.

[34] Quoted in <u>Observer</u>, June 6, 1830.

[35] '<u>Che Sara, Sara; or Lord John Russell And The Jews</u> (1848), pp. 10-11.

[36] <u>Jewish Chronicle</u>, March 26, 1852.

[37] <u>Jewish Chronicle</u>, December 10, 1852.

[38] Even the liberal Macaulay had his sneers at his Jewish friends. In 1831 he described a ball at Goldsmid's house as follows: "Yesterday night I went to the Jews ... The Company was not as we exclusives think quite a thing. There was a little too much of St. Mary Axe's about it ...

Jewesses by dozens, and Jews by scores ... I walked home quietly, but it was some time before I could get sleep. The sound of fiddles was in mine ears, and gaudy dresses and black hairs, and Jewish noses were fluctuating up and down mine eyes." T. B. Macaulay to his sister Hannah, June 8, 1831 in Thomas Pinney, ed. The Letters Of Thomas Babington Macaulay (Cambridge, 1974), Vol. II, pp. 34-36.

[39] Jewish Chronicle, February 25, 1848.

[40] Times, March 27, 1857.

[41] Jewish Chronicle, July 28, 1858.

[42] On A. L. Green see Alex M. Jacob, "Aaron Levy Green, 1821-1883", Trans. J. H. S. E. XXV (1977), 87-106; See Green's pamphlet Dr. Croly Versus Civil And Religious Liberty (Bristol, 1850).

[43] The Hebrew Review And Magazine of Rabbinical Literature, Vol. III (1836), p. 1.

[44] The Hebrew Review, p. 114

[45] D. Salomons, A Short Statement On Behalf Of His Majesty's Subjects Professing The Jewish Religion (1835), p.26.

[46] Jewish Chronicle, February 7, 1845. See also a letter signed by I.L.L. in the issue of May 10, 1852.

[47] Lucy Cohen, Arthur Cohen, A Memoir By His Daughter For His Descendants (London, 1917); Israel Finestein, "Arthur Cohen, Q. C. 1829-1914", in John Shaftesley, ed. Remember The Days (London, 1964), pp. 279-302.

[48] Israel Finestein, "Anglo Jewish Opinion ...", 125ff.

[49] On the persistent efforts to expand education during the mid-Victorian period see, London Board of Religious Education, Catalogue Of A Cenentary Exhibition Of Anglo-Jewish Education Held At The J. F. S. Secondary School (December, 1960).

[50] Abrahams, pp. 164-5.

[51] Jewish Chronicle, April 28, 1857.

[52] Lord Holland to I. L. Goldsmid, June 29, 1833, in Abrahams, p. 166.

[53] Voice of Jacob, March 6, 1844.

[54] Ibid.

[55] Jewish Chronicle, October 1, 1844.

[56] Ibid.

[57] Corporation of London Record Office, Proceedings Of The Court Of Aldermen, Vol. 248 (1843-44), f. 437. The petition is signed by: Lewis Isaac (Jewish), Moses Jacobs (J), A. Saul, James Thomson, John Robins, Jr., Isaac Isaacs (J), George Myers (J), Ch. F. Warman (J), Lewis Lazarus (J), Asher Isaacs (J), John Marton (J), Sam watkins.

[58] Jewish Chronicle, November 1, 1844.

[59] Jewish Chronicle, July 23, 1847.

[60] Jewish Chronicle, August 6, 1847.

[61] Ibid.

[62] Jewish Chronicle, February 4, 1848.

[63] Jewish Chronicle, April 28, 1848.

[64] Mocatta Miscellaneous Papers, Box IV, items 6, 8, 10, 11, 13, 14.

[65] Jewish Chronicle, June 27, 1852.

[66] Jewish Chronicle, June 18, 1852.

[67] Jewish Chronicle, July 2, 1852.

[68] Jewish Chronicle, April 28, 1853.

[69] Jewish Chronicle, March 27, 1857.

[70] Jewish Chronicle, April 3, 1857.

[71] <u>Jewish Chronicle</u>, April 10, 1857.

[72] <u>Jewish Chronicle</u>, April 7, 1857.

[73] <u>Jewish Chronicle</u>, April 17, 1857.

[74] <u>Jewish Chronicle</u>, October 2, 1857.

[75] <u>Jewish Chronicle</u>, November 6, 1857.

[76] <u>Jewish Chronicle</u>, May 2, 1859.

Chapter 3

THE STRUGGLE FOR JEWISH EMANCIPATION, 1828-1860

The Early Years, 1828-1840

The campaign for the removal of Jewish disabilities
began in 1828 in connection with the repeal of the Test
and Corporation Acts. When the repeal was first debated
in the House of Commons the aim was to abolish the
requirement of taking the sacrament of the Lord's Supper
in an Anglican church. The Tories, however, insisted on
substituting for this religious test a declaration that
candidates for national or municipal offices would never
use their power to injure or weaken the established
church. Although most Protestant Dissenters resented
this declaration, their United Committee decided to yield
to Tory pressure because the influential Home Secretary,
Sir Robert Peel, made the enactment of this declaration
a condition of his support for repeal. The new piece of
legislation was also seen as removing the necessity of
the legal protection granted to Nonconformists by the
annual Indemnity Acts, which had previously enabled both
them and Jews to postpone taking the oaths upon entering
office.

When Isaac Lyon Goldsmid first heard about the
proposition to enact a new declaration and to insert in
it the words 'on a true faith of a Christian', he was
startled. The new declaration, proposed by Edward
Copelston, Bishop of Llandaff, in the House of Lords, left
the Jews in a markedly more disadvantageous position than
previously. Goldsmid observed that "by the passing of
the measure of 1828 the Indemnity Act became a nullity;
and in lieu of a test which was dispensed with from year
to year, another test was introduced that was not to be
dispensed with, to which all dissenters could submit except
the Hebrews, who were thus exceptionally disqualified in
a direct and positive manner."[1]

The new clause angered the Jewish leadership who
immediately enlisted its non-Jewish sympathizers to protest.
I. L. Goldsmid asked the Duke of Sussex, Lord Holland and
Henry Brougham to raise opposition in Parliament. Lord
Holland's protest is recorded in the Journals of the
House of Lords, specifying that the insertion of the
objectionable words "imply an opinion in which I can
never conscientiously concur, that a particular faith
in matters of religion is necessary to the honest dis-
charge of duties purely political and temporal."[2] Lord
Bexley, a leading Philo-Judean despite his High Tory
convictions, was handed a petition from the Board of
Deputies for delivery to the Lords. The Deputies asked

the peers to redress the grievance caused by the enactment of the new declaration.[3] But too strong a protest
could endanger the passage of the Bill, so the Goldsmids
were persuaded by Lord Holland to accept it despite the
injustices it inflicted on Jewish subjects. The
Dissenters' United Committee also decided to put up with
the proposed measure and ceased agitating.[4] John Bowring
of the Dissenting Deputies sent a sympathetic letter to
Goldsmid on behalf of the entire committee, in which he
expressed his disagreement with the new legislation and
promised support for the future.

The damage caused by the repeal and the growing unrest among Roman Catholics stirred the Jewish Deputies
to action. Efforts to coordinate activities with Catholics
and Dissenters had already begun in 1828. On June 26,
Moses Montefiore and Nathan Mayer Rothschild met with
various committees of Nonconformists at the Duke of
Norfolk's house. Similar meetings were held on subsequent
occasions. In addition, Jewish leaders actively lobbied
in Parliament with Moses Montefiore, Nathan Mayer Rothschild
and Isaac Lyon Goldsmid using all their social and
commercial contacts to promote the issue. In March, 1829
Goldsmid was admitted to a conference of the Deputies at
the President's house where he informed the Deputies of
the support assured by Lord Holland, Lansdowne, Suffield
and Messers. Baring, Gurney, Martin and others. Goldsmid
urged Montefiore, who was less enthusiastic about Jewish
organized efforts on behalf of emancipation, to use his
own contacts to promote the cause. He called upon the
Deputies to agitate for Jewish freedom by enlisting non-
Jewish sympathizers.[5] The Deputies, however, decided
not to commit themselves at this stage and their President,
Moses Mocatta, rejected Goldsmid's proposition for total
commitment without first checking the views of the Government on the subject. Only on April 16, after Rothschild
reported conversations with Wellington and Lyndhurst and
their 'not unfavourable' position, did the Deputies decide
to endorse the cause. Rothschild strongly advised that
in the meantime nothing should be publicized or advertised
through the press, "as any controversy on the subject would
be fatal."[6]

Rothschild's caution and discretion was character-
istic. Mayer Amschel's son came to Manchester in 1797,
dealing in cotton goods, but he moved to London in 1803.
In 1806 he married Hannah, daughter of Levi Barnet Cohen
and sister-in-law of Montefiore. Thus, he became associated
with the most prestigious Anglo-Jewish family. In London,
he rapidly became the outstanding figure on the Stock
Enxhange. Because of his crucial role in financing
Wellington's Spanish campaigns during the Napoleonic Wars,
he had good contacts with the Prime Minister, and his

interventions of behalf of emancipation were of great value. Both Rothschild and Goldsmid, the two non-Deputies who had participated in the meeting at Mocatta's house, recommended a petition be drawn up and presented to the Lords. Consequently, the Board instructed its solicitor, H. P. Pearce, to prepare a petition for their approval. The petition was ready at the beginning of May and passed on to Lord Bexley. During the early days of May the Deputies resolved to draft a bill of their own. The bill was submitted to the Duke of Sussex, Lord Bexley and Dr. Lushington, but the latter discovered strong opposition from Wellington. Since the Government would not support it, there was no reason to push the matter during the current session. Sussex, Bexley and Lushington agreed the Bill should be dropped for the time being and that the Jews themselves ought to contact the Prime Minister and solicit his consent to put forth a bill during the next session.[7]

Wellington's attitude was of primary importance and is therefore worthy of special attention. His 1829 opposition to Jewish freedom was not the first occasion on which he manifested negative feelings. In 1828, he rejected Rothschild's proposal for a measure to enable Jews to own freehold land and to vote for Members of Parliament. This measure was unsuccessfully moved by the prominent politician and philosopher Sir James Mackintosh. The Duke also ignored a petition from Goldsmid in which the latter raised the problem of his son's eligibility to serve as barrister. Wellington gave the Deputies the impression that he was 'not unfavourable' to Jewish emancipation, but was obliged to postpone the issue because of circumstances. In 1829 he intimated that the Deputies ought not to pursue the matter without his consent, which he denied at present; otherwise, he would not support their claim as long as he was in office. In fact, he was entirely opposed to Jewish freedom as he was to all unnecessary reforms. Since the number of British Jews was small, Wellington believed the issue was not worth the effort. His negative attitude to social change, unless forced to reform, contrasted with the position taken by George Canning, whom he and Peel thought pursued reform 'con amore'.[8] Certainly, one of the main blocks supporting Jewish emancipation was identified by an anonymous pamphleteer as the Canningites, especially William Huskisson and the brothers Grant.[9]

Wellington played his game shrewdly. He assured the Jews he was not indifferent to their emancipation, at the same time attempting to avoid the subject. Montefiore described in his diary a February, 1829 meeting of Rothschild with the Prime Minister concerning financial affairs. Rothschild tried to raise the Jewish question but the

Duke managed to avoid the topic.[10] On February 12,
Montefiore, Goldsmid and Rothschild met the Duke once again
and though the latter promised nothing, "Mr. Montefiore[11]
had no doubt the Duke would take no part against them."

Until 1830, Lord Holland was convinced the Premier
had no objection to Jewish relief in principle. Both
Holland and Lushington believed in the good will of the[12]
ministry and consequently advocated a low key approach.
The only active participant who guessed Wellington's real
intentions was Goldsmid. He realized that Wellington and
Peel would oppose any relief measure for British Jews
"to win back some of the ground they had lost with the
High Tory party by reason of recent concessions to the[13]
Roman Catholics."   Hence, Goldsmid was sure that the
aim would not be achieved through parlimentary tactics
alone and he wanted to agitate outside the legislature
by stirring his 'city and Catholic friends'. Lord Holland,
however, disagreed with his Jewish friend at this point.
In a letter of May, 1829 Holland stated that "any
assistance or public cooperation of the sort from religious
bodies, Catholics or Protestant, would, till the consequences of the late conflict have a little subsided,[14]
be unreasonable and premature and possibly injurious."

In February 1830, the Board of Deputies met again
and resolved to draw up another petition to both Houses
of Parliament. A committee of five was appointed to
continue the negotiations with the Government: included
were Rothschild, Goldsmid, Montefiore, Mocatta and Joshua
Van Oven. The Board adopted a moderate line of action,
proclaiming that "the right to sit in Parliament should
not form so conspicuous a feature in the new bill, provided the privilege can be obtained in any other measure."[15]
The petitions were prepared and signed by Christians as
well as Jews and copies were distributed in various
bankers' and merchants' offices in London. In the City,
a subcommittee of Deputies met daily at the King's Head
Tavern in the Poultry, while in Liverpool, the leading
communal member, M. L. Mozley, stirred the public to[16]
support the Jewish effort.

The Deputies hoped to entrust the new relief bill
to their declared sympathizer Charles Grant (1778-1886,
later Baron Glenelg), M. P. for Inverness and member of
Lord Grey's and Melbourne's cabinets. But the latter
appears to have backed out and instead, his brother Robert
agreed to take care of the measure. Robert Grant's
association with the Jewish cause dissatisfied his
Inverness constituents, so he had to resign his seat. He
contested a parliamentary vacancy in Norwich and won this
seat by 2277 votes. This was the first test of a constituency's readiness to support Jewish emancipation and

fortunately, the results strengthened the cause. Lord Holland wrote I. L. Goldsmid that this was an indication of possible success and therefore he was optimistic about the prospects of the first Jewish relief bill.[17]

When the first bill for the removal of the Jewish disabilities was introduced in the House of Commons on April 5, 1830, it immediately gained the support of four distinct political sections. The most important group of sympathizers was composed of Whigs and was led by Lord Holland. Henry Richard Vassall Fox, the third Baron Holland (1773-1840) took his seat in the House of Lords in 1798, where he became at once the recognized exponent of the policy of his uncle, Charles James Fox. Lord Holland resisted in the most determined manner the sus- pension of the Habeas Corpus Act, openly denounced the union with Ireland as unjust and championed the cause of Catholic emancipation. He advocated the emancipation of the slaves in the West Indies and constantly supported all measures against slave trade. Lord Holland became Chancellor of the Duchy of Lancaster in Grey's adminis- tration, an office he held, with short intervals, till his death. But his influence was greater in his capacity as a social leader of the Whigs and in his lifetime, Holland House became the center of Whig aristocratic socializing. Holland was described by contemporaries as witty, humorous, a lover of anecdotes, friendly, vivid and above all, compassionate, generous and charitable to the helpless and the oppressed.

Religious freedom and civil rights constituted the pillars of his philosophy. Holland's Whigishness was nourished by the traditional philosophy of his party and heavily influenced by the secularist tradition of the European Enlightenment. He was not sure that his well- known libertarian views would prove an asset to the campaign for Jewish emancipation. In 1830, he urged Goldsmid to consult Lord Bexley and pass on to him a petition to Parliament: "I think he would present your case most effectively. I have no objection to speak to him, but I am not clear that the appreciation of such a Latitudinarian as I could help you with Church of England men or would be of much use."[18]

Despite his liberality, Lord Holland was deeply affected by the Whig elitism. He did not believe in Jewish agitation and did not conceal his dislike for popular participation in the struggle. The question of Jewish emancipation was then an anachronism, so he trusted it would be solved sooner or later through in- dividual efforts and without much agitation. Therefore he favored parliamentary measures alone. Jewish emancipation, for Lord Holland, was a problem for the governing elite; it should not concern the masses. He wrote of this to Goldsmid in 1830: "But the difficulty lies in raising general attention to your cause, without giving it a character which it in no sense deserved of an encroachment, an attack upon our establishment. The apprehension of the later inconveniences, very reasonably distress you from resorting to meetings, petitions & numerous popular publications."[19] He constantly discouraged his militant Jewish friend from using popular agitation in pursuit of the cause.

On the other hand, Lord Holland contributed his political experience and important connections to the campaign. Holland House became the center of advocacy of Jewish emancipation, to some extent because of Holland's personal relationship with Goldsmid. Holland House habitues such as Henry Brougham, Thomas Babington Macaulay, Sir James Mackintosh and Lord John Russell were immediately enlisted in the ranks of supporters.

A second group of sympathizers, as has been suggested, comprised the former followers of Canning, led after his death by William Huskisson. The latter collaborated with Goldsmid in founding University College and was widely known for his commitment to the establishment of religious freedom. Huskisson presented a petition from the inhabitants of Liverpool in 1830 and while doing so, he took the opportunity "to express the opinion which I have always held of the impolicy and injustice of imposing civil disabilties on account of religious opinions."[20] The Huskissonites, whether they became Tories or Whigs, strongly supported the cause after their leader's accidental death in September, 1830 and the most notable among them were the brothers Grant. Charles Grant was involved in the earlier years of the struggle. For example, he tried hard to persuade the Duke of Richmond to vote for the first relief bill.[21] His brother Robert, a Whig politician, member of Grey's cabinet and subsequently, an East India administrator, supported Jewish freedom both as a liberal and as a member of the London Society for Promoting Christianity among the Jews. Doubtless, Robert Grant was deeply influenced by religious motives, but his public advocacy was primarily based on secular grounds. Grant was so devoted to the Jewish cause he sacrificed his Scottish constituency and, after his election for Norwich, refused to accept the financial aid offered by a number of wealthy Jews to defray his election expenditure. His involvement was disinterested and his actions dictated by humanitarian sentiments.

A third party of friends consisted of Tories who promoted Jewish emancipation on purely religious grounds. They were led by Lord Bexley, formerly Nicholas Vansittart (1766-1851). For twenty-five years he sat in the House

of Commons and in Grenville's administration, following
Pitt's death, he took the Secretaryship of the Treasury.
During this office he was the first to summon Rothschild
to the assistance of the Treasury. In 1812, he became
Chancellor of Exchequer in Perceval's Government, when
he introduced a number of reforms in taxation and finances.
In 1823, he was created Baron Bexley and during the same
period, he was active as member of the London Society
and founder of the Philo-Judean group. Bexley never
concealed his conversionist expectations of the Jews after
emancipation was achieved.

Equally sincere about the hope for Jewish conversion
to Christianity was the Liberal Connop Thirlwall (1797-
1875), historian and Bishop of St. David's. As a
Cambridge tutor, he supported the admission of Dissenters
to higher degrees, an opinion for which he had to resign.
As the Bishop of St. David's he supported Maynooth Grant
(1845), the removal of Jewish disabilities and the disestablishment of the Church in Ireland. He was known for
his scholarly work and intellectual abilities.

Some prominent Evangelicals were influenced by similar arguments and so lent their support.[22] Zachary
Macaulay (1768-1838), champion of the abolition of the
slave trade, member of the Clapham Sect and editor of its
organ, the Christian Observer, for many years, openly
sympathized with the Jewish claim.[23] Macaulay expressed
his feelings in a letter addressed to I. L. Goldsmid.[24]

Finally, credit should be given to Radical circles
for their interest in Jewish emancipation. Naturally,
the Radicals advanced secularist arguments that Jewish
relief would further weaken the Church; they wanted to
see the Church less powerful as a result of religious
freedom. Prominent Radical spokesmen on behalf of
emancipation were Sir William Moleswoth, Arthur James
Roebuck, Joseph Hume, George Grote, Ralph Bernal Osborne
and John Bright. While the Chartist sympathizer Thomas
Duncombe chose to endorse the cause, Feargus O'Conner
became its staunch enemy and constantly attacked it
in the Northern Star. London Radicals played an important role, most notably William Thornborrow, Charles
Pearson, Sir George Carrol, David Wire and Samuel Gurney.
The Radicals promoted Jewish liberty and voted constantly
for it, even though they had difficulties understanding
the Jewish dilemma: Roebuck, for example, wondered on
a number of occasions why Lionel de Rothschild could
not take the oath 'on the true faith of a Christian'
and let others think whatever they liked. If he himself
were a Jew, he said in the House of Commons, he would
have taken the oath in the manner prescribed by law and
disregarded all conscientious objections.[25] A similar

position was taken by the Radical Westminster Review, whose contributor and subsequently proprietor, Colonel Thomas Perronet Thompson (1783-1869), promised support as early as 1833.[26]

Robert Grant's 1830 Bill proposed to repeal the civil disabilities affecting British subjects who professed the Jewish religion. By its provisions, "all civil rights, franchises and privileges ... offices, places, employments, trusts and confidences" that had been open to Roman Catholics would hitherto be opened to Jews. "To our infinite surprise", admitted John Cam Hobhouse, "we divided 115 to 97" and the Bill passed the first reading.[27] But the victory was short lived. The Duke of Gloucester and his wife, Duchess Sophia, went to the King and asked him to intervene against the passage of the second reading. George IV, who opposed Jewish emancipation in principle, made his resistance known to the House of Commons and evidently, his stance reinforced the reluctance of its Members. Another attempt to influence the division prior to the second reading was made by N. M. Rothschild, who, according to the Observer of April 18, 1830, tried to persuade Wellington to allow the ministers of his Government to vote according to their own opinions. The Prime Minister refused to grant the request. Thus on May 17, 1830 the Bill was defeated in the House of Commons on its second reading by a majority of 228 to 165.

The debates in the House were later described by Hobhouse as follows:

> The second reading of the Jews' Relief Bill came in on the House of Commons, when Sir R. Peel made his first appearance since his father's death and spoke against the Bill. Brougham's was the speech of the night. He was most successful but was not well heard. Too deep and too learned for the multitude. His reference to Gibbon and Bolingbroke as professed infidels, though admirably introduced, failed of effect.[28]

Henry Brougham (1778-1868) was enlisted to the campaign by Goldsmid, with whom the former collaborated during the formation of University College. Brougham became Goldsmid's friend and frequently borrowed money from the Jewish financier. In return, Goldsmid secured the support of a remarkable parliamentarian and one of the most eloquent speakers of the age. Brougham was a brilliant Whig politician, a barrister, writer and founder of Edinburgh Review. In 1830 he was created Baron Brougham and Vaux and subsequently sworn as Lord Chancellor. In his new office (1830-1834), Brougham worked with remarkable energy, encouraging law reforms and taking a leading part in all the business of the House. His involvement in the parliamentary struggle for emancipation added prestige to the Jewish campaign.

Attempts to pursue the cause of emancipation after the 1830 defeat were neglected after Wellington's fall because of the preoccupation with the Great Reform Bill. Another reason for leaving the matter at the time was the unsympathetic attitude of the new Prime Minister, Earl Grey. In 1832, Grey sent a chilly note to Lord Holland declining the latter's request to pass a relief measure during the current session.[29] Thus, despite the considerable presence of friendly politicians in the Government (Holland and the brothers Grant sat in the Cabinet; Brougham was Lord Chancellor), the issue was not pursued energetically.

The Jewish Deputies resolved, after the 1830 defeat, to neglect the cause for the time being. Lord Holland and the Duke of Sussex agreed with this policy, but the radical emancipationists wanted to act at once. Encouraged by the admission of Jews to the freedom of the City, Joshua Van Oven, Joseph Micholls and Louis Lucas urged the Board to take immediate steps to continue the struggle.[30] But the Deputies again responded negatively, so the radicals decided to act on their own. On February 7, 1831, L. Keyser appealed to the Deputies asking whether they would again petition Parliament. When he received a negative reply, Keyser requested that drafts of previous bills and petitions be forwarded to Goldsmid, who might continue the agitation of the cause.[31]

During the next few years, Goldsmid undertook the responsibility for the struggle. I. L. Goldsmid (1778-1859) was a retired businessman who had made a large fortune, partly in financing railway construction and the London docks. Since his retirement, he dedicated most of his time to philanthropy, public service and the struggle for civil rights. Goldsmid was an ambitious man who fought for social acceptance of Jews in Victorian Britain. In the 1820s he collaborated with a group of English radicals in the foundation of the non-sectarian University of London. Radical in political views, dynamic, controversial and aggressive, Goldsmid pursued the cause relentlessly. His hot temper and impulsiveness often raised the eyebrows of Jews and their sympathizers. The vehemence of the corpulent and opinionated Goldsmid became notorious during the course of the struggle and in later years he became one of the most controversial characters inside the Anglo-Jewish community.

Aided by his son, Francis Henry, and by Bernard
Van Oven, he labored on behalf of emancipation and lobbied
actively in Parliament. Goldsmid appealed to opponents
such as Sir Rober Inglis, Spencer Perceval, Earl Grey,
the Duke of Wellington, the Archbishop of Canterbury and
the Bishop of Rochester. He reminded potential supporters,
like Hobhouse, of the need to be in the House during the
divisions over Jewish relief bills.[32] A Member of the
House who had been approached by Goldsmid even apologized
to him for his absence during a 1833 division. I. L.
Goldsmid agitated constantly outside Parliament and never
let the country forget the Jewish grievance. On April
27, 1830, for example, he spoke on the Jewish disabilities
to the Port of London Society for Promoting Religion
among Seamen.[33] No less devoted was Francis Henry, whose
commitment was described by his biographer as follows:
"Night after night he was seen in the lobby, way-laying
Members as their passage to or from the House, now freely
obtaining and now earnestly entreating promises of
support."[34]

Meanwhile the Board of Deputies did not entirely
ignore the campaign. On February 9, 1831, their President,
Moses Mocatta, suggested that the Deputies appoint a
sub-committee authorized to take action in case of
emergency. The retired businessman Mocatta (1768-1857),
who had devoted his leisure to scholarship, publication
and Jewish education, was not indifferent to the cause
of emancipation. He argued that the Deputies might be
approached by the Government and might, in this case,
have to respond at once. Since he did not wish to solely
take responsibility, Mocatta wanted the appointment of
a sub-committee.[35] Clearly, he did not intend to forget
the issue. A few days later, the Deputies were asked by
I. L. Goldsmid to join a deputation to Robert Grant for
further deliberations on the subject. The Board delegated
Mocatta, Montefiore and Van Oven to accompany Goldsmid.
Unfortunately, from February, 1831 till May, 1834 the
proceedings of the Board were not recorded, so we do not
know the Deputies' position during that period. Montefiore's diaries indicate that his own attitude became
rather reserved. Evidently his skepticism arose from
the realization that the cause generated a much stronger
public opposition than he had anticipated. The King, the
prime minister, the peers, the bishops and a good portion
of the Commons were still unfavorable to the removal of
the disabilities. Under these terms, Montefiore probably
preferred to temporarily leave the matter.

On April 7, 1833, on the motion of Robert Grant,
the reformed House of Commons resolved itself into committee to discuss the removal of the Jewish disabilities.
The chamber was not full, the atmosphere was relaxed and

the debate did not generate a great deal of attention.
The motion was agreed to without a division and on
May 22 the second reading was moved and carried by a
majority of 159 to 52.[36] At the end of July, the Bill
was given a third reading in the Commons and on August 1
it was read a first time in the Lords on the motion of
Lord Bexley. The Duke of Sussex, Lord Melbourne, Lord
Brougham, the Marquis of Westminster, the Archbishop of
Dublin and the Bishop of Chichester gave their strong
support. The opposition was led by the Archbishop of
Canterbury and the Bishop of London. The Earl of
Winchelsea and his personal enemy, the Duke of Wellington,
both expressed their disapproval. The Duke of Gloucester
followed suit. An eyewitness of the debate, Lord Holland,
described the event most vividly:

> The Archbishop of Dublin, very ably and with great
> propriety as well as force of argument, supported
> the bill, as did Maltby, Bishop of Chichester.
> Canterbury and London opposed it on grounds silly
> enough but very narrow, and in a tone and temper
> very different and much milder than the lay lords,
> including Winchelsea and the Duke of Wellington.
> The latter of whom delivered one of the worst and
> perhaps most injudicious speeches we have yet heard
> from him; every word of it implied or avowed that
> no relaxation of exclusive laws should ever be made
> but under the pressure of necessity, i.e. intimi-
> dation, and that the repeal of test act as well as
> of Catholic disabilities had been granted to the
> formidable number of petitioners and their deter-
> mined manner of demanding relief, not to the reason
> of justice of their cause. The burden of proof lay,
> according to his Grace's notable philosophy, on those
> who claimed, not on those refused constitutional
> rights. A more inveterate worshiper of power and a
> more bigoted enemy of fundamental principle of pol-
> itical liberty certainly never existed. His theory
> of human society is truly that of an enemy. All right
> and authority in the chiefs, obedience, the sole
> duty of the mass, and every enjoyment or, as he termed
> it in his speech 'indulgence', to be measured by the
> convenience of the commanders, not by the wants or
> wishes of the army, who are the means not the object,
> formed to obey not to think, act or enjoy. I re-
> solved to enter my protest as containing principles
> so opposite to those avowed by Wellington in the
> debate. Lord Segrave avowed himself anxious to
> uphold Christianity and therefore charitably voted
> to exclude the Jews. One of the Newspapers remarked
> that they often observed his Lordship's proceedings,
> which were busy enough in propagation, but they have
> never been aware till then that it was Xtianity he
> was propagating on.[37]

Ignoring the result of the Lords' division, five days
later, on August 6, 1833, the Marquis of Westminster gave
notice of his intention to renew the question in the next
session. Robert Grosvenor, second Earl Grosvenor and
first Marquis of Westminster (1767-1845), was one of the
leading Whig advocates of Jewish emancipation in the Upper
House. From his childhood he took an active part in public
affairs and supported Pitt till his death, when he seceded
from the Tory party. For the rest of his life he remained
faithful to the Whigs, defending both the Anti-Corn Law
League and the Reform Bill. His aid to the Jewish campaign
was of great value during this stage.

Early in 1834, Robert Grant once more introduced a
relief measure in the House of Commons. The Bill, like
its predecessors, proposed a total removal of all civil
disabilities under which Jewish subjects still labored.
Opposition in the House of Commons remained vocal, but
the measure was carried through all its stages. During
its progress through the Commons, popular support was
demonstrated by a number of petitions. First, Lord Durham
presented the Lords a petition in favor, signed by 23,398
merchants, bankers and traders of the City. Then Lord
Brougham brought in a petition from Edinburgh, signed
by 6200 persons.

The Bill was introduced in the Lords by the Marquis
of Westminster on May 21. In his speech, the Marquis tried
to persuade the peers to approve of the measure because
the Jews were not hostile to Christianity, and even when
in possession of power they would not harm the established
church. He promised that Jewish emancipation would be the
most effectual step which could be taken to win the Jews
over to Christianity. Lord Bexley and Earl Radnor provided
similar arguments in support, but the majority remained
unconvinced. Even the Marquis of Bute, a Scottish philanthropist who later espoused the Jewish cause, voted against
this bill. The Lords defeated the new proposition and
reactionaries such as Malmesbury, Winchelsea and Westmeath
dominated the scene. Thus, the Jewish Civil Disabilities
Bill was rejected by 130 to 38 votes.[38]

Meanwhile, British Jews obtained a number of civil
rights. In 1833, a declaratory act finally established
their right to own freehold land. In January, 1833,
Francis Henry Goldsmid was called to the bar, becoming the
first Jew ever thus honored. The decision by the Lincoln
Inn's Benchers followed long discussions on how the oaths
should be administered. Finally, a formal method was
devised by the Benchers. Their senior, Sir Launcelot
Shadwell, eminent barrister and conveyancer, insisted on
the oath being taken on a special volume of the Old
Testament (Mikraot Gedolot) fetched from his own library

for that purpose.[39]   The year 1835 was marked by further
progress toward full emancipation: a Parliamentary enactment legalized Jews' right to the electoral franchise
by removing the sixth section of 5 & 6 Will. IV, c. 36.
Hence, oaths were no longer required at the polls during
elections.   On November 17, of the same year, the first
Jewish juryman, John Simon (1818-1897), a Jamaican-born
barrister, was sworn on the Old Testament as a member of
the grand jury at the Kirkdale Quarter Sessions.

The most important development of the year, however,
was the Sheriff's Declaration Act that passed into law to
solve a particular grievance. On June 24, 1835, the mayor,
aldermen and liverymen of the several companies of the
City assembled in the Common Hall at the Guildhall to
elect two sheriffs for London and Middlesex.[40]   The election
was won by John Lainson and David Salomons. It was confirmed
by the Lord Mayor, Henry Winchester, the Law Recorder and
several of the aldermen present on the occasion. No one
raised any legal question or expressed any doubts. A few
days later, however, Salomons was required to take the
declaration prescribed by law. Naturally he refused, but
could not obtain protection through the annual Indemnity
Act.

Consequently, the issue was raised in Parliament by
the Attorney General, Sir John Campbell. The problem was
attacked by the Sheriff's Declaration Bill which provided
that no one elected to the office of sheriff of any city
being also a county, like London, should be liable to the
operation of the declaration in question. Campbell, who
took charge of the bill in the Lower House, ten years
later testified that as early as 1835 he had wanted complete relief for Jews, but had he gone further at that time
he might have risked the limited measure. Perhaps this
was the self-justification of a highly conservative person
who, despite his liberalism, would never take a leading part
on questions of reform. Campbell always stood on the side
of moderation and restraint with regard to changes.
Campbell (1779-1861), who in 1841 was raised to the peerage,
was known as legal biographer, Lord Chief Justice and
Lord Chancellor. He was one of the most prominent jurists
of the age and he rendered important services to the Whig
administration during his office as Attorney General from
1834 to 1841. He stood on the side of reform on the great
questions of Catholic emancipation, the repeal of the
Test Act, the suppression of slavery and Parliamentary
reform. He also sympathized with Jewish emancipation, but
his support was cautious and reserved.

Early in the year, David Salomons approached the new
premier, Sir Robert Peel, who had recently declared his
belief in freedom of conscience in his Tamworth Manifesto.[41]

In response to the Prime Minister's appeal to his
constituency prior to the general election, Salomons wondered why Jews should be excluded from the civil liberty
Peel so ardently espoused. Probably following Lord Holland's
idea, Salomons noted a contradiction between Peel's manifesto and the real actions. Peel's answer was brief and
cold, as if concealing embarrassment: "His Majesty's
Government does not propose to introduce any measure in
Parliament with reference to the civil capacities of the
Jewish subjects of his Majesty."

Whereas Peel and most Tories remained hostile, the
Whigs became more committed: the Sheriff's Declaration
Act was endorsed by Peel's successor, Lord Melbourne and
therefore it received greater support both in the Commons
and Lords. According to his biographer, Lord David Cecil,
Melbourne maintained that all religious tests and civil
disabilities were ineffectual, and therefore unnecessary.[42]
On May 2, 1835 Melbourne wrote I. L. Goldsmid: "I beg
leave to acquaint you that upon that petition or upon
any measure founded on it, I shall pursue the same course
as upon former similar occasions by giving it my individual
support."[43] Melbourne should be credited for backing
the enfranchisement of British Jews, in response to
Goldsmid's appeal after the return of Whigs to office
in April, 1835.

Late in the year 1835, the problem of municipal offices
came to the fore once again: on November 19, David
Salomons was elected alderman for the Aldgate Ward, the
number of votes for him having outnumbered those for John
Humphrey and James Law Jones. But in the Court of
Aldermen the problem of the oath rose once more.[44]
Salomons refused to make a declaration containing the
objectionable words, but the Court insisted that he make
it in the manner prescribed by law. The mayor of London
listened on December 27 to Salomons' grievance, but
offered no solution. Consequently, the election was nul-
lified by the Court and Salomons' rival, John Humphrey,
was declared the alderman for the ward. Salomons
immediately appealed to the electors, a considerable number
of whom were Jewish, and this meeting, held at the London
Tavern on December 27, ended with a resolution that the
matter should be pursued in the courts.

In addition to the courts, Salomons decided to try
legislation. Early in 1836, he approached the Chancellor
of Exchequer, Thomas Spring Rice, and asked him to move
a comprehensive relief measure in the Commons. Salomons
acted on his own and disregarded the Deputies, who had
refused to go along with his appeal to the courts. When
the Deputies heard about the new bill, they protested
politely against the introduction of a measure without

consultation with "the Jews as a body from some authorized organ."[45] (The Board of Deputies could claim such a position since the enactment of the Marriage Registration Act of 1836, which gave it statutory recognition.) But the Deputies nonetheless requested a copy of the Bill from the Chancellor and resolved to collaborate with Salomons on the promotion of the cause. Salomons and his followers were invited to confer with the Deputies on June 13 at Montefiore's house in Park Lane. The meeting included Salomons, the Goldsmids, and Bernard Van Oven. It concluded with a plan for cooperation, for which a sub-committee of Deputies and non-Deputies was appointed and the president, Montefiore, promised his best endeavors on its behalf. Early in July 1836 the Deputies petitioned the Archbishop of Dublin and solicited his support in the House of Lords.[46]

Spring Rice's Bill was read for the first time in the Commons on June 13 and was supported by the bulk of the petitions. The opposition was not active, probably reckoning on a veto of the peers.[47] The Bill reached the Lords on August 19 and was read for the first time, but due to the lateness of the session, the Marquis of Westminster decided not to push it forward. Westminster, who moved the Bill in the Upper House, promised to continue his efforts on another occasion.

In the fall of 1837 a Municipal Officer's Declaration Bill was introduced in the House of Commons by the representative of Leeds, Edward Baines, for the admission of Quakers, Moravians and Separatists to municipal offices. Baines (1774-1848) was the owner of the Leeds Mercury and M. P. for that city during the years 1834-1841. He was a prominent agitator in the cause of Dissent for the abolition of church rates and civil disabilities. Now he tried to solve the grievance of three denominations whose members were admitted to Parliament (from 1833) but were excluded from municipal and national offices. Baines' Bill was designed to alter the declaration contained in 9 Geo. IV, c. 17, required upon entry into municipal offices. The Morning Chronicle at once suggested that the measure ought to be extended in scope for the relief of Jewish subjects as well.[48]

Even the Deputies realized this was a rare opportunity, and decided to act immediately. In their meeting on November 29, they resolved to approach Baines and ask him to include Jews in his Bill.[49] But Baines was afraid of the risk and declined the request. Salomons, however, managed to convince the Radical Member for the City, historian on Greece, George Grote (1794-1871) to introduce an amendment to the proposed Bill. Grote was a Radical Benthamite who took a leading part in the foundation of University College. He entered Parliament in 1832 and sat there till 1841, first in the Liberal ranks but later, discouraged with the Liberal zeal for reforms, he split with the party and headed the independent group of Philosophical radicals. Being independent of the Liberals, he was in a position to make an unpopular move for the advancement of the goal.

At the same time, Montefiore led a deputation to the Duke of Sussex at Kensington Palace, but the Duke promised he would support the amendment only if it would not harm the cause of Dissenters.[50] A petition was taken to Melbourne and Lansdowne for presentation to Parliament, but fear that the entire measure might be endangered by the controversial Jewish demand made both politicians refuse to commit themselves despite their sympathy with the Jews. Even Lord John Russell responded unfavorably this time, so the Deputies decided to take one final chance with Peel. On December 4, Lionel and Nathaniel de Rothschild, David Salomons and Moses Montefiore were to meet Peel in Westminster but when they arrived, only Salomons and Montefiore were allowed to enter with a petition from the Jewish community. Somehow they failed to locate Peel, so the debate on Grote's amendment began without his hearing the Jewish view. Jewish emancipation was defeated once again.

The major victory for Jewish freedom during the year 1837 was Montefiore's election as sheriff of London and Middlesex, thus following Salomons and becoming the second professing Jew elected to that office. Montefiore did not want the honor, but he was persuaded by the Radical businessman William Thornborrow to offer his candidacy for the sake of promoting civil emancipation. Thornborrow disclosed in a pamphlet how he had labored for the election of a Dissenter and a Roman Catholic as sheriffs of the City in 1834,[51] and how he had pushed for Salomons' election in 1835. In 1837 he stood behind Montefiore's candidacy and even tried to obtain a knighthood for him. But Lord Holland, whom Thornborrow addressed for this purpose, thought the time was not yet ripe for such ventures. The election had public significance for the campaign, as Sir John Campbell observed during the Sheriffs Inauguration Dinner:

> I am happy to say that the ancient prejudices founded on difference of religious belief are fast waning away, and I hope the time is at hand when objections on such grounds will altogether cease to operate. It is the desire of her Majesty's Government to promote such a state of things by all the means in their power. For my part, my opinion is that so far from injuring the constitution, it will tend materially to uphold and strengthen it.[52]

On November 16, on the occasion of the Queen's visit to
the City, Montefiore was knighted with the other sheriffs
and thus, another step toward equalizing the status of
Jews was taken. Montefiore was the first professing Jew
to be honored in that way during the nineteenth century.

The years 1836-1840 marked the end of the first
phase of the struggle for Jewish emancipation. Three
major activists had passed away during the course of
these years: N. M. Rothschild, Sir Robert Grant and
Lord Holland. Rothschild's death in July, 1836 was a
severe blow to the campaign. Rothschild preferred to
avoid the limelight because of his foreign origin, appearance and accent, but his enthusiasm and devotion were
of great value. Both Jewish Deputies and dissidents
respected his prudent, tactful and conciliatory attitude.
A year later, Sir Robert Grant died. Grant ended his
involvement in the struggle in 1834, with his departure
for India as an East India administrator in Madras. But
the community at large, as well as Continental Jews
interested in emancipation, felt grateful for his unselfish
participation.[53] The most dramatic loss was Lord Holland's
death in 1840. In addition to his public support, Holland
possessed political experience which the Jews lacked.
As the architect of the early phase of the campaign he
insisted the issue never become a party question. In
1830, he suggested that the first relief measure be moved
by the Tory churchman Lord Bexley, who offered the chance
of gaining the confidence of the Evangelical party and
the High Church Tories. Although himself a devoted Whig,
he did not attempt to profit politically by advocating
this cause. He disregarded party interests and placed
the good of the cause above everything else. These three
losses marked an end to the first generation of
emancipationists and to the preliminary phase in the
struggle for Jewish freedom.

Compromises With Tories, 1840-1847

The municipal offices' problem raised by David
Salomons was in the forefront of Jewish attention from
1838. The Board of Deputies declined to concur with
Salomons' suggestion to appeal to the courts, so he
acted alone. He appealed to the Court of King's Bench
about the refusal to admit him to the Court of Aldermen.
King's Bench decided favorably on Salomons' appeal, but
the case was lost in the Court of Exchequer after an
appeal of the Aldermen. In January, 1839, Salomons urged
the Deputies to turn to the House of Lords in its capacity as the highest court of appeals of the realm. The
Deputies voted against this idea and in response, Salomons
resigned his membership on the Board. Salomons' exclusion
from the Aldermanic seat became an anachronism as Jews

were increasingly admitted to various municipal offices
in provincial towns, the declaration containing the
objectionable words not usually being enforced by the
returning officers. Salomons himself admitted that Jews
"were permitted to exercise many privileges which the
strict application of disqualifying statutes would not
allow."[54]

The restrictions on Jewish appointments in 1835
to municipal offices in the City of London was already
out of line with practices elsewhere in the country. In
1830, Phineas Levy, a navy agent of Devonport, had been
elected to the local Board of Commissioners, the fore-
runner of the Devonport Town Council. Eight years later,
Abraham Abraham, a Southampton silversmith, was elected
to the local town council and three years later became
sheriff. In 1835, David Barnett, a jeweler of Russian
origin, was elected to the Birmingham City Council and
thus began a long municipal career. Barnett was
allowed to enter office without making a declaration
because of the precedent set by the Southampton Town
Council. In 1841, Emanuel Emanuel, a silversmith from
Portsmouth, was elected to the city council, and in Hull
during the same year, Bethel Jacobs, also a jeweler, was
elected for the third successive year to the municipal
office of Governor of the Workhouse of the city.[55]

Under these circumstances, the Member for Exeter,
Edward Divett, introduced a bill in 1841 to enable the
admission of Jews to municipal offices. Divett proposed
to exempt Jews from pronouncing the words 'on the true
faith of a Christian' when making the 1828 declaration.
The Bill passed its three readings in the House of
Commons without difficulty, partly due to the Government's
support. The third reading attracted some public attention
because of a debate between Gladstone and Macaulay.
Gladstone strongly opposed the measure, maintaining that
the removal of municipal disabilities would necessitate
Jewish admission to Parliament. He could understand the
acceptance of Roman Catholics within the scope of
constitutional rights, but could not see how a provision
for Jews would be compatible with the Christian character
of the House. Furthermore, he did not think the issue
worthy of a lengthy discussion, because the number of
Jewish subjects living in the country was insignificant.
Macaulay, in response, pointed to the necessity of removing
the Jewish disabilities for constitutional purposes.
It was absurd that the law should be disregarded in some
parts of the country before it has been amended by Parliament. As to the argument concerning the number of Jews
residing in England, Macaulay's response was particularly
sharp. This argument, he claimed, was immoral, because
a denial of civil rights was proposed on the basis of

an irrelevant principle. He scorned Gladstone's
self-righteousness and stood up for the cherished
tradition of freedom of conscience. But the argument proved
academic; the Bill was defeated in the Lords by a majority
of 98 to 64 votes on the third reading.[56]

The year 1841 saw the general election which ended
with a Tory victory. In the City, however, Lord John
Russell managed to get elected, to a great extent because
of Jewish support. During the election, Russell was heavily
attacked by his Tory opponents. A diatribe titled A New
Song To A Old Tune, written by one of his rivals, included
the following threat to Lord John:

> From Parliament
> They have you sent,
> As surely you'll remember
> We wont have you.
> You little Jew
> You homeopathic Member.[57]

For the Jewish electors, Russell was an ideal
representative. Jewish emancipation was not only an
opportunity for promoting his personal interests, but a
cause to which he had been fully committed from the early
years of the struggle. The son of the sixth Duke of
Bedford was deeply influenced by Lord Holland, with whom
he had travelled to Portugal in 1808 and with whom he
had collaborated throughout his entire career. Russell
(1792-1878) moved the repeal of the Test and Corporation
Acts in the House of Commons in 1828; he gave strong support
to Catholic emancipation and was the hero of the struggle
for the Great Reform Bill. In 1834 he introduced the
Dissenter's Marriage Bill to enable Dissenting ministers
to celebrate marriages in places of worship licensed for
that purpose, and during the same year he called for
extensive reforms of the Anglican establishment in Ireland.

Few people were as involved as Lord John in the
campaign for religious freedom. Small and delicate in
constitution, broadly educated, mild mannered and soft
spoken, he was popular enough to push the matter forward.
Russell's personal interest in the cause was vividly
depicted by I. L. Goldsmid who especially addressed the
Jewish electors of London on behalf of Russell's candidacy.[58]
The election cemented the London alliance between the Whig
politician and the Jewish community; henceforth, Lord John
Russell became the leading champion of the cause in
Parliament. David Salomons recorded the sentiments
entertained toward Russell in 1845, when he wrote him from
Tunbridge Wells to thank the Whig statesman for his advocacy: "No one can have read your speech in the late
debate without feeling the utmost participation. It is
delightful to me to know that there is a friendly statesman in the House of Commons who faithfully advocates the

cause of truth."[59]

Two years later, the Tories might have seen once again
that, by objecting to Jewish emancipation, they infuriated
the Jewish electors of the City. During a City by-election,
held in October, 1843, the Conservative candidate Thomas
Baring was confronted by a strong Liberal opposition,
which emphasized anti-Corn Law propaganda. Thomas Baring
(1799-1873) was the director of the family's banking
house, Conservative politician and confidant of Lord
Derby. He wanted to strike a blow at the League, so the
election was important both for him and the party.
In a letter to the Duke of Wellington, Peel said that a
Radical victory in the City would be a League triumph.
He therefore asked the Duke to intervene with the Rothschilds and press Lionel, in particular, to remain neutral
during this contest: "Baron Rothschild is an important
man. He told Baron Kielmansegge that he had not committed
himself and that he could command a thousand votes. There
are, I believe, not less than twelve thousand Jewish
votes. All we can hope for is his neutrality."[60] Wellington promised Peel to have a word with Rothschild's
wife and with his mother, but he warned the Prime Minister
that the two ladies would in return ask for some[61]
concessions for the cause of emancipation. Baring,
reckoning that the Jews would vote against, hoped that
many of them would not appear at the poll as the election
fell on the Sabbath.[62] But London Jewry was determined
to demonstrate its dedication to emancipation and voted
in great numbers. Baring was defeated, a reminder to
Peel of the power of Jewish electors in perhaps the most[63]
important constituency in the country.

In September, 1844, David Salomons stood for alderman
of Portsoken Ward. His only competitor was Francis Graham
Moon (1769-1871), a famous printseller, publisher and man
of literary taste who received the patronage of the English
and many European courts. Salomons won the seat by a
majority of 236 to 168 votes. But he did not present
himself before the Court of Aldermen when the results of
the election were formally announced. Not until two days
later did he appear before the Court to claim his seat,
probably after deliberation on the pursuit of his cause.
The Court offered, as a compromise, that Salomons would
take the declaration as a Separatist, but he refused.
Salomons insisted on his right to be admitted to the Court
as a professing Jew. When the negotiations reached a
dead end, Salomons asked the Aldermen to postpone the
proceedings on his election for a few days to enable him[64]
consultation with lawyers then absent from the City.
But his request was denied and the Court ordered him
to take the declaration at once. Salomons rejected the
ultimatum, so the Court declared his election null and

void. Moon was sworn as alderman for the Portsoken Ward
instead.

Salomons immediately reacted. He appealed to his
electors, many of whom were Jews, and urged them to file
a protest with the Lord Mayor. He himself protested
vehemently against the exclusion: "I, the undersigned
David Salomons, do hereby respectfully declare and protest
that I have been duly elected and that I now am the
Alderman of this Ward in the room and stead of Thomas
Johnson, Esquire, who has resigned the said office, and
that the precept of your Lordship by virtue of which this
Wardmote has been convened and is now holden and all the
proceedings thereunder is, are and will be illegal and   65
void by reason that the said office is now full as aforesaid."

On November 6, 1844, Salomons addressed the Prime
Minister with a letter urging Peel to take action on
behalf of his cause. Salomons had been in touch with
Peel from 1843 and now, when a tangible grievance had
arisen, he urged Government intervention.[66] But Peel
was in no hurry to commit himself. Early in 1845 Salomons
had an interview with him, explaining to Peel the serious-
ness of the situation. Peel promised to notify Salomons
by letter of his decision, but when the promised response
did not come, Salomons again wrote to the Premier. In
this letter he warned the Tory statesman that if action
were deferred, both Jews and their sympathizers would
agitate against the discrimination imposed on them by
the law of their country:

At the interview with which you so kindly
honoured me some time ago, you were pleased to in-
timate that about this period a communication from
yourself should inform me of the views & intentions
of the Government. Believe me, sir, that I have
been looking forward with increasing interest &
with fervent hope to the present moment, when I
expected to be honoured with your commands. Having
stated confidentially to private & discreet friends
the possibility the Gov. might themselves initiate
a measure of relief, we have by our united influence
been enabled to delay until now any further manifestation of feeling, whether on the part of the
Jewish community or on that of our own fellow-citizens
in the city of London. We have thus restrained public
actions for a time & become open to a charge of
infirmness, altogether at variance with our real
sentiments. But we are no longer able to resist
the pressure for a more active demonstration to be
made on our behalf. The humiliation to which we
were subjected by the conduct of the Court of
Aldermen, the limitation of the rights of the electors

involved in that illiberal decision, the disadvantageous position in which we stand, when
compared with other named dissenters, all tend
to make some immediate forward move, imperative.[67]

Peel must have been touched by this bitter and
passionate address, for he finally decided to take up the
question. On February 22, he asked Lord Chancellor
Lyndhurst to assume responsibility for a bill to admit
Jews into municipal offices.[68] To that end, Lyndhurst
was also appointed chairman of a Royal Commission instructed
to investigate the disabilities imposed on non-Anglicans
for religious opinion. Its report, submitted on May 30,
1845, included a comprehensive survey of the history of
Anglo-Jewry and a detailed account of all the statutes
and acts which imposed penalties on non-Anglicans for
dissenting religious beliefs. The Royal Commission
recommended the repeal of the law forbidding Jews to own
land, the admission of Jews to corporate offices and the
substitution for religious tests of a declaration unrelated
to religious opinions.[69] In consequence of the report,
Lyndhurst introduced into the House of Lords a Jewish
Disabilities Removal Bill. The range of the Bill was
limited to municipal restrictions and Lyndhurst assured
the peers that it would not be widened in scope to remove
parliamentary limitations, so it passed the Upper House
with little opposition.

Lyndhurst himself would have liked to solve the problem
of Jewish admission to Parliament on the same occasion,
but as he later explained, he was afraid to risk the passage
of the limited relief measure in view of the vocal opposition
in both Houses of Parliament.[70] Although bound by party
lines, Lyndhurst did not conceal his sympathy with Jewish
emancipation arising from his 1837 marriage to Georgina,
daughter of Louis Goldsmith. Born John Singleton Copley
(1772-1863), he was a man of vigor, gaiety and humor.
He was known for his superb memory, artistic taste and
capacity for hard work. As one of the most brilliant
lawyers of the period, he managed to build a spectacular
career. In 1818 he entered Parliament and a year later
was appointed Solicitor General. The attractive, sensitive
and eloquent Member rapidly gained a reputation as a de-
bater and parliamentarian. Subsequently he was raised
to the peerage and appointed Lord Chancellor (1826-1830),
during a period in which he exercised enormous influence
on Wellington, Peel and the entire party.

While the issue was debated in Westminster, the Board
of Deputies promoted it outside the legislature. A
committee of five Deputies, including Montefiore, Salomons
and Lionel de Rothschild, took charge of the campaign and
opened a public subscription to defray the expenses involved.[71]

On February 18, 1845 the Board decided to bring the Bill
to public attention and on the following day the sub-committee in charge had an interview with the Premier. To
their dismay, the Deputies learned that Peel had already
been approached by the Reform Congregation headed by the
Goldsmids. The latter insisted that British Jews would
not be satisfied with less than complete emancipation.
Peel was inclined to take advantage of the difference of
opinion inside the Jewish community and shelve the issue,
but Montefiore convinced him to see Goldsmid and make up
his mind later. Peel was also persuaded to present a
petition from the Deputies to the House of Commons. The
Prime Minister told the Deputies he would inform them of
his decision after he had seen Goldsmid. On March 7, 1845,
Salomons and Rothschild were invited once more to see
Peel, and the Prime Minister told them of his decision
to introduce the Municipal Disabilities Removal Bill.
Peel showed them a copy of the Bill and the Jewish Deputies
found it satisfactory. They were perfectly happy with a
partial relief measure and agreed with Peel that the
question of Parliamentary representation ought to be
dealt with separately. The Deputies thanked Peel for
his exertion on their behalf.[72] In May, probably at his
request, they prepared another petition and passed it to
Peel for delivery to the Commons.[73]

During these developments, another pressure for the
comprehensive settlement of the Jewish question, including
admission to Parliament, was put before the Committee of
the Protestant Dissenting Deputies. The Dissenting
Deputies agreed with Goldsmid that the matter ought to be
solved once and for all, so on April 28 they petitioned
Parliament and stated their desire in unequivocal terms.[74]
This request horrified Gladstone, the leading opponent of
the municipal measure in the House of Commons. Peel,
however, assured the Commons that he had no intention of
introducing a comprehensive settlement.[75]

On July 31, 1845, "An Act For The Relief Of Persons
Of The Jewish Religion Elected To Municipal Offices" (8
& 9, Vict., c. 52) received the Royal Assent; the municipal disabilities were finally removed from the Statute
Book. A second bill passed into law as 9 & 10 Vict. c.59
in August, effected the other recommendations of Lyndhurst's
Royal Commission. The Religious Opinion Relief Act
removed the Statutum de Judaismo and repealed the Act of
1702, compelling Jews to finance their children during a
Protestant education. The Act also placed English Jews
in the same position as other Dissenters with respect
to schools, places of worship and charities.

The termination of Peel's tenure of office in July
1846 put an end to Jewish collaboration with the Tories.

Peel's break with the party and its take-over by the
Protectionists precluded any future settlement with the
approval of the Conservatives. The 1846 break led to a
polarization of the old pre-1846 Conservative party toward
Jewish emancipation: whereas the Protectionists found the
opposition to Jewish freedom a unifying element, the
Peelites became more receptive to the Jewish claims.
Jewish opinion gave Peel great credit for his endeavors.
Despite their attraction to the Liberal party, Jewish
leaders had to admit that Peel's treatment of their cause
was effective and that his actions were praiseworthy.
David Salomons, the staunch Liberal, felt grateful to Peel
and did not fail to express his sentiments after being
sworn Alderman for Cordwainer Ward in 1847. Salomons
wrote Peel:

> I have this day been admitted to a seat in the
> Court of Aldermen. On two previous occasions, I was
> elected an Alderman but unable to qualify according
> to the form of the Court. It is to the remedial measure
> proposed by the Gov. of which you were the distin-
> guished head, that I am now enabled to qualify to
> take my place in the wardmote of the city, where my
> family lived for many many years. Appreciating as
> I do most highly the confidence given to me by my
> fellow citizens, I am at the same time most forcibly
> reminded of the appeal I made to you on my last
> failure. You received me most amiably. On public
> grounds, you promised to consider the subject & on
> the responsibility of your Gov. you afterwards sup-
> ported & applied a remedy. In the first opportunity
> that has presented itself, your kind & enlightened
> measure has been sanctified by an almost unanimous
> act of approval, without as within, the walls of the
> Court of Aldermen. I beg to tender to you, sir, the
> warmest expression of my gratitude for this act of
> your official life; to offer my warmest prayer that
> you may be long found to assist in the councils of
> Britain & in the enjoyment of all earthly blessings.[76]

A second letter from Salomons to Peel in May 1849,
after Peel's son's maiden speech in Parliament in favor
of admitting Rothschild to the House, similarly conveyed
the high regard entertained by Jewish emancipationists for
the great Tory statesman.[77]

A second major event that transformed the course of
the campaign was the 1847 election of Baron Rothschild
(1808-1879), head of the family banking house at New Court,
who was responsible for many government loans, including
those for the relief of the Irish famine, the Crimean
War and the purchase of the Khedive's Suez Canal shares.

His various philanthropic ventures made him popular in
the City and he had no difficulties getting elected Member
of Parliament. Rothschild was a devoted Liberal and an
ardent free trader and by virtue of being the only Jewish
candidate who won a seat in the election, his leadership
linked the Jewish and Liberal causes.[78] Certainly, for
the rest of the period of political emancipation, most
British Jews agitated their cause within the ranks of the
Liberal party.

The Struggle For Parliamentary Representation, 1847-1856.

In July 1847, the Board of Deputies was notified of
Rothschild's intention to contest a seat in Parliament.
Rothschild campaigned for his election in the City, stressing
his belief in religious freedom, free trade, imposition of
property taxes and opposition to church rates. Accepting
Rothschild's total commitment to the Liberal party, the
Deputies, regardless of their political affiliations, de-
cided to endorse his cause and labor for his election.
The Board appointed seven Deputies to serve on a committee
to promote his candidacy. Included were Israel Barned,
Simon Samuel, Jonas Levy, S. H. Ellis, John Salmon, Samuel
Cohen and Moses Montefiore. The Deputies resolved "that
each member of the Board be requested to use his influence
for the promotion of the success of the object."[79] On
July 30, the Liberal party scored a significant victory
as three of its candidates for the City of London, Lord
John Russell, James Pattison and Lionel de Rothschild were
elected Members of Parliament.

Following this victory, Russell moved a Jewish
Disabilities Bill in the Commons to solve Rothschild's
problem by enacting a special oath for Jews, just as
Parliament designed an oath for Roman Catholics in 1829.
The motion was followed by one of the most important
debates in the history of the struggle. To the amazement
of the House, Gladstone announced on December 16 that he
had changed his mind and would support the admission of
Jews to Parliament. "I state, with deep regret, so far
as regards my relation to that learned body (Oxford),
that not without pain indeed, it is my intention, because
I feel it to be my duty, to support the measure which
we are now assembled to discuss."[80]

No less surprising was Peel's first public expression
of support of the admission of Jews to the legislature:
only on February 11, 1847, he had admitted that he gave a
silent vote on the first occasion on which the matter
was discussed 'with great reluctance'. In December,
however, Peel decided to endorse a cause which placed him
"in painful collision with many with whom he had almost
invariably acted."

Benjamin Disraeli delivered an eloquent speech in which he pointed to the affinity of Judaism to Christianity. He would therefore not take upon himself "the awful responsibility of excluding from the legislature those who are of the religion in the bosom of which my Lord and Saviour was born."[81] Disraeli claimed the Jews were natural born Tories, whose conservatism predominated over their political views. He reaffirmed his belief that Jews deserved emancipation because they were Jews and that they had a better claim than Roman Catholics, Unitarians or Quakers. His speech generated violent responses both from Tories and Liberals; it was not well received and Disraeli resumed his seat amid shouts and expressions of anger.

But the most astonishing moment during the debate came when Lord George Bentinck, the leader of the Protectionist party, delivered a supportive speech. The fifth child and second surviving son of the fourth Duke of Portland shaped his political views under the impact of his uncle Canning, under whom he served as secretary and to whom he was strongly attached. Bentinck (1802- 1848) was tall and well-built, physically attractive and well known for his skill in every kind of sport. He was a bold rider, good hunter and a remarkable cricketer. He excelled on the turf and had won a number of riding races and derbies. After becoming M.P. in the Conservative interest, Lord George sometimes came to the House from a run, with his scarlet coat not wholly hidden by a white overcoat. As a politician, Bentinck's deficiency was that he took public affairs as a kind of sport. In his political views, he was known for his objections to court influences, his love of religious liberty and his trust in the people. In many respects, Bentinck was an 1689 Whig rather than a nineteenth century Tory. Yet, he was affiliated with the Protectionist party. Though a bad speaker, whose arguments had to be read in order to sound convincing, he appealed to the public. Good humored, blunt, outspoken and eccentric, he could publicly reproach Peel with the presence of Prince Albert in the House of Commons on the first night of the 1845 session. During the early recess of the same year, he accepted the leadership of the Protectionist party on condition that he would relinquish it when he discovered a better man for the post and that he would be free to act as he thought right on religious questions.

Prior to the division on the Jewish question, Bentinck was asked by Stanley to give a silent vote. He decided instead to speak out against religious intolerance.[82] Lord George retained his old Whigishness with regard to religious freedom, although he admitted he had little sympathy for the Jews. When Jacob A. Franklin asked him to become involved in the struggle, Bentinck replied that he had not given the cause enough consideration.

His attitude was faithfully recorded when he said:

> As for the question itself, I look upon it just
> of about as much national importance as Lord
> Ellenborough's divorce bill or the Duke of Beaufort's
> Marriage Bill; indeed I am here over-estimating the
> importance of the Jew Bill and as for the Jews them-
> selves, I don't care two strokes about them and
> heartily wish they were all back in the Holy Land.[83]

However, he could not compromise at this point with the
reactionary members of his own party, people such as
Inglis, Spooner, Plumptre and Sibthorp.

Immediately after the division, William Beresford
(1768-1854), one of the whips, a General who served under
Wellington and became his political supporter, took it
upon himself to tell Bentinck that he could no longer be
regarded as a party leader. The blunt and outspoken
Beresford was expressing his personal view, but Bentinck
wrote Disraeli that he felt rejected by the entire party,
so he decided to resign. In January 1848, Lord George
sent his resignation to George Bankes (1788-1856), M.P.
for Dorsetshire and one of the more influential Protectionists.[84] The letter was read at a meeting of the
Protectionist party, where Beresford was severely criticized
for having written to Bentinck before consulting with
other members.[85] A number of Protectionists tried to
convince Bentinck to withdraw his resignation, among them
Bankes and Lord Granby. But Stanley did not show sufficient enthusiasm for the idea and evidently the majority
did not want Bentinck back. A new leader had to be chosen,
but Lord Granby, the new choice, was not competent enough
and not really willing to assume the leadership. At the
beginning of the session, Lord George walked up to the
head of the second bench below the gangway and this
signified that he was no longer the leader of the party.
Disraeli, who generally sat by the side of Lord George,
was thus left to occupy the usual place of the opposition
leader.[86] One of the most brilliant political careers
in the nineteenth century was thus firmly launched.

During the debates in Parliament, the Board of Deputies
campaigned vigorously for the cause. On December 29, 1847,
Montefiore read two letters at a meeting of the Deputies,
both from I. L. Goldsmid giving suggestions for the effective
waging of the campaign. Goldsmid recommended petitioning
Parliament, personal contact with M.P.s and an agitation
of public opinion in support of the Jewish claim. Since
the Parliamentary debates of December had attracted wide
attention and the question had galvanized national importance
for the the first time, the opportunity had to be exploited.
The Deputies' responses to these suggestions were not

recorded in their minutes, but the proceedings of the Board clearly reflect the collaboration of the two parties.[87] The Board resolved unanimously to invite all Jewish congregations in the country to petition Parliament and also decided to appoint a sub-committee to direct agitation. The Board submitted its own petitions to Lord John Russell and Lord Lansdowne for presentation to both Houses of Parliament.

January to May, 1848, saw a strenuous campaign to stir the public, and the Jewish community was electrified. A sub-committee of Deputies met three times a week at Baron Rothschild's offices in New Court, St. Swithin's Lane, to promote signatures for petitions and correspond with provincial congregations. The response was gratifying. In February, the best attended meeting in support of the cause was held at Sussex Hall, under the auspices of the Jewish Association For The Removal Of Civil And Religious Disabilities. People flocked to the hall by the hundreds and there was not enough room. Meanwhile, petitions from all over the country flooded Parliament; they were sent from mayors and town councils of Worcester, Portsmouth, Yarmouth, Leicester, Canterbury, Truro, Hull, Bristol, Falmouth, Manchester, Birmingham, Edinburgh, Cambridge, Liverpool, Dublin, Norwich, Southampton, Portsea, Brighton, Ipswich, as well as from a considerable number of smaller towns and counties. The London boroughs of Southwark, Lambeth, Tower Hamlets, Finsbury, Westminster, Chelsea and Aldgate sent petitions of their own. The number of signatures collected in favor of the Bill was 251,863 and the number of those against it only 62,611.

Despite the opposition of Tories and the reluctance of many Liberals, the Bill passed its second reading in February by a majority of 277 to 204. The Commons could not remain deaf to these public manifestations of support. But when the Bill reached the Lords in April, 1848, chances for its passage into law diminished. Not only did the bishops and the Conservative peers oppose it, but also a large portion of the Liberals was still undecided. The attitude recorded by the eighth Duke of Argyll was probably not untypical, even though he later espoused Jewish emancipation wholeheartedly:

> It was a very unfavourable opportunity for me, because I could not be enthusiastic either way. I had difficulties in making up my mind how to vote. There were several arguments on both sides which I rejected altogether ... I was therefore in favour of leaving constituencies free to exercise their own judgement as to the religion of their Members. It is needless to say that this was a position unfavourable to effective speaking, because unfavourable to the energy of strong convictions.[88]

Thus, no leading Liberal politician could have been astonished in May 1848, when the Bill was lost on the second reading in the Lords by a majority of 163 to 125.

But for the Jewish electors the defeat was a great disappointment and frustration was increased by some fierce anti-Jewish remarks made by the Bishop of Oxford, Samuel Wilberforce. The Jewish Chronicle expressed the general mood in its editorial of June 2, 1848:

> We must confess we were not prepared. Such words might have graced the lips of a Spanish inquisitor in those ages, which the nineteenth century stigmatizes with the epithet of 'dark'. Their Lordships were pleased to term the question under consideration a religious and a Christian question, but their proceedings savour much more of superstition and a spirit of persecution than of true religion and so called Christian charity.

On January 31, 1849 a meeting of the Liberal electors of the City was held at the London Tavern to consider how to deal with the rebuff Rothschild had met. Raikes Currie, the chairman, advised a moderate line of action, but David Wire (1801-1860), a senior partner in a City firm of solicitors, Radical politician and a well know philanthropist, took the opposite line. He called for the abolition of all religious tests and advocated active agitation for that purpose. The meeting resolved to urge Lord John Russell to press the issue and if Parliament did not respond, then the City electors would have to turn to less peaceful methods. For the moment, they decided to leave the City's fourth seat unfilled and to continue supporting Rothschild in the following election.[89]

Early in June, London had a chance to demonstrate its loyalty to Rothschild when a City by-election was held. The Tory candidate for the City was Lord John Manners (1815-1888), the second son of the fifth Duke of Rutland, Disraeli's personal friend and member of the Young England movement. Manners testified to the popular enthusiasm on Rothschild's behalf: "the row was prodigious; the mob made Rothschild inaudible by applauding, not by groaning."[90] Raikes Currie publicly scorned the ardent Protectionist for his staunch support of the rights of the church, the agricultural interest and the Tithe Redemption Trust. Currie described Manners' views as yearnings for the restoration of medieval institutions in the political reality of the nineteenth century. Lord John hardly had a chance to deliver a speech, usually being received with yells, goarns and whistles. When the poll was declared, Lord John Manners had a majority of three thousand votes against him.

The following session, Russell tried once more to
solve the Jewish problem by introducing an Oaths Bill
which sought to simplify or abolish the various oaths
required upon admission to make them acceptable to Jews
and less offensive to Roman Catholics. Gladstone welcomed the measure, not only as a remedy to the Jewish
grievance, but also because he identified with the need
to simplify the oaths and adjust their content to the circumstances. Henry Goulburn again opposed, but Peel in
supporting the motion indicated that he would be prepared
to go further and enable Jews to hold some other civil
offices from which they were still barred by the required
oaths. But the 1849 motion drew little interest: "The
speakers felt, no doubt, a great difficulty in giving their
respective arguments the attraction of novelty; most of
what was said, pro and contra, having been repeated a
dozen times before, and with greater force and eloquence
than on the present occasion", the Jewish Chronicle
reported on May 11, 1849. The Bill passed the third
reading in the Commons by a vote of 272 to 206 (June 11),
but was again defeated by the Lords.

In March 1850, the representative of Oxford, William
Page Wood, moved for a select committee to search the
Journals of the House to see if Rothschild's case had
no precedent. Wood compared Rothschild's exclusion with
Joseph Pease's refusal to take the oaths in 1833. The
Quaker M.P. insisted on affirming, instead of taking the
oaths in the manner prescribed by the law because of
conscientious scruples. Wood also wondered how it was
that the courts were allowed to tender the oaths in a
manner acceptable to Jews, while Parliament, which was
also a branch of the judiciary, did not recognize such
procedures. The Commons agreed to appoint the Select
Committee, but the report of the Select Committee On
The Oaths of Members indicated that Pease did not take
the oaths in 1833 due to a special dispensation which
strictly limited the affirmation to Quakers. In other
words, Jews could not be included in the legal provision
by which Pease was exempted from taking the oath.

However, the year 1850 saw some progress toward
political emancipation. Rothschild was returned to Parliament for the third time and stood before the table of the
House on July 26, 1850. He asked to be sworn on the Old
Testament and this request generated a debate on the
motion of Joseph Hume, Radical Member for Montrose and
founder of University College. After an adjournment and
three divisions, the request was conceded. The following
day Lionel de Rothschild returned to Westminster to take
the three oaths on the Old Testament. For the first time,
he could subscribe to the oaths of supremacy and allegiance
and their taking was considered perfectly legal by the

Speaker of the House. Another obstacle on his path was
finally removed. Subsequently he took the oath of
abjuration, but omitted the objectionable words from
the pronunciation of the oath. The Speaker found this
unsatisfactory and ordered Rothschild to withdraw. A
proposal was introduced at that point that Rothschild be
seated by a Resolution of the Commons, but the majority
of M.P.s objected to the attempt to by-pass the Lords.
The Attorney General, Sir John Romilly, moved a resolution
on behalf of the Government that Rothschild should not
be allowed to take his seat unless he was sworn in the
manner prescribed by the law. The Government resolved to
redress Rothschild's grievance by direct legislation but
would not go along with attempts to circumvent the
statute. At the same time, the Premier, Lord John Russell,
promised that the matter would be pursued in the forthcoming
session and he carried a resolution to that effect.

Early in 1851, Page Wood raised the question once
more. But Russell refused to fix a definite date for the
Jewish problem so long as the Papal Agression Bill was
pending. The Jewish Chronicle was outraged by Russell's
response and condemned the reluctance of the Prime Minister.[91]
Tension between Anglo-Jewry and the Liberal champion of
emancipation grew steadily and when rumors were spread
about a possible change in the ministry, the Jewish newspaper declared that the replacement of the Liberals would
not affect the cause in the least. "Should Lord John
Russell succeed in forming a ministry and come again
into office, we have little or nothing to expect from the
procrastinating spirit in which he deals with all questions
of reform."[92]

Finally, Russell yielded to pressure and introduced
an Oath of Abjuration (Jews) Bill, proposing to tender the
oath to Jews without pronouncing the objectionable words.
Russell had to defend his Bill on May 1, 1851, when it was
read for the second time (thereby missing the jubilant
opening of the Great Exhibition at the Crystal Palace).
His presence in the Parliament was necessary because the
opposition only waited for an opportunity to defeat the
measure in the absence of many supporters from the House.
This Bill was read a second time by a majority of 202 to
177 and then passed on to the Upper House, where it was
thrown out by 144 to 108 votes. Seven bishops were enlisted to head the opposition to Jewish relief in the
House of Lords.

But Rothschild's failure did not terminate Jewish
efforts to advance political emancipation. David Salomons
pursued his own election for a parliamentary seat and in
July, 1851, succeeded in obtaining the representation of
Greenwich. He defeated the City Radical David Wire, also

a strong advocate of religious freedom and a champion of
emancipation. Wire backed Rothschild during his election
campaigns in the City and supported Salomons in 1844,
after his rejection from the Court of Aldermen. He had a
particular interest in the Holy Land, and in 1840 he
accompanied Montefiore on his journey to Palestine. But
in 1851, he and Salomons contested a vacancy created by
the decease of E. G. Barnard, former Liberal M.P. for
Greenwich.[93] Both candidates appealed to the electors
with similar statements, expressing their support of
extension of suffrage, free trade, education for the people
and religious liberty. Wire did not attack Salomons
directly, but he claimed that the Jewish candidate would
not be allowed to take his seat if elected for Parliament.
Salomons, on the other hand, was backed by John Abel Smith,
who had personal contacts in this constituency. Smith
(1801-1871) was a prominent banker, M.P. for Chichester
and a staunch Liberal. He took an active part in the
struggle for the Great Reform Bill and in public he was
identified as the leading Liberal champion of Jewish
emancipation. Wire, however, was widely attacked as being
unfit for election. He alienated many electors by his
denunciation of Papal Agression and by his failure to
appeal to such local interests as the dockyard workers'.
When the poll was declared, Salomons had 2169 votes and
Wire 1278.

David Salomons appeared in the House of Commons on
July 18, a day after the defeat of Russell's Bill. He
stood in front of the table of the House and asked to be
sworn on the Old Testament. Then he took the oaths of
supremacy and allegiance in the usual form and like
Rothschild, omitted the objectionable words from the oath
of abjuration. The Speaker then announced that Salomons
had not taken the oath in an acceptable manner and therefore ordered him to withdraw. Salomons accordingly withdrew
below the bar but pressed his claims on the Commons through
Sir Benjamin Hall. The Member for Marylebone, subsequently
Baron Llanover, was widely known as a champion of religious
liberty because of his consistent attacks on church rates.
Hall (1802-1867) insisted on the right of the Welsh to
have church services in their own language and took an
active part in the cause of ecclesiastical reform. He
constantly called attention to the great abuses existing
in the management of ecclesiastical property and in the
distribution of church patronage. For Salomons he was the
best available advocate. Naturally, he was requested to
speak for Salomons and in this capacity he rose and asked
whether the elected Member for Greenwich would be sued
by the Government if he took his seat in the House. In
the absence of the Prime Minister, the question was left
after some discussion, unanswered and the House adjourned.[94]
None of the Members present on the occasion suspected that

the debate would later become one of the most sensational events of the session.

The following Monday, July 21, Hall repeated the question. Russell replied that the Government would not prosecute in such a case. Salomons thereupon entered the chamber amidst general confusion. Russell himself was astonished, not anticipating that Salomons would make such a move. The Speaker at once ordered Salomons to leave the chamber and the Premier moved that "Mr. Alderman Salomons be ordered to withdraw from the House." At this moment, however, two Radical Members, Ralph Bernal Osborne and Chisholm Anstey, moved an amendment that "David Salomons, having taken the oaths prescribed by Law in the manner which is binding on his conscience, is entitled to take his seat in this House." The amendment was lost in a division, but during the debate John Cam Hobhouse called upon Salomons to state to the House the course which he intended to pursue. Salomons rose amidst excitement and cries of 'withdraw', on the one side, and cheering on the other side, and addressed the Commons. A second amendment of Anstey, similar to the first, was lost, while Russell's original motion was carried by a majority of 150. Salomons voted on both occasions. He was then requested by the Speaker to withdraw, but he remained seated. Consequently, the Speaker directed the Sergeant-at-Arms to remove him and only when the Sergeant touched him, did Salomons retire below the bar.

Even for seasoned veterans who had seen turbulent sessions in the House, the excitement and unrest of the current debate was unusual. When things calmed a bit, the Premier announced that on the next day he would move a resolution similar to that carried the year before on Baron Rothschild's case, "that David Salomons, Esq. is not entitled to sit or vote in this House until he shall have taken the Oath of Abjuration in the form appointed by the Law." Bernal Osborne then asked whether Salomons, having taken his seat, voted three times and spoken in the House in defiance of the law, would be prosecuted by the Government. Russell replied in the negative and the House then adjourned.

Lord John Russell brought forward his motion on the next day, July 22. A number of amendments and resolutions were debated on that occasion, most notably an amendment moved by the Attorney General, Sir Richard Bethell, that Baron Rothschild and David Salomons, having taken the three oaths "in the manner which this House is bound by Law to administer", were entitled to take their seats. Russell was evidently astonished, if not enraged, that a member of his own Cabinet took a position so antagonistic to the Government's. Sir Richard Bethell (1800-1873), later

Lord Westbury, felt deeply committed to the cause of
religious freedom and was dependent on Rothschild in
his Aylesbury constituency. He was a conservative man,
despite his Liberal affiliation and reforming zeal, but
on questions of personal liberty, such as the admission
of Jews to Parliament and the abolition of tests in the
universities, he was at one with the progressive
elements of the Liberal party. Nobody had the right to
expect Bethell to keep silent on such an occasion.
Unfortunately, his amendment was lost by 118 to 71 votes.
Another zealous reformer, anti-slavery champion and Anti-
Corn Law leader, George Thompson (1804-1878), proposed
an amendment that the House exercise its privileges to
alter the oaths so that Salomons could take his seat.
But at this point the Commons closed the debate and the
House adjourned.

On the following Monday, July 28, the Speaker read
a letter he had received from Salomons, stating that two
actions had been commenced against him and that he was
advised to use as evidence the proceedings in the House.
The Commons were also presented with two petitions, one
from Greenwich and the other from the City, both praying
that their representatives should be heard at the bar.
The two petitions were denied and after defeating Thompson's
amendment of July 22, the House supported Russell's previous
motion by a majority of 123 to 55.[95]

Two actions for penalties were commenced against
David Salomons, one of which was subsequently withdrawn.
The other came up for trial in the Court of Exchequer on
December 9, before Baron Martin and a special Jury. However, the judge felt that as the case involved complicated
legal questions it ought to be referred for a Special
Verdict in the full Court of Exchequer. The full Court
heard the case on January 26 and 28, 1852. It was presided
over by Baron Pollock, the Lord Chief Justice, Baron
Parke, Baron Alderson and Baron Martin. Sir Fitzroy Kelly,
Q.C. acted as leading counsel for the defendant. Judgement was not given until April 19, when three of the four
judges found Salomons guilty of the offense. The three
judges, including Chief Justice Pollock, maintained that
the words in question were part of the oath. The fourth,
Baron Martin, disagreed with this construction and held
that as the oath of abjuration was originally designed for
Roman Catholics, not for Jews, it could not pertain to
Jewish subjects.[96] David Salomons appealed against this
decision to the Court of Exchequer Chamber, which in May,
1852, unanimously affirmed the verdict of the lower court.
The Chief Justice, Lord Campbell, deplored the status of
the law, which he himself regarded as anachronistic. But
he was bound to uphold it and the Court therefore confirmed
the judgment against Salomons.

The defendant was not discouraged and turned to the highest court of appeal in the realm, the House of Lords, but before the issue was brought before the peers, David Salomons lost his Greenwich seat in the general election and decided to give up the appeal. The election was held in Greenwich in July, 1852, and was won by the Protectionist candidate Peter Rolt and the Liberal Montague Chambers. Salomons' campaign emphasized the opinion given by Baron Martin in the full Court of Exchequer, but this time public opinion was not in his favor, as suggested by the Kentish And Surrey Mercury:

> Really, Mr. Salomons, it is too much to require from a community to which you were an entire stranger and who have shown so large a degree of sympathy in your favor. If you believed you could succeed in your appeal from the decision of the House of Commons and the decision of the courts of law, there might be some slight ground for your acting in disregard of your positive pledge that you would resign if you could not both take and retain your seat.[97]

But since there was no chance of his succeeding, the newspaper advised Salomons to retire from the campaign.

Having failed in the courts, Salomons was fined 500 pounds and was liable to disqualification for all national and municipal offices and for representation in Parliament. But the Tory Government of Lord Derby, which took over for a short time, decided to make a concession. On May 4, 1852, a fortnight after the decision of the Court of Exchequer was given, Lord Lyndhurst introduced into the House of Lords a Disabilities Repeal Bill the aim of which was the abolition of the penalties, with the exception of the fine. Lord Derby, the Premier, gave the Bill his personal support and after short debates it passed into law. The Act received the Royal Assent on June 30 and due to its retroactive operation, Salomons was able to become Lord Mayor of London in 1855 and M.P. in 1859.

Lord John Russell's rigid formalism, when applied to the Jewish question, alienated a good number of Radicals and embittered many of the Jewish emancipationists. During the City election of 1852, two Liberal candidates, George Thompson and A. S. Ayrton, called upon the Jewish community not to vote for Russell because of 'his want of energy and zeal in this cause'.[98] Salomons expressed his disapproval of Russell's course at a public meeting in Greenwich in May 1852. But Lionel de Rothschild, who publicly disagreed with Salomons' actions in Parliament, continued to defend Russell. Both Russell and Rothschild were returned as representatives for the City, many Jewish electors voting for Lord John despite the propaganda against him.

Why did Russell, the champion of religious liberty
and advocate of Jewish freedom, neglect the issue during
his premiership?   Two arguments can be advanced in defense
of Russell's neglect of the Jewish question during that
period: first, the instability of his government and the
turmoil in the country during the years 1846-1851; secondly, the reluctance of many Liberals to pursue the cause
vigorously.

A brief glance at the events during Russell's tenure
of office indicates clearly that circumstances were not
favorable for Jewish emancipation.   Russell took office
in July 1846, heading a weak coalition of Liberals and
Peelites.   There were 325 Liberals in the House, 226
Protectionists and 105 Conservative Free-Traders.   The
coalition thus really depended on the animosity between
Protectionists and Peelites.⁹⁹   The difficulties Russell
encountered were enormous: Ireland was on the verge of
starvation and revolt; everywhere in Europe the rebellions
which finally culminated in 1848 were beginning to stir,
and in Britain, the Chartist agitation became violent.
In December 1847, the Government passed the Irish Coercion
Bill in Parliament, which increased its unpopularity
among Liberals.   In September 1850, the Papal Bull which
divided England into Roman Catholic Sees, threw the country
into a state of excitement.   The passage of Russell's
Papal Aggression Bill into law directly affected the
treatment of the Jewish question, as Russell himself
explained in the Commons.   In 1851, Palmerston was forced
out of the Government upon the demand of the Queen and
Prince Consort.   Thus, the Palmerstonian wing was alienated
from the party, and Palmerston himself tried to strike a
bargain with the Protectionists.   The budget of the same
year was unpopular and in February, 1851, the Whig
Palmerstonian Peter Locke King succeeded in passing, with
the help of the Radicals, a measure for the extension of
the franchise, in spite of the Ministry's opposition.
The Government was too weak to contest the Lords or even
put forth controversial measures under these circumstances.

The second argument in defense of Lord John Russell
is the reluctance of many Liberals to stand wholeheartedly
behind the Jewish cause.   Russell was often criticized by
members of his own party for his excessive energy in this
matter.   A remarkable example is the Duke of Argyll's
attitude toward Russell's attempts to promote Jewish emancipation during the 1848 session.   In a letter to an
unknown correspondent, Argyll said:

> I can't help expressing to you, as I have done to
> others, my sense of inconvenience and danger of the
> course Lord John Russell threatens to take in sending
> up a second Jew Bill during the same session, under

a change of form at a time when everything depends
on good feeling being preserved between the various
branches of our Constitution. I think it most un-
justifiable to express so distinctly disrespect to
the deliberate opinion of the House of Lords, given
after a good debate and with no mixture of party
spirit. It will place the peers in this position:
either they must incur the discredit of giving a
vote one day, which by a deliberate opinion they
have refused to give the previous day, or they must
take a course involving the danger of raising bad
feeling between the two Houses. I can see no justification for such a course on such a question and I
do trust the attempt will be stopped in the Commons.
If it comes to the peers this session again, I should
have no hesitation in voting against it, so will
many who voted for the Bill before.[100]

The beginning of the 1853 session was marked by a
shift in the Peelite position toward the Jewish claim.
So far, the Peelites had been split over this issue:
Peel himself and a small group of followers had tended
since 1848-49 to look sympathetically on the Jewish claim
and went as far as agreeing to the admission of Jews to
some national offices. The majority of the party, however,
remained hostile or indifferent until the establishment
of the coalition with the Liberals. Early in 1853, a
considerable number of Peelites, including the Prime Minister,
Lord Aberdeen, announced their public support for Jewish
relief. In February 1853, Russell, Foreign Secretary in
the coalition Government, moved that the House resolve
itself into committee to discuss the removal of the Jewish
disabilities. The motion was carried by 234 to 205 votes
and on March 1, Russell introduced his Jewish Disabilities
Bill. During the second reading, a prominent Peelite,
Lord Drumlanrig, made a short speech in which he explained
his decision to vote for the measure, despite his past
opposition. Another Peelite, Sidney Herbert, welcomed
the Bill most warmly. Then, two other party members entered
the debate, the third Sir Robert Peel, whose anti-Jewish
remarks scandalized the House, and his Peelite colleague,
Henry Fitzroy, who rebuked the former for his speech but
expressed his own objections.[101] Despite this conspicuous
change, Aberdeen still felt that the Government did not
give full and unanimous backing to the measure, as he clearly
wrote to Russell after the second reading: "Indeed, to
say the truth, I had not the least notion of the Government
being so united on the subject; for I think it was half
formed before you were aware of the change that had taken
place in my own case."[102]

The shift was indeed too sudden, but still it had a
considerable impact on the proceedings in Parliament. The

third reading was carried in a large House on April 15, by a majority of 288 to 230. The Irish Independents voted with the Government, as did 32 Peelites and 10 Conservatives, including Disraeli and young Lord Stanley. At the beginning of May, the peers rejected the Jewish Disabilities Removal Bill by a majority of 49 (164 against 115), the majority being led by the Earl of Shaftesbury. The most eminent advocates were Lord Aberdeen, Lord Brougham, the Duke of Argyll, the Archbishop of Dublin and the Bishop of St. David's. The problem was, as the Hebrew Observer rightly commented, that (except for three leaders) the Protectionists were virtually unanimous in their resistance. As a matter of fact, "the only common line of policy which was to keep together the agriculturist party was avowedly that of civil exclusion of Jews on grounds of difference of religious belief."[103] At the same time, the Liberals remained luke-warm and timid, an attitude that was particularly notable in the Upper House:

> The majority in the House of Lords is greater by fourteen votes than that of last year: Lord Granville (the intimate friend of Baron Rothschild) was shut out by mistake with three proxies; and the Duke of Norfolk, also with three, was just in time to be too late. The Marquis of Westminster stayed away on purpose to mark his disgust at Lord Aberdeen for having neglected to make him a gold stick in waiting. But Lord Lyndhurst first time voted for the bill and the Duke of Wellington followed his good example. The Archbishop of York was absent without a pair, although he had supported the measure on all previous occasions. The Duke of Cambridge ventured on the occasion to muster in votes against the Ministers ...[104]

The Jewish electors and the Liberal politicians of the City were confused. In May they sent a deputation to the Paymaster General's Office in Whitehall to meet Lord John Russell for the sake of deliberation on the future course of the struggle. Russell could only advise them to wait and see what would happen to a new bill introduced on May 31 in the House of Lords by Lyndhurst. The new measure proposed to consolidate the oaths of supremacy, allegiance and abjuration into a single oath, but did not omit the words 'on the true faith of a Christian'. It only dropped the abjuration of the allegiance to the descendants of James II. Lyndhurst himself hoped the Bill would be amended in the Commons in favor of the Jews.[105] So did Lord John Russell. Lord Derby allowed the Bill to be read a second time on condition that it would not include the Jews. But on the motion to go into committee, two nights afterwards, both Derby and Ellenborough, who anticipated an amendment in the Commons, raised objections. Thus the Bill was defeated and as a result, a number of

City Liberals began pressing Baron Lionel de Rothschild
to vacate his seat. The proposition was made by Aldermen
Sidney and Bower in a meeting of the electors of Billingsgate ward, but the Jewish emancipationist Henry Keeling
managed to persuade the electors to give Rothschild another
chance and he carried a resolution to that effect.[106]

Lord John Russell renewed his efforts on behalf of
the cause at the beginning of 1854. He gave notice of his
intention in the House of Commons in January and fixed
February 6 as the date for a new motion. Public opinion
was skeptical about the worth of another attempt in the
legislature, and the Times caught the general mood in its
editorial of February 10, 1854:

> If Lord John Russell had anything new to say or to
> do; if we could discover a single new argument; if
> he is ready to resign should the bill not pass the
> House; if Lord Aberdeen will recommend dissolution
> of Parliament or the creation of a hundred new peers;
> in any of these cases it will be worth his while,
> and not an insult to himself and the House to bring
> on this bill. Without some serious threat of this
> sort, the Jews know well enough they have no chance
> in the Lords. Lord John Russell has no such heroic
> intention. He intends to sacrifice the Jews but not
> himself. By the time their names, their virtues,
> and their history have been before the public for
> five or six weeks, and a certain contemporary has
> exhausted upon them its own very copious vocabulary
> of abuse, suddenly but by no means unexpectedly,
> the bill will be thrown out and Lord John Russell
> will sit down to dinner with no less appetite than
> usual.

Perhaps in view of the gloomy prospects, Lord John
resorted to a radical solution which distressed Parliament
and Government. Russell introduced an Oaths Bill which
would unite the three current oaths and abolish the special
oath designed for Roman Catholics in 1829. The Catholic
Oath enraged many English Catholics because they had to
swear a denial of the Pope's temporal and civil jurisdiction within the realm. Russell seized this opportunity
to right the situation and his newly proposed oath deleted
the offensive rejection of ecclesiastical or temporal
authority of any foreign prince, person or prelate. Of
significance to the Jews, the words 'on the true faith of
a Christian' were not contained in the new oath and therefore its passage would have allowed their admission into
Parliament. The Oaths Bill was read a first time without
a division, but the opposition warned that the storm was
yet to come. For the moment, the only serious protest
was expressed by Sir Frederick Thesiger, a leading Tory

opponent of Jewish Emancipation. Thesiger was appointed
Solicitor General by Peel in 1844 and a year later became Attorney General, a post he resumed under Lord
Derby's first administration in 1852. He represented
Abingdon from 1844 to 1852 and Stamford from 1852 till
his creation in the peerage. As Lord Chelmsford, he was
Lord Chancellor in Derby's second (1858) and third
administrations (1866-1868). Thesiger's membership in
various Conservative cabinets made his opinion highly
influential.

Worse than Thesiger's resentment and the reaction
in the House was the violent public response. In March
1854, prior to the second reading in the Commons, a turbulent group in Liverpool protested and demonstrated against
the new parliamentary initiative.[107] The leading spirit
behind the agitation was Dr. Hugh McNeile of St. Jude's,
Liverpool, the spokesman of the extreme wing of English
Protestantism, who had hysterically warned against the
expansion of Popery in the country since the Papal Bull
of 1850 and now took up the Jewish danger. A local Jewish
barrister attended the meeting to defend Russell and the
Roman Catholic community, but he was attacked physically
and had to run away. The violent meeting ended in confusion and disorder.

Public demonstrations of this sort evidently reinforced
the unsympathetic Commons in its determination to defeat
the measure. Even the Liberals felt that the concession
for Roman Catholics went too far. In vain did Russell try
to persuade them that the only subject before the Commons
was admission of Jews to Parliament, and that the Bill
did nothing more for Catholics than embody the provisions
of different acts already in existence. The Commons
listened instead to Disraeli, who again announced his
support of the Jewish cause, but would not make a single
gesture in favor of English Catholics. Thus the Bill was
defeated by 251 to 247 votes, the first time since 1830
that a Jewish relief measure had been thrown out by the
Commons. The Anglo-Jewish press blamed Russell for an
imprudent strategy, and observers like David Marks advocated
detaching the Jewish grievance from the Catholic cause.
Doubtless the association with the Roman Catholic cause
did cause the setback in the Commons, but it strengthened
the moral claim of freedom of conscience of the entire
campaign.

Russell was too discouraged or perhaps too busy with
the Crimean War to resume an active role in the campaign.
In June 1855, in response to a question from John Abel
Smith, he informed the House that neither he nor Palmerston intended to introduce a new measure for Jewish relief.
But the setbacks in Parliament were in part offset by the
satisfaction derived from Salomons' election as Lord Mayor

of London on September 29, 1855. Salomons' election
to this illustrious office and the dignity with which he
filled it were a reminder to the Lords that Jews could
not be entirely excluded from the service of their country.
His mayoralty might have reassured even as reluctant an
observer as the Prince Consort, who felt uneasy about the[108]
Lord Mayor coming from 'beyond the pale of Christianity'.
Salomons paid his own tribute to the principle of religious
freedom by removing from the Fish Street Monument, which
commemorated the end of the Great Fire of 1666, the in-[109]
scription blaming the Roman Catholics for the fire.
This mayoralty was another step toward full Jewish
integration into the civil and political life in their
country.

The next attempt was made by the free trader Thomas
Milner Gibson (1806-1884), M.P. for Manchester, President
of the Board of Trade in Russell's cabinet and subsequently
an opponent of the Crimean War. Milner Gibson wanted to
abolish the oath of abjuration and decided to move his
bill without waiting for ministerial support. He was
aided by the London Liberal Registration Association, most
notably by Raikes Currie and Thomas Slingsby Duncombe
(1796-1861), M.P. for Finsbury, sympathizer with the
Chartists and spokesman for civil, political and religious
liberties. The Association held a meeting in the London
Tavern on March 2, 1856, expressing its determination
to pursue the cause regardless of Palmerston's or Russell's
opinion. Palmerston decided to give full support to the
Bill and he spoke for it during the second reading on
April 9.[110] This time Disraeli backed it too, although
he would have preferred to retain the oath with its
objectionable words and give the Jews a special exemption.
Russell and Milner Gibson did their share in defending
the Bill and the second reading passed without difficulty
by a majority of 230 to 195. A concession was made by
substituting for the oath of abjuration a new oath to
secure the Protestant succession to the crown, but this was
not objectionable to the Jews.

Early in June, during a debate over the third reading
of the amended Bill, Disraeli, Stanley and a good number
of Tories joined the Liberals to defeat an amendment by
Sir Frederick Thesiger to undermine the measure. The
House of Lords was as stubborn as ever and rejected the
Bill on its second reading, despite the efforts of Lyndhurst
and Clarendon to persuade them to compromise with the Commons.
The advocates hoped that by linking the Jewish question
with the need to reform the oaths they might overcome
the peers' resistance, but they were wrong. Derby responded
to all the arguments about the need for revising the oaths
by introducing an Oath of Abjuration Amendment Bill which
would eliminate the abjuration, but at the same time, retain

the disqualifying words. Naturally, the Commons defeated
the revised version of their original Bill and consequently
the Jewish cause was again shelved.

From the Jewish standpoint, things looked gloomy
at the end of 1856. The two Houses of Parliament were
sharply divided in their opinions on Jewish emancipation,
but the Lower House was not committed enough to coerce
the Lords. Under these circumstances the solution to the
problem seemed beyond immediate grasp. A radical change
was needed to stir the Liberals to resort to extreme
action. Fortunately, such a shift was effected by the
general election of 1857.

The Solution, 1857-1860

The dissolution of Parliament in March 1857 and the
general election that ensued marked the turning point in
the history of the Jewish campaign. For the first time,
the determination and influence of the Jewish electors
was publicly demonstrated to British politicians. Not
only did London Jewry support Liberalism at the polls,
but they also drew a considerable amount of non-Jewish
support that endorsed their emancipation. The powerful
Jewish demonstration of 1857 clarified to both Liberals
and Tories that the electors of perhaps the most influential constituency in the country could no longer
be ignored.

The occasion for the general election was provided
by Palmerston's Chinese policy, which aroused intense
opposition in the House of Commons. In March 1857, on
Cobden's motion, Palmerston was defeated by sixteen votes
and went to the country with a patriotic issue which
seemed immensely popular. There seemed no chance that
Lord John Russell, who opposed the jingo cry, would retain
his seat. Even Cobden and Bright were defeated in their
own constituencies and the coutry returned Palmerston
with a majority of seventy-nine. Prior to City election,
Lord John Russell's chances seemed so dim that the Liberal
committee of the City did not even consider his candidacy.
On top of everything, Russell's Liberal and Radical rivals
attacked him in their propaganda, appealing to the Liberal
electorate with arguments such as:

> The objection to the selection of a Lord and a
> statesman for the representation of this commercial
> city is not pro re nata. It has been raised from
> time to time ever since Lord John Russell was elected,
> by Tories as well as by Whigs, and by the highest
> as well as by the humblest order of the constituency.
> The enormous and infinitely diversified commercial
> element comprehended within this great community

suggest it, as a piece of plain English common
sense, that these should be watched over by men
themselves engaged in and alone capable of fully
understanding the concerns they are engaged to guard
and promote.[111]

The Liberal Registration Association, led by the
Radical Representative of Orkney and Shetland and subs-
tantial London merchant, Arthur Anderson (1792-1851), made
efforts to attract Jewish voters who had traditionally
supported Russell. Mass meetings, appeals in the Jewish
press and pamphlets were used to persuade London Jews
that Russell was not doing enough for their cause. But
metropolitan Jewry was unconvinced and preferred to
stick to Lord John, the general opinion being "that Lord
John Russell, as a Liberal, has no doubt in many points
disappointed his party, but he has yet accomplished more
than any other Liberal Member." Jewish emancipation saved
(this time) Russell's political career, a reminder to
Palmerston that the issue had broad political implications.
A similar demonstration of Jewish dedication to the struggle
was manifested in provincial towns such as Liverpool,
Plymouth, Bristol and in Middlesex. The Government was
defeated in the House of Commons due to its foreign policy,
but the principle of religious liberty played a vital
role in the 1857 election.

It would seem that Palmerston was getting the message
from the constituencies. As early as May 15, the Prime
Minister himself introduced an Oaths Bill in the House of
Commons. The proposed measure did not touch the Catholic
oath, but only consolidated the oath of allegiance and
parts of the oaths of supremacy and abjuration applicable
to the circumstances by dropping the sections relevant
to the Pretender. The Bill was drafted in response to
an appeal from the Jewish Board of Deputies, whose new
President, Isaac Foligno, was highly interested in the
promotion of political emancipation. Foligno wrote a
letter to the Premier urging him to devise a relief
measure and Palmerston acknowledged its receipt and granted an interview to a deputation from the Board. In this
interview, the Prime Minister expressed his sympathy with
Anglo-Jewry and consented to deliver a petition to the
Commons. The Deputies thereupon launched a national
campaign, appealing to Jewish congregations and influential
individuals. Consequently, petitions from Jewish communities
and public institutions started flowing into Westminster.[112]

Things, however, became more complicated as Roman
Catholic politicians decided to take advantage of the
opportunity for promoting their own cause. After the
second reading of Palmerston's Oaths Bill, their deputation
waited on the Prime Minister for the purpose of persuading

him to include them in the scope of his Bill. But
Palmerston explained to the deputation that he could not
take care of their grievance on this occasion, despite
his sympathy. He warned that pressure of this sort might
risk Jewish relief. A number of Catholic M.P.s consequently
threatened to vote against it if their grievance was not
also settled. An amendment to the Bill was moved in the
House of Commons in June, when the Members went into
Committee, but the amendment was lost by 290 votes. Another amendment, aiming at the defeat of the entire measure,
was pushed forward by Sir Frederick Thesiger but rejected
at once. It was thrown out by a majority that included
a leading Tory, Sir John Pakington, who took the occasion
to announce his support for the first time. Pakington,
later First Baron Hampton (1799-1880), was a staunch churchman himself, but he was tolerant in religious matters and
his views on issues like nonsectarian education were
progressive. He served in various Tory cabinets and was
known as a conscientious administrator. His declaration
of support was an important and prestigious gain to the
Jewish campaign.

At the report stage, the Government agreed to the
insertion of clauses in Palmerston's Bill preventing
Jews from holding the high offices of state from which
Roman Catholics were excluded by the Act of 1829. Another clause prevented Jews from exercising any
ecclesiastical patronage attached to offices they might
hold. The Oaths Bill, like its predecessors, treated
the problem of national offices, in addition to the
question of representation in Parliament. The third
reading passed by a majority of 291 to 168, so the Oaths
Bill moved to the Upper House. It reached the Lords in
July and was introduced by the Earl of Granville, who
urged the peers to compromise with the Commons. The
Catholic lords either supported or abstained from voting
against the measure, the Duke of Norfolk speaking publicly
in its favor. Lyndhurst delivered a remarkable speech in
its support, but the opposition had the powerful advocacy
of Lord Derby who managed to defeat the Oaths Bill by
171 to 139 votes by taking advantage of the prevalent
conservatism of the peers.

This time, however, a group of Liberals and Radicals
resolved not to give in. On July 13, Lewis Dillwyn, M.P.
for Swansea, Palmerston's supporter and advocate of abolishing
church rates and removing all religious disabilities, gave
notice in the House of Commons that he would move that
Baron Rothschild be allowed to take his seat by taking
the oath without the objectionable words. Dillwyn wanted
the House to pass a Resolution of its own in defiance of
the Upper House. Francis Henry Goldsmid urged Lord John
Russell to pursue the same path, insisting that "the House

of Commons would be quite right in proceeding by Resolution".[113] But the cautious and reluctant Lord Campbell pressed Russell not to take such a step. On July 29 he wrote Russell:

> Hoping you will continue to resist the coup d'etat of introducing the Jews into the House of Commons by Resolution, instead of waiting for a constitutional and legal consummation of our wishes; adducing arguments that 'on the true faith of a Christian' is part of which is to be sworn by Members of Parliament, I propose (with such men as Roebuck) the resolution that it will be a breach of privilege to bring an action against a Jew for not using the above oath. It would be a bare-faced attempt by one House to make laws against the wish of the other without the consent of the crown.[114]

Campbell twice warned Russell that the seating of Rothschild by Resolution of the Commons would be dangerous and entirely unconstitutional. Russell decided to again try legislation, hoping that the threat of Resolution would soften the peers. A week after Palmerston's Oath Bill was lost in the House of Lords, on July 24, he gave notice in the Commons of a new measure different in form, but not in substance, from its predecessor. The Commons allowed Russell, by a majority of 92 votes, to introduce the first stage of his Oaths Validity Act Amendment Bill, aimed at the alteration of the oaths.

Meanwhile, on June 16, a meeting of M.P.s and politicians favorable to Jewish emancipation was held at the King's Arms Hotel, Palace Yard, to discuss the issue in detail. The participants felt that the Liberal Party was not sufficiently committed and that more radical steps were needed at that point. Dillwyn continued to suggest the seating of Rothschild in the House through a Resolution of the Commons, but others felt legislation ought to be tried again, and they persuaded Dillwyn to withdraw his motion in the Commons. Rothschild announced that should he be repulsed by the House after another election he would not stand again, but he agreed to one more attempt to force the issue by taking the Chiltern Hundreds. Edward Horseman lamented the lack of determination on the part of the ministry and held Palmerston responsible for the neglect of religious freedom.[115] The eminent Peelite Sir James Graham reminded the participants how effective Peel was after he had committed himself to the cause. Graham reprimanded the Liberals for their apathy. Arthur Roebuck did not like the idea of a Resolution, but he saw little hope of the Lords accepting the current proposition, after constantly defeating similar measures. Finally, the meeting resolved to again try legislation, fearing a Resolution proposal might alienate too many potential supporters.

On July 27, Russell's Bill was discussed in the House
of Commons. Immediately after the motion, the Tory M.P.
for Midhurst and Derby's home secretary in three cabinets,
Spencer Walpole (1806-1898) rose to suggest that Russell's
new Bill was identical in content to the previously defeated
measure of Lord Palmerston. The reintroduction, he claimed,
was an evasion of the rules of Parliament. This argument
effectively attacked the measure and led to its abandonment,
for though it was successfully carried through the first
reading by a majority of 246 to 154, Russell feared that
the Lords would use the pretext for throwing it out.

Having failed again, Russell tried another course.
On August 3, 1857, at the suggestion of the Attorney General,
Sir Richard Bethel, he raised the question of an act of
William IV, the Statutory Declaration Act of 1835, which
had authorized the universities of Oxford and Cambridge and
other bodies to make statutes allowing the substitution
of a declaration for any required oath or affirmation.
Russell wondered whether this could apply to the House of
Commons and asked that a committee of enquiry should be
appointed to discuss this possibility. The committee was
appointed and instructed to find out whether, under the terms
of the Act in question, a declaration could be designed in
place of the oath of abjuration.[116] The Committee decided
by a narrow majority that the Act did not fit the interpretation of the Attorney General and Lord John Russell.
The Committee was especially influenced by Lord Campbell's
opinion that a Resolution to seat Jews by allowing them to
omit the objectionable words would be unconstitutional, even
if based on 5 & 6 William IV, c. 62, s. 8. The only way
to change the oath was by a direct legislation of Parliament.

Lord John Russell introduced another relief bill on
December 10, 1857. The Bill provided that one simple oath
should be taken by non-Catholic Members of both Houses.
The objectionable words were included in the new oath, but
Jews were given an exemption by a separate clause (the
fifth clause). In his speech Russell described the proceedings in the Select Committee of the Commons and argued that
they, rather than the courts, "were fully competent to
decide whether a Member who has taken the oath or the
declaration, as the case may be, is eligible to sit in this
House." But he did not wish to discuss the question at
that moment. He repeated that his object "is to bring in
a bill and to endeavour to obtain for it the assent of the
whole legislature; but at the same time, I shall not be
prepared to abandon the rights of the House of Commons,
as they have been ably stated by very high legal authorities,
believing them to be in conformity with the liberty of the
subject and the privilege of the House."[117] This was a
distinct threat that he had a Resolution in mind.

Sir Frederick Thesiger, who spoke after Russell, hoped Russell would deliberate carefully before taking a dangerous step that would lead to a collision with the courts. Dillwyn then rose to give his immediate support to Russell, although he had little hope for the new Bill. All attempts to solve the crisis by means of conciliation had thus far failed, so the Commons "would be bound to assert the right conferred on them by law and by precedent of interpreting the law affecting their own privileges for themselves." William Cox, M.P. for Finsbury, a Liberal Palmerstonian and staunch opponent of church rates, was also confident that if Russell proposed the Resolution, "he would get plenty of hon. Members on that side of the House to go into the lobby with him."[118]

The new Bill was carried in the House through all its stages without a division. On February 10, 1858, the House resolved itself into committee to discuss the different clauses of the Bill. Sir Frederick Thesiger moved for the omission of clause five, which gave the Jews exemption from pronouncing the objectionable words incorporated in the proposed oath. This motion was defeated by 294 to 144 votes, a majority of 153, which was larger than any other in the history of the campaign. The Liberals became determined to solve the problem once and for all.

The House of Lords received the Bill on April 27 and passed it through all its stages without a division in a period of less than two weeks. But when the Bill was discussed in the committee of the Upper House, clause five and one other minor clause were dropped by an amendment. The amended Bill infuriated the Commons who decided, by a majority of 113, to disagree with the amendments. A committee was appointed to draw up a list of reasons to be assigned to the Lords for disagreement. Thomas Duncombe at once suggested that Baron Rothschild should serve on the committee. He was able to show that early in the eighteenth century, Sir Joseph Jekyll had been appointed to a committee in secrecy before taking the oaths at the bar. The precedent was strong and the proposition was accepted by the Commons.

On May 13, Lord John Russell brought in the report of the amendments. Nine reasons were read by the clerk of the House. First, the oaths were not intended for the exclusion of Jews. Secondly, the refusal to admit Jews was contrary to the principle of religious freedom. Third, the tenets of Judaism were not opposed to or incompatible with the principle of religious liberty. Fourth, nobody could prove that Jews were unfit to serve in the House. Fifth, the country was favorable to the removal of the disabilities. Sixth, the Jewish relief Bill was endorsed by Members of both Houses of Parliament, who recognized the 'injustice and

expediency of measures for the relief of the Jews'.
Seventh, the exclusion violated the rights of the constituencies to be represented by candidates they had
elected. Eighth, the omission of the fifth clause would
result in the exclusion of Jews from several offices to which
they had been already admitted. And finally, the Commons
stated that the amendment would alter the intention of other
clauses and of the title of the Bill.[119] The reasons were
delivered to the Lords at a conference of the two Houses
and they were printed in the Journals of the House of Lords.
At the same time, the Commons returned their original Bill
to the peers.

On the last day of May, the Lords met to consider the
reasons of the other House. The debate was opened by Lord
Lucan (1800-1888), a Conservative supporter of Derby and
former military commander of a cavalry division during
the Crimean War, who was responsible for the blunder in
the battlefield. Lucan introduced a suggestion for the
restoration of harmony between the two branches of the
legislature by proposing that an act be passed to enable
each House to determine the form of oath to be tendered
to its own Members. Derby was confused and undetermined.
As a Whig, he had been able to vote for Jewish emancipation
in 1830, but having switched to the Conservative Party, he
chose to maintain opposition to Jewish freedom as a means
of unifying the party. By yielding to the Commons, Derby
would have had to acknowledge a defeat both of the Lords
and the Tories. At the moment he did not want to give up
the opposition to Jewish emancipation, so he called upon
the peers to consider the question very carefully, because
a great constitutional principle was at stake.[120] He
concluded that "we should be sacrificing the principles
and opinions of this House if we did not insist upon the
Amendments we have made at the same time, intimating that
we shall be ready to give attentive and dispassionate
consideration to a Bill which may hereafter be introduced
on the subject."[121] Lucan's amendment was dropped, but the
possibility of direct legislation to redress the Jewish
grievance was no longer out of question for Lord Derby.

Derby had convinced the Lords to insist on their
amendments to the Commons' Bill and a committee was appointed
to propose reasons for such amendments. But the pressure on
the Tory leader increased to such an extent that he had no
choice but to capitulate. On the same division, the Earl
of Stanhope, who led the opposition to Milner Gibson's
Bill of 1856, announced he would support Lucan's compromise.
The Standard, Derby's source of public support, also switched
to agreement with Jewish emancipation; so did the Atlas
and the Clerical Journal, the organ of the High Church
Party. The erosion of the Tory resistance in Parliament
became obvious. In March, the Morning Advertiser reported

that a number of so far staunch Tory opponents had altered
their position. Among them were: The Earl of Dalkeith,
Lord Haddo, the Earl of Lisburne, Sir R. Gore Booth, Sir J.
Yarde Buller, Sir George Foster, Sir W. Payne Galway, Sir
E. C. Karrison and Sir E. L. B. Lytton. Others, who had
generally abstained from this question, began appearing and
voting on the side opposite the Government's. Included were:
Thomas Baring, William Mackinnon, William Brown, Colonel
Smith, Colonel Tynte, A. Beresford Hope, Mr. Bangshaw and
Mr. Butt.[122]

Derby, however, wanted to settle the question on his
own terms and had to magnify the effect of a Liberal defeat.
On July 12, reasons for the peers' amendments were introduced and debated in the House of Lords. The Upper House
insisted on pressing the amendments, first because the
objectionable words, although not directly designed for
Jews, were phrased to secure the Christian qualification
for admission. Secondly, Jews had never been eligible for
admission to either House of Parliament. The third reason
was that exclusion from Parliament on religious grounds
was legitimized in the Act of the Settlement and in other
instances. Fourth, the non-profession of Christianity was
a moral disqualification for representation in Parliament,
and the fifth reason was that Parliament ought to remain
an exclusive Christian assembly. The old and familiar
rhetoric was thus repeated as a gesture to assert the
Lords' constitutional position, even if it had become clear
that the settlement was inevitable.

The debate over the amendments, however, did not prevent
both Lord Lucan and Lyndhurst from introducing a bill of his
own. For some technical reasons, Lucan's bill was found
more attractive and pursued by the Lords as the solution
to the Jewish grievance. The Bill was carried through its
third reading without a division on July 12 and on the same
day, the peers approved their amendments to the Commons'
previously defeated Oaths Bill. Both Lucan's Bill and the
amendments were sent to the Lower House at the same time.

In the Commons, Russell indicated that by doing what
they had done, the Lords agreed to Rothschild's admission
and gave reasons why such a bill ought not to pass. The
contradiction was ridiculous. It was as derogatory to their
own dignity as to the Commons'. But this was not enough
to convince many M.P.s to settle the issue on the Lords'
terms. When the House went into committee, on July 19,
a number of Members refused to support Lucan's Bill, as they
found the entire procedure disrespectful. C. Gilpin said
he though "that this was a miserable compromise. It did
not respect the conscientious scruples of either side of
the House, but was thrown among them in a manner which was
discreditable to those who had thrown it among them."

Arthur Roebuck shared the wide feelings of indignation
at the Bill, but Thomas Duncombe tried to persuade his
colleagues "that the Bill was not so contemptible as some
hon. Members seem to consider, for they must remember the
circumstances under which the Bill passed."

Russell then said it appeared to him "a matter of
doubt, whether in agreeing in the course proposed by the
House of Lords we should not place some Resolution on our
Journals in which, without answering the Reasons adopted
by that House, we might state our reasons for not taking
notice of those reasons, saying, for instance, that as the
Lords have passed a Bill carrying into effect the object of
the House of Commons, it is not necessary to consider their
reasons." He proposed to disregard the Lords' amendments
but at the same time accept the compromise offered by Lord
Lucan. The Commons took this path on July 21, 1858.

After the Commons' agreement to the Lords' solution,
two separate bills were carried to implement the settlement.
On Friday, July 23, 1858, two Bills received the Royal
Assent in the House of Lords: the first, an 'Act To
Substitute One Oath For The Oaths Of Allegiance, Supremacy
And Abjuration And For The Relief Of Her Majesty's Subjects
Professing The Jewish Religion', 21 & 22 Vict. c. 48; the
second, 'An Act To Provide For The Relief Of Her Majesty's
Subjects Professing The Jewish Religion', 21 & 22 Vict.
c. 49. The first Act consolidated the oaths of supremacy,
allegiance and abjuration into one simplified and updated
oath, to be taken upon admission to Parliament or entry into
national office. Jews were not exempted from taking the
new oath under the provisions of this Act. The second Act
excused Jewish subjects from pronouncing the objectionable
words when the new oath was tendered to them, after the
relevant bodies passed a resolution of their own to that
effect. In other words, each branch of the legislature
was entitled from now on, to pass a Resolution of its own
to administer the newly enacted oath in the manner it found
appropriate.

The following day, Baron Lionel de Rothschild appeared
at the table of the House and asked to be sworn an M.P.
The Commons had previously passed a Resolution to administer
the oath to him without the objectionable words, so he could
legally take it without saying 'on the true faith of a
Christian.' Rothschild was accompanied to the table by
Russell and Abel Smith and could celebrate the end of a
crucial phase of the struggle for Jewish emancipation.

The Parliamentary settlement of the question was
received by the Jewish public with a certain ambivalence.
Generally, British Jewry regarded Rothschild's admission
to Parliament a triumph for their cause. But there were

voices expressing criticism and reservation. A letter
to the editor of Jewish Chronicle published on July 23,
1858, reflected the indignation of a correspondent from
Bristol, who refused to subscribe to the testimonial
offered to Rothschild: "There is nothing in the passing
of the Oaths Bill as it is, accompanied by the disgraceful
and insulting reasons of the Lords, for the Jew either to
triumph or to rejoice at." An editorial published in the
same issue tried to reassure the critics by disagreeing
with "many Jews who were indignant at the disgraceful
manner in which the concession was made by the peers."
During the mass meeting of Anglo-Jewry for the commemoration
of the event on July 26 at the London Tavern, the ardent
emancipationist George Jessell admitted that the form in
which the concession had been made "bore an ugly appearance
and was of a most ungracious character."

Among some keen activists the mood was not exactly
jubilant. Furthermore, the issue was not entirely settled
because Lucan's compromise only authorized each House to
pass a resolution of its own to administer the oath in the
manner it found fitting. But what would happen if an unsympathetic House denied a Jewish request for the alteration
of the oath? A highly reactionary House of Commons could
legally deny Jewish admission to Parliament by refusing to
pass the necessary Resolution. The Jews felt they ought
to continue the agitation. An editorial in Jewish Chronicle
(April 3, 1859) urged the continuation of the Jewish alliance
with the Liberals on behalf of the cause: "An imbecile
House of Peers has cemented the connections between the
Jews and the Liberals, which have previously been voluntarily
forming among them. The former moral dependence has now
become a reality through the continued good will of the
Liberals." The collaboration of the two bodies can be seen
in three election campaigns that followed.

At the end of August 1858, David Salomons offered his
candidacy for the borough of Greenwich as a Liberal representative. The Tories counted on a split among Liberals over
the question of parliamentary reform and hoped to secure an
easy victory for their own candidate. Salomons stood for
the extension of the suffrage, the secret ballot and against
church rates. He was returned by a majority of 889 votes,
primarily due to the support of Dissenters who were attracted
by his opposition to church rates. Meanwhile, a vacancy
had been created in the representation of the borough of
Hythe, Folkstone and Sandgate in Yorkshire. Baron Mayer
de Rothschild contested the seat. In his address to the
electors he emphasized that "he is, as he always had been,
a Liberal and should he be elected, it would be his earnest
endeavour to enforce, to the extent of his ability", the
political program of the Liberal Party. He was returned
unopposed.

During the 1859 election, British Jews once again demonstrated their loyalty to the Party. The most important event from a Jewish point of view was the return of Francis Henry Goldsmid by the electors of Reading. This election was accompanied by an agitated struggle in which another Liberal candidate, Mr. Benson, appealed to the Liberal electors to vote against Goldsmid on account of his religion. Benson's strategy did not lead to the desired results and he was defeated by 662 to 560 votes. Goldsmid was supported by a good number of Tories, but he himself regarded the results as a Liberal victory, an interpretation clearly reflected in his address to his constituents:

> I hasten most cordially to thank you for having elected me as one of your representatives in the House of Commons. Considering the vigorous exertions of the Conservative party in your borough, and the influences brought to bear against me, especially the attempt to persuade the Liberal electors that it was their religious duty to desert their political principles, I think that the sense and the firmness with which these endeavours and influences were resisted and the victory which, under such circumstances, the Liberal party has achieved, are things of which they may well be proud.[123]

Nor did the Liberals abandon the Jews. On March 3, 1859, Thomas Duncombe raised in the House of Commons the question of changing the Resolution pertaining to Jewish Members into a Standing Order, in order to avoid the necessity of annual renewal. Duncombe wondered whether the Resolution had to be passed each session and if redundant procedures could be spared. Benjamin Disraeli, however, feared that any change of procedure might upset the delicate compromise reached between the two Houses of Parliament. In the end, the House appointed a Select Committee to check the law and find a solution to the problem raised by Duncombe. The Committee recommended on April 11, 1859 that a Standing Order be passed in the House four days after the swearing of new Members and it would be valid until repealed. Still, this was an action of the Commons and not a law passed by the entire Parliament. In the next session, Duncombe tried to carry a measure to implement what was so far a Commons' Resolution as Parliament's Standing Order. This time the response was favorable, and on August 6, 1860, Duncombe's measure became the Jews' Act Amendment Bill, 23 & 24 Vict. c. 63.[124]

The civil and political disabilities were finally removed. As far as the law was concerned, British Jews were now full and equal citizens. But they still had to face the challenge of social integration and to labor for their acceptance by their fellow-countrymen. The elimination of the anomalous discrimination against Jews from the Statute Book was only a first step toward a broad emancipation. In the meantime, English Jews could justly rejoice in an unqualified victory.

Notes

[1] D. Marks & A. Loewy, eds. Memoir Of Sir Francis Henry Goldsmid, Bart. (London, 1882), p. 21.

[2] Protest signed by Lord Holland and others, Journal of House of Lords, Vol. 60, p. 247; April 28, 1828.

[3] Minutes Of Board Of Deputies, Vol. I (November 1760-April 1828), f. 36; April 28, 1828.

[4] Letter of John Bowring to I. L. Goldsmid in Abrahams, p. 132.

[5] Minutes Of Board Of Deputies, Vol. II (March 1828-January 1838), ff. 3-5.

[6] Minutes, ff. 7-8.

[7] Minutes, ff. 18-19, 24-27.

[8] See Wellington to Peel, April 6, 1830, in C. S. Parker, Sir Robert Peel From His Private Papers (London, 1899), Vol. II, pp. 145-146. "The political importance of the question is one of feeling. This Christian community will not much like to have Jewish magistrates and rulers. In another view it is of importance, as it will be opposed by the Bishops in the House of Lords, and by those Lords who dislike innovation. It besides gives a false colouring and throws ridicule upon the great measures of 1828 and 1829, which it resembles only in name."

[9] Progress Of Jewish Emancipation Since 1829 (1947), p. 4.

[10] Diaries Of Sir Moses And Lady Montefiore, Vol. I, p. 78.

[11] Diaries, p. 79.

[12] Lord Holland to I. L. Goldsmid, May 12, 1829, in Abrahams, pp. 143-144.

[13] Memoirs Of Sir Francis Henry Goldsmid, p. 38.

[14] Abrahams, p. 144.

[15] C. H. L. Emanuel, A Century And A Half Of Jewish History, Extracts From The Minutes Of The Board Of Deputies (London, 1920), pp. 15-16.

[16]Minutes, Vol. II, ff. 30-49; Lord Holland to I. L. Goldsmid, May 26, 1830, in Letter Book Of I. L. Goldsmid (page number is missing).

[17]Letter Book, f. 143 and also an anonymous 1830 letter to Lord Holland on f. 186.

[18]Lord Holland to I. L. Goldsmid, June 29, 1830 in Letter Book, f. 128.

[19]Lord Holland to I. L. Goldsmid, April 13, 1830 in Letter Book, p. 133.

[20]The Speeches Of The Right Hon. William Huskisson, (London, 1906), Vol. III, p. 565.

[21]Charles Grant to I. L. Goldsmid, September, 1829, Letter Book, f. 33.

[22]Zachary Macaulay to I. L. Goldsmid, March 2, 1829, Letter Book, f. 33.

[23]Progress Of Jewish Emancipation Since 1829, p. 4.

[24]Lord George Bentinck, in a letter to Disraeli of December 24, 1847, talked about massive support of the Granvillite faction; Disraeli Papers, Hughenden Manor, Box 89, B/XX/Be/45.

[25]Progress Of Jewish Emancipation Since 1829, p. 4.

[26]T. Perronet Thompson to I. L. Goldsmid, February 12, 1829, Letter Book, f. 324.

[27]Lady Dorchester, ed. Recollection Of A Long Life By Lord Broughton (London, 1910), Vol. IV, p. 16.

[28]Dorchester, Recollection, p. 22.

[29]Earl Grey to Lord Holland, in Abrahams, p. 163.

[30]Minutes Of The Board Of Deputies, Vol. II, ff. 71-77.

[31]Minutes, ff. 78-81.

[32] I. L. Goldsmid to Hobhouse, May 14, 1830, Broughton Papers, British Library ADD MSS 36466, f. 138. See Goldsmid's sample letter written on June 19, 1833 in his Letter Book, f. 322: "Sir, the House of Commons will be moved this evening to go into committee on the Jewish Civil Disabilities Bill, even if the question should come at a late hour. I take the liberty earnestly to solicit the favour of your attendance on this occasion in order to prevent the necessity of any further postponement, as the opponents of the Bill appear to be endeavouring to defeat by delay a measure in favour of which the House has already expressed so decidedly an opinion."

[33] Letter Book, f. 33a.

[34] Memoirs Of Sir Francis Henry Goldsmid, pp. 44-45.

[35] Minutes, Vol. II, ff. 82-85.

[36] Hansard, Third Series, Vol. 20, pp. 44-45; August 1, 1833.

[37] Abraham D. Kreigel, ed. The Holland House Diaries, 1831-1840. The Diary of Henry Richard Vassall Fox, Third Lord Holland, With Extracts From The Diaries Of Dr. John Allen (London, 1976) pp. 236-7.

[38] Hansard, Third Series, Vol. 23, pp. 1158-76; May 21, 1834.

[39] Memoir Of Sir Francis Henry Goldsmid, pp. 16-17.

[40] Corporation of London Record Office, Common Hall Book, Vol. 10, ff. 378-379.

[41] David Salomons to Peel, February 17, 1835, Peel Papers, B. L. ADD MSS 40414, f. 351; Peel to Salomons, February 26, 1835, Peel Papers, B. L. ADD MSS 40414, f. 353. Salomons' letter to Peel was signed by a number of Jewish emancipationists. A copy of the same letter in Holland's handwriting, probably the original, appears in I. L. Goldsmid's Letter Book.

[42] Lord David Cecil, Melbourne (London, 1934), p. 210.

[43] Melbourne to Goldsmid, in Abrahams, p. 171.

[44] Corporation of London Record Office, Proceedings Of The Court Of Aldermen, Vol. 240, ff. 15-16. Four Letters

To The Editor Of Morning Chronicle, Signed By Britannicus (December, 1835).

[45] Minutes, Vol. II, ff. 105-108.

[46] Minutes, ff. 111-112, 120-123.

[47] Hansard, Third Series, Vol. 33, pp. 1227-38, May 31, 1836; Vol. 35, pp. 867-75, August 3, 1836; Vol. 35, pp. 1236-9, August 15, 1836.

[48] Morning Chronicle, November 30, 1837.

[49] Minutes, Vol. II, ff. 129-132.

[50] Diaries Of Sir Moses And Lady Montefiore, Vol. I, p. 128.

[51] William Thornborrow, Advocacy Of Jewish Freedom (London, 1848).

[52] Lucien Wolf, Essays In Jewish History (London, 1935), p. 315.

[53] Letter Of The Frankfurt Jewish Community to Sir Robert Grant and his reply, Morning Chronicle, February 4, 1835.

[54] David Salomons, A Short Statement On Behalf Of His Majesty's Subjects Professing The Jewish Religion, p. 21.

[55] Israel Finestein, A Short History Of Anglo-Jewry, p. 86.

[56] Hansard, Third Series, Vol. 56, pp. 84-89, March 10, 1841; Vol. 57, pp. 754-68, March 31, 1841; Vol. 58, pp. 1048-9, June 3, 1841; Vol. 58, pp. 1449-58, June 11, 1841.

[57] A New Song To A Old Tune, (London, 1841).

[58] Address From I. L. Goldsmid To The Jewish Electors Of The City Of London (June 18, 1841).

[59] David Salomons to Lord John Russell, August 1, 1845, Russell Papers, Public Record Office, Vol. 13V, f. 326.

[60] Peel to Wellington, October 10, 1843, in C. S. Parker, Sir Robert Peel From His Private Papers, Vol. II, p. 570.

[61] Wellington to Peel, October 12, 1843 in Parker, p. 571.

[62] Voice of Jacob, October 27, 1843.

[63] Ibid.

[64] Corporation of London Record Office, Proceedings Of The Court Of Aldermen (1843-44), Vol. 248, ff. 406-7, 411-13, 435.

[65] Proceedings, f. 435.

[66] David Salomons to Peel, November 6, 1844, Peel Papers, B. L. ADD MSS 40553, ff. 298-300. Also Salomons to Peel, May 13, 1833, B. L. ADD MSS 40544, f. 217 and Salomons to Peel, November 8, 1843, B. L. ADD MSS 40535, ff. 245-257.

[67] Salomons to Peel, February 9, 1845, Peel Papers, B. L. ADD MSS 40559, f. 233.

[68] Peel to Lyndhurst, February 22, 1845, Peel Papers, B. L. ADD MSS 40422, ff. 263-4.

[69] First Report Of Her Majesty's Commissioners For Revising And Consolidating The Criminal Law, Appointed February 22, 1845, Dated May 30, 1845 in Parliamentary Papers, February 4-August 9 (XIV), 631, pp. 1-160.

[70] Lord Campbell, Lives Of Lord Chancellors And Keepers Of The Great Seal Of England, From The Earliest Time To The Reign Of Queen Victoria, 1845-1869 (1869), Vol. VIII, pp. 155-6.

[71] Minutes, Vol. V (May 1841-February 1846), ff. 308-310.

[72] Minutes, ff. 309-310.

[73] Minutes, ff. 310-311.

[74] Bernard Lord Manning, The Protestant Dissenting Deputies (Cambridge, 1952), p. 212.

[75] Hansard, Third Series, Vol. 78, pp. 515-27, March 10, 1845; Vol. 78, pp. 885-6, March 14, 1845; Vol. 82, pp. 622-43, July 17, 1845; Vol. 82, pp. 869-701, July 21, 1845.

[76] Salomons to Peel, December 14, 1847, Peel Papers, B. L. ADD MSS 40599, ff. 487-8.

[77] Salomons to Peel, May 8, 1849, Peel Papers, B. L. ADD MSS 40609, f. 340.

[78] Other Jewish candidates who tried their luck in the 1847 election but failed were F. H. Goldsmid (Yarmouth), I. L. Goldsmid (Beverly), D. Salomons (Marylebone), and Mayer Rothschild (Hythe). David Salomons stood for Shoreham in 1837, but failed.

[79] Minutes, Vol. VI, ff. 64-66.

[80] Hansard, Third Series, Vo. 95, p. 1282, December 16, 1847.

[81] Hansard, Third Series, Vol. 95, pp. 1234-1332, December 16, 1847; On Disraeli's involvement in the campaign see my article "Benjamin Disraeli and the Emancipation Of The Jews", Disraeli Newsletter, Vol. 5, No.1, 26-46.

[82] Robert Stewart, The Politics Of Protection, Lord Derby And The Protectionist Party, 1841-1852 (Cambridge, 1971).

[83] Quoted by Sir Henry D'Avigdor Goldsmid, "Lord George Bentinck And The Jews", Trans. J. H. S. E. Vol. 23 (1971), 44-52; See Maurice Myres, "Some MS Sidelights On Anglo-Jewish Emancipation", Trans. J. H. S. E. Vol. 6 (1912), 241-2: Lord George Bentinck to Jacob A. Franklin, January 6, 1848: "For the reasons I have referred to being lukewarm on the subject, I have not given it that deep attention or study which I might have devoted to it."

[84] Lord George Bentinck to Disraeli, January 10, 1848, Disraeli Papers, Hughenden Manor, B/XX/Be/47 and November 3, 1847, B/XX/Be/40.

[85] Earl of Malmesbury, Memoirs Of An Ex-Minister, An Autobiography (London, 1884), Vol. I, pp. 205-6.

[86]Louis J. Jennings, The Correspondence And Diaries
Of The Late Right Hon. John Wilson Croker, L.L.D., F. R. S.
Secretary To The Admirality From 1809 To 1830 (London, 1885),
Vol. III, pp. 139-140; Charles Whibley, Lord John Manners
And His Friends (London, 1925), Vol. I, p. 283.

[87]On Jewish efforts on behalf of the 1847-48 Bill see
Minutes, Vol. 6, ff. 64-66, 102-116; Lucien Wolf, Sir Moses
Montefiore, A Centennial Biography With Selections From
Letters And Journals (New York, 1885), pp. 141-144.

[88]Dowager Duchess of Argyll, ed. Autobiography And
Memoirs of George Douglas, Eighth Duke Of Argyll (London, 1906)
Vol. I, p. 303. The debates are in Hansard, Third Series,
Vol. 96, pp. 460-540, February 11, 1848; Vol. 97, pp. 1215-
50, April 3, 1848; Vol. 98, pp. 606-70, May 4, 1848.

[89]Jewish Chronicle, February 9, 1849.

[90]Charles Whibley, Lord John Manners And His Friends,
Vol. I, pp. 15-18.

[91]Jewish Chronicle, February 14, 1851.

[92]Jewish Chronicle, February 28, 1851.

[93]Based on Kentish And Surrey Mercury, June 21, 1851
and June 28, 1851. See also election posters located in the
Greenwich Local History Center.

[94]Hansard, Third Series, Vol. 118, pp. 979-986, July 18,
1851; Vol. 118, pp. 1143-1217, July 21, 1851; Vol. 118, pp.
1318-66, July 22, 1851.

[95]Hansard, Third Series, Vol. 118, pp. 1573-1629,
July 28, 1851.

[96]Proceedings against Salomons in the courts are given
in August Goldsmid, ed., Report Of The Case Miller Versus
Salomons, M.P. With A Summary Of The Parliamentary Proceedings
In The House Of Commons (London, 1830).

[97]Kentish And Surrey Mercury, July 19, 1852.

[98]Jewish Chronicle, May 7, 1852.

[99]See Desmond MacCarthy & Agatha Russell, eds. Lady John
Russell, A Memoir With Selections From Her Diaries And
Correspondence (London, 1910), pp. 167-170.

[100]Duke of Argyll to anonymous correspondent, June 5, 1848, Jewish Museum Papers, London, MS 882.

[101]See J. B. Conacher, The Aberdeen Coalition, 1852-55: A Study In Mid-Nineteenth Century Party Politics (Cambridge, 1968).

[102]Aberdeen to Russell, February 27, 1853, Aberdeen Papers, B. L. ADD MSS 43070, ff. 298-9.

[103]Hebrew Observer, April 15, 1853.

[104]Hebrew Observer, May 13, 1853.

[105]Sir Theodore Martin, The Life Of Lord Lyndhurst, From Letters And Papers In Possession Of His Family (London, 1883), pp. 451-453.

[106]Jewish Chronicle, August 3, 1853.

[107]Jewish Chronicle, March 3, 1854.

[108]Hannah F. Cohen, Changing Faces, A Memoir Of Louisa Lady Cohen (London, 1937), p. 48.

[109]Albert M. Hyamson, David Salomons (London, 1939), p. 68.

[110]Hansard, Third Series, Vol. 141, pp. 703-759, April 9, 1856; Vol. 142, pp. 595-605, May 23, 1856; Vol. 142, pp. 1165-97, June 9, 1856.

[111]Jewish Chronicle, March 27, 1857.

[112]Minutes, Vol. IX, ff. 222-223.

[113]F. H. Goldsmid to Russell, July 20, 1857, Russell Papers, P. R. O. Vol. 13D, ff. 21-22.

[114]Lord Campbell to Russell, July 20, 1857, Russell Papers, P. R. O. Vol. 13D, f. 23. Also Lord Campbell to Russell, July 27, 1857, Russell Papers, Vol. 13D, ff. 39-42.

[115]Jewish Chronicle, July 24, 1857.

[116]Hansard, Third Series, Vol. 147, pp. 993-60, August 3, 1857; Vol. 147, pp. 1010-20, August 4, 1857.

[117]See Polly Pinsker, "English Opinion And Jewish Emancipation, 1830-60", Jewish Social Studies XIV (1952), 51-95. Hansard, Third Series, Vol. 147, p. 273, December 10, 1857.

[118]Hansard, Third Series, Vol. 149, pp. 1749-97, April 27, 1858.

[119]Hansard, Third Series, Vol. 149, pp. 1749-97, April 27, 1858.

[120]Pinsker, p. 85.

[121]Hansard, Third Series, Vol. 150, p. 1269, May 31, 1858.

[122]Morning Advertiser, March 23, 1858.

[123]Jewish Chronicle, January 13, 1860.

[124]Hansard, Third Series, Vol. 157, pp. 960-3, March 20, 1860; Vol. 158, pp. 1916-9, April 18, 1860; Vol. 159, pp. 1734-50, July 12, 1860, p. 687, August 6, 1860; Vol. 160, pp. 1346-7, August 15, 1860.

Chapter 4

THE PUBLIC DEBATE

For over thirty years, the Jewish question was constantly debated in public. The issue was discussed by all
important organs of opinion; newspapers, periodicals,
pamphlets as well as parliamentary sessions. The early years
of the struggle for Jewish freedom attracted considerable
interest, but as the question dragged on without reaching
a settlement, the debate became tedious for many. Even
staunch supporters of the Jewish cause found the repetition
of the arguments from both sides boring. One can sympathize
with Macaulay's response to Lord John Russell's request for
an expression of support during the debate over his 1858
Oaths Bill:

> As for the Jews, I shall content myself with giving
> them my vote in silence. You would not, I am sure,
> advise me to make any debut in the House of Lords on
> a subject long worn out; on a subject which has gone
> to the debating societies; on a subject on which I
> made my maiden speech in the Commons twenty-eight
> years ago; on a subject on which I have harangued and
> written till I am weary and on which I have nothing
> to say but what has long been in print, and has been
> read, reviewed, quoted, praised and abused both in
> England and America. If ever I do strain my voice in
> Parliament, it shall be in order to tell the Lords
> something that I have not told all the world twenty
> times before.[1]

To spare the reader similar boredom, the public debate
will be presented in this chapter in a topical rather than
a chronological order. The main arguments pertaining to
Jewish emancipation can be reduced to three or four. The
first argument was that the uniqueness and particularity
of the Jewish people justified their exclusion from the
British nation and the rights of citizenship. The Jews
were a separate nation with distinct collective aspirations
of their own, so the argument went. They refused to assimilate themselves to the non-Jewish population, preferring
alienation from the Christian public.

The response was the liberal view that religious
disabilities constituted a persecution, no matter how
insignificant and unimportant they might appear. Judaism,
the advocates claimed, was a religion, not a nationality.
Because the Jews filled all civic duties honorably, there
was no reason to deprive them in this respect. The opponents
replied that Christianity was part and parcel of the
constitution. All social and political institutions, including the law, were imbued with the spirit of Christianity.
Jews were not fit to legislate for a Christian commonwealth
as their faith was antagonistic to the religion of the

majority. If admitted to Parliament, they might abuse
their position to injure the national church or even help
to pass anti-Christian legislation.

Finally, the advocates advanced the technical argument that the legal restrictions were inconsistent and no
longer compatible with the law or with the actual proceedings.
They created all kinds of anomalies and anachronisms that
a modern law could not tolerate.

The most popular anti-emancipationist argument was
that the Jews were aliens and wished to remain so throughout their residence in the country. To prove his claim that
Jews were foreigners, the representative of Oxford University,
Sir Robert Inglis, contended in the House of Commons that
Jewish primary loyalties were reserved for their co-religionists rather than countrymen. "The fact was," he told the
Commons on May 22, 1833, "that a Jew could never be made
an Englishman, even though he be born here. So long as
he looked forward to another kingdom, his sympathies would
be given more to a Jew in Paris and in Warsaw, than to a
person residing in the same or in the next country to him."[2]
Moreover, the Jews did not behave as patriotic citizens in
peace or wartime. As an example, Inglis said that London
Jewry had furnished Napoleon with a loan to help him fight
their own country. He referred to the Jamaican merchant
Alexander Lindo, and even though Inglis twisted the facts
to produce a misleading impression, his point was clear and
the argument that Jews were foreigners was often repeated
in Parliament.

Lord Derby contended in the same vein that Jews were
never devoted wholeheartedly to national causes, that they
had collective aspirations of their own, based on Messianic
hopes for a restoration to the Holy Land. He claimed that
they were a nation within a nation and that they did not
intermingle with the Christian population.[3] For this reason,
Derby stated in 1857, the exclusion of Jews from the benefits
of citizenship were entirely justified.

In response to these insinuations, the advocates replied
that international affiliations were not uncommon in English
history and were not, in other cases, perceived as contradictory to national loyalty. Lord John Russell mentioned
in Parliament, in reference to the question, the Catholic
attachments to the Papal establishment, which possessed
temporal power and had secular interests of its own.[4]
Macaulay wrote in his Civil Disabilities Of The Jews that
"the English Puritans, under Charles I, prevailed on the
Scotch to invade England. Do Protestant Dissenters of our
own time wish to see the Church put down by an invasion of
foreign Calvinists? ... Some of the most illustrious public
men England ever had were inclined to take refuge from the

tyranny of Laud in North America. Was this because
Presbyterians are incapable of loving their country?"[5]
And W. J. Fox, the Member for Oldham, pointed out to the
House that Jews fought in the ranks of the Prussian army
against Napoleon at Waterloo, even though the French
Emperor emancipated them and equalized them in rank and
status.[6]

   The Jews denied all charges of contradiction between
their religious opinions and national obligations. Francis
Henry Goldsmid stated in one of his pamphlets that "they do
not, as seem to have been imagined, they cannot believe that
they have now any political existence or political interest
distinct from those of the country in which they live."[7]
To prove his point, Goldsmid turned to the Scriptures:
"I do not perceive that he could rely upon any higher authority
than the conduct of the Prophets during the captivity. And
this will teach the Jew that to serve the State and Government
which protect him is a duty, not a crime; for Jeremaiah
more than once enjoined cheerful submission to Babylon, and
Nehemaiah and Daniel were ministers and servants of
Babylonian and Persian kings."[8] Thus, truly pietist Jews
ought to approve of political emancipation.

   This argument contradicted Inglis' accusation that
orthodox Jews wished to remain unemancipated, because
participation in public life would lead to a violation of
the tenets of Judaism. The argument of Jewish foreignness
was absurd because it was not applied to parallel situations.
Bernard Van Oven therefore emphasized that "the British Jew
is as dictinct from the French Jew just as the British
descendant of any one of the Barons who came over with the
Conqueror was distinct from the French descendant of the
brother of the same baron who stayed in Normandy."[9]

   The advocates rejected the attempt to prove Jewish
alienation with Messianic legends. These aspirations had
little real appeal in the nineteenth century because of their
supernatural and irrational character. Consequently, it
appeared to Lord John Russell "an outrage on common sense
to say that expectations so indefinite and remote (Messianic)
have the slightest practical influence on the conduct of
their relations with existing things."[10] Zionist programs
had not yet been formulated and English Jews necessarily
regarded Britain as their only homeland. The only voices in
support of Jewish restoration to Zion were Christian pietists.
Goldsmid rightly asserted that such Messianic hopes were
founded on Adventist visions popular among Christians rather
than Jews.[11] Then how could British Jews be blamed of
divided loyalties?

   The second major argument in favor of emancipation was
that representation in Parliament was a constitutional right

of every citizen, at least within the limits of property qualification. The exclusion of natural-born subjects and tax-payers were therefore an infringement of the constitution. Lord Lyndhurst expressed this view quite explicitly in a speech he delivered in the House of Lords on July 10, 1857: "You cannot insert the disabilities with the view of excluding natural born subjects, the Jews, from sitting in Parliament, for you have constitutionally no right to do so. If you wish to exclude the Jews, I repeat it again, exclude them by a direct act of legislation. Unless you do so, you cannot, according to the law and constitutional principle, effect that object."[12] Sir Robert Peel made the same point in a speech he delivered in February 1848, the first time he publicly endorsed Jewish admission to Parliament.[13] The legal restrictions imposed on natural-born subjects was not an abstract deprivation but a penalty for religious opinion. There was no provision in the law for thus penalizing blameless citizens. Similarly, Lord John Russell stated to the House of Commons: "My belief is that the imposing of a penalty, the imposing of a disability on man because he is of a different religion, is in principle exactly the same as imposing further penalties, the same as imposing fine and imprisonment, and even inflicting punishment of death itself."[14]

Jews were penalized, according to liberal views, because of a lingering prejudice that prevailed in certain influential circles. William Hazlitt claimed that the harassment of Jews in Papal Rome was not substantially different from the imposition of civil disabilities in Britain. The two kinds of discrimination, although dissimilar in quality and degree, originated in bigotry. Hazlitt felt appalled by the manifestations of hostility derived from prejudice and he expressed his feelings acutely in his stirring appeal to his contemporaries:

> How truly has it been said of prejudice, that it has the singular ability of accommodating itself to all the possible varieties of the human mind. Some passions and vices are but thinly scattered among mankind and find only here and there a fitness of reception. But prejudice, like the spider, makes everywhere its home. It has neither taste nor choice of place and all that it requires is room. There is scarcely a situation, except fire and water, in which a spider will not live. So let the mind be as naked as the walls of an empty and forsaken tenement, gloomy as a dungeon or ornamented with the richest abilities of thinking; let it be hot, cold, dark or light, lonely or inhabited, still prejudice, if undisturbed, will fill it with cobwebs and live on. If the one prepares his food by poisoning it to her palate and her use, the other does the same, and as several of our passions are strongly characterized

by the animal world, prejudice may be denominated
the spider of the mind.[15]

In Hazlitt's view, the equalization of Jews with the
rest of the population was beneficial to the emancipators
as well. It would liberate the latter from the oppression
of prejudice, and this was a precondition to enlightenment
and human progress toward perfection.

The radical Westminster Review followed the same path.
It urged the removal of Jewish disabilities on universalistic
grounds and denounced the sordid motivation of the opponents
of the cause. Their reason for retaining the privations
was sheer bigotry.[16] "There is a moral stain in the permission of persecution, a species of complicity in living in
a country where it takes place ... Civilized men show
deference in each other's tastes and fancies, even though
they may not be convinced of their being reasonable and
necessary. It is a base thing to take advantage of a man's
honest prejudice to oppress him."[17]

The result of such prejudices was that Jews internal-
ized some of the derogatory feelings expressed in public.
If all red-haired men were discriminated against as Jews
were, Macaulay explained, all would develop anti-social
qualities. In countries where Jews were given a fair chance
to integrate, they had already proven their loyalty, talent
and productivity. In France, Belgium, Holland and Denmark
emancipation had been effected, and the results in all were
satisfactory. Even in various dependencies of the British
crown, Canada, Barbados and Jamaica, Jews lived on terms
of equality with their countrymen. In every case, Jews
showed their adaptability to the environment.[18] Thus, the
only reason for the Jewish failure to cultivate was the
oppressive condition in which Jews were placed. Had they
been offered a chance, they too would distinguish themselves
in the cultural, political and social activities of their
country. J. S. Buckingham presented the argument in a radical
manner when he told Members of Parliament on May 22, 1833
that like all men, "Jews were the creatures of circumstances
and of the legislation under which they lived. Whatever of
inferiority or disqualification remained to adhere to them,
it was in our power to remove; as by placing them on a level
with ourselves in the employment of every civil and political
right, they would soon become our equals in every moral
and intellectual respect."[19]

But reactionary foes disagreed with the notion of
natural rights upon which the advocacy of the cause had been
based and maintained that no such rights existed. Sir
Robert Inglis said in Parliament that political power was
no man's due. It belonged to the sovereign, who could
distribute or deny it completely. Political power could

be allocated in greater proportions to some and in lesser
to others. This principle applied to a legal disqualification
from the franchise of paupers, women and lunatics. Similarly,
political activity could exclude non-Christians within the
framework of existing laws. It was, under some circumstances,
a normal and legitimate deprivation based on constitutional
grounds.[20]

No less controversial was the argument that the
admission of Jews to Parliament would unChristianize it.
For enemies of Jewish relief, the constitution was designed
to safeguard and promote Christianity. In view of the
alleged antagonistic attitude of Jews toward Christianity,
it was inconceivable that Jews would be eligible to legislate for the country.[21] Gladstone articulated this thought
in the House of Commons on March 31, 1841:

> If Christianity was a great pervading principle of
> their law, if the glory of God was proposed in their
> daily worship as the principal ground of their acts,
> if also most great questions which came before them
> were intimately associated with the distinctive
> principles of Christianity, he conceived himself at
> perfect liberty to pronounce that those who as
> conscientious men rejected Christianity as a fable
> and imposture, could not be competent to enter on the
> consideration of such subjects.[22]

Trying to elaborate on the implications of Christianity
for the preservation of the constitution, James Whiteside
explained to the House how Jewish M.P.s might be prevented
from fulfilling their parliamentary duties. Whiteside was
the Tory Member for Enniskillen, Solicitor General for Ireland
in 1852 and writer of works on Italy and ancient Rome. As
one might expect, his speeches were persuasive and his arguments intelligent. First he wondered what would be the
response if a Jew chose to denounce Christianity in Parliament and find protection in his parliamentary privilege.
Or what would be the effect on parliamentary efficiency,
if Jewish Members abstained from the House on the Sabbath?
In England, he went on, Christianity was interwoven with
the Common Law, and the constitution was based on it. Was
it not indicative that each session began with the Anglican
prayers? Was there a divorce administered outside the
jurisdiction of the church?[23]

But the supporters of Jewish emancipation could easily
meet these questions. There was no danger of blasphemy on
the part of Jewish Members, because it was punishable and
parliamentary privilege offered no protection for this offense.
The Bishop of London, Campbell Tait, saw no reason why Jews'
admission to Parliament should unChristianize it. The
religious feelings of the nation were strongly enough embedded

to persist regardless of the composition of the legislature.
Colonel Cockburn wondered ironically whether "the devotional
feeling of Sir Robert Inglis would be in the slightest degree
diminished if a Jew were to take his seat by the side of
the Hon. Member?"[24]

Jews would not Judaize Parliament because the number
of Jewish Members likely to be returned would always be
small. And when a Jew was elected to Parliament, he would
always represent a predominantly Christian constituency.
Baron Rothschild, for example, did not represent a Jewish
interest but the London electorate. As for the absence from
sessions on the Sabbath, that would not prevent the Commons
from carrying out their duties. Even if a few Jewish
M.P.s were missing on these occasions, there would always
be enough Members to participate in parliamentary sessions
and committees.

The most forceful argument used by supporters to meet
the attack in the name of Christianity was that the country
was not Christian. Since the resettlement of Jews in the
seventeenth century, the population could no longer be
considered exclusively Christian, so there was no reason
its legislature should be so. Putting the argument in
further historical perspective, it was clear that the
constitution in recent times had never stressed Christianity
as such. If it had, why had Roman Catholics or Protestant
Dissenters, who were good Christians, been denied toleration
and excluded from the benefits of the constitution for so
long? Bernard Van Oven advanced this argument most pointedly:

> This is not a Christian country, and Christianity is
> not a part and parcel of the constitution. On this
> point I will venture to repeat the arguments used
> fifteen years ago, and which I am not aware have been
> refuted. It can no longer be asserted with any
> appearance of reason that Christianity is part and
> parcel of the law of the land, for what is Christianity?
> At least what is being regarded as a portion of the
> Common Law? From the time of Elizabeth until very lately,
> Christianity was understood to mean Episcopacy, the
> Protestant reformed Church of England: all else was
> excluded, that, and that alone, constituted part and
> parcel of the law of the land: but about three years
> since, this definition was enlarged, and it was ad-
> mitted to include all Protestants of whatever
> denomination ... In one short year (1829), this barrier
> gave way, the line of distinction vanished, and Christian
> Catholicism was included in the definitions which made
> Christianity part and parcel of the law of the land.[25]

Even the conservative Gentleman's Magazine had to
agree with the Jewish emancipationists on this point. In

an editorial commenting on one of Goldsmid's pamphlets,
the magazine justified the Jewish claim.[26]   If Roman
Catholics had been emancipated, there was no reason why
Jews should still be discriminated against. "England
certainly meant, at the time of the Reformation, to be a
Christian Protestant country. The multiplication of sects
in Cromwell's time did not alter this character of the
constitution. Our modern Liberals have violated its integrity; it has ceased to be Protestant. Therefore, Mr.
Goldsmid's arguments are, in our opinion, fair and Jews have
as just a claim to sit in Parliament as Papists, and so
Mohametans." The Reactionary and bigoted periodical admitted that the Jews had a case, even though it disliked
the extension of religious liberty in the country.

Jews would neither unChristianize the country nor
threaten Christian interests because their faith discouraged
proselytism. Bernard Van Oven tried to prove this with
quotations from rabbinic sources and an anonymous Jewess
explained the fact to Lord Winchelsea in a letter to the
Times.[27]   In this letter she wrote:

Faithful to their creed, they do not, either directly
or indirectly, endeavour to undermine the religious
opinions of others. Why should they make the attempt?
They are taught to believe that Almighty God, the foun-
tain of all blessings, judges all human beings
according to their work, and that the pious and
righteous on earth, whatever be their race or faith,
may all hope to enter into the kingdom of heaven.

Another Jewish emancipationist repeated the argument even
more clearly: "It is important to recollect that the Jewish
religion is not, and by its very nature cannot be a prosely-
tizing religion; and it has been established on the most
trustworthy authority."[28]

Even if the constitution were Christian and even if
Jews would unChristianize Parliament or Judaize the country,
the oaths in their current form would not protect the religion
of the majority. Various speakers contended in Parliament
that the oaths had little to do with Christianity, especially
the oath of abjuration, the main barrier in Rothschild's
way. By taking the oath, a person did not declare he was
a Christian; he only announced that he abjured allegiance
to the Pretender or his descendants and swore that he recognized the Hanoverian right to reign in the country.[29]
Furthermore, the oaths were a weak test of personal religious
beliefs. Henry Brougham argued brilliantly in 1833; Edward
Gibbon took his declaration 'on the true faith of a Christian'
and not only sat in Parliament, but also held office under
George III. He sat on the Treasury benches under a High
Church government then in existence. Nobody paid attention

to his antagonistic attitude toward religion and Deists
like him served a 'Christian' government and sat in a
'Christian' legislature. This was a demonstration that the
oaths could not secure the Christian character of Parliament.

The main reason for objecting to Jewish emancipation
was the harm anticipated to the union of church and state.
Sir Robert Inglis once explained that the various relief
acts recently passed for the several religious denominations
signified a gradual separation of church from state. The
repeal of the Test Acts and the Roman Catholic emancipation
were sufficiently dangerous; Jewish relief would further
dissolve this union.[30] Bishop Samuel Wilberforce predicted
that upon admission to Parliament, Jewish Members would
take direct steps against the establishment of the Anglican
church.[31]

Even for this accusation advocates had some convincing
replies. Jews were less likely than Protestant Dissenters
or Roman Catholics to injure the Anglican establishment.
British Jews were not concerned with the difference between
various Christian sects or which, if any, should be established. Lord Brougham told the Lords that Jews were
qualified for full citizenship because the M.P.s "had let
in Dissenters, who were opposed to a church establishment,
while the conscientious Jew might have no such objection.
But that was not all. They have let Roman Catholics who
were not only against the establishment, but who were in
favour of another establishment ..."[32] The Jews were not
affiliated with an organized religious hierarchy, so they
could recognize the supremacy of the crown over the
established church. Some of them even paid church rates
(after the 1853 Braintree Decision of the courts, which
partially exempted Nonconformists from paying church rates),
to demonstrate they bore no hostility to the national church.

The final major argument pronounced during the public
debate was that the disabilities contradicted one another,
they obstructed other laws and constitutional principles and
were incompatible with the modern world. The disabilities
created anomalies within the law that a modern legal system
could not tolerate.

Perhaps the most obvious anomaly was that a Jew could
be elected sheriff or appointed juryman, but until 1845
was barred from the minor corporate offices. The Marquis
of Lansdowne asked the Lords on March 10, 1845 to consider
the implications of such a contradiction:

And what was more injurious to the public interest,
while it was unjust to individuals, than that one of
the most respectable men in England (David Salomons),
one who had been entrusted to fill the responsible

office of sheriff, who in some counties was ad-
missable as Magistrate, while in others he was
excluded; for even in this point the law was
anomalous and inconsistent. Why should not that man,
when elected as Alderman, be allowed to take part in
municipal proceedings in that capacity?[33]

Lansdowne touched on a fundamental inconsistency: Jews
served as aldermen and magistrates in various provincial
towns and counties long before the law had been amended in
Parliament, but they were still excluded from the same
offices in the city of London.[34] How could an equitable
constitution accept such a violation in the uniform
application of its laws? Lord Lyndhurst summarized the
argument when he told the Lords that "the object which I
have in view is to get rid of this anomaly and to place the
law upon a distinct footing that every man may know the
ground upon which he stands and that there may for the future
be no difference of construction and no practical difference
in the admission of persons to office between the corporation[35]
of the city of London and other corporations of the Empire."

Macaulay showed that the disabilities were divorced from
reality because they failed to deny Jews political power.
Exclusion from Parliament or national offices could not deprive
them of power. Political influence, he claimed, depended
on wealth and it was impossible to prevent rich Jews from
using their means in public life. As Victorian politics
were notoriously corrupt, Jews had little trouble influencing
the polity. "Gatton and Old Sarum may be the property of
the Hebrew. An elector of Penrhyn will take ten pounds
from Shylock rather than nine pounds nineteen shillings and
eleven pence three farthings from Antonio."[36] Macaulay
used popular stereotypes to elucidate his point, and one
can easily imagine how uncomfortable English Jews must
have been when reading advocacies such as this.

Jewish emancipationists stressed that the disabilities
stood in sharp contradiction with other laws, or at least,
with other constitutional principles. Time and again they
indicated that the discrimination against them was a
product of mere chance, or rather, misfortune. As Goldsmid
once remarked, "the Jew has been accidently affected by laws
of which he was not the object; and his situation is as
full of inconsistencies as it might be expected that a work
of chance could be."[37] In 1853, David Salomons demonstrated
the same idea when he reminded the Lords that their refusal
to administer the oaths in a manner most binding on his
conscience was a violation of a constitutional theory which
had already been affirmed by Parliament. Consequently, he
maintained, "the constructive disability, which you wish
to perpetuate, is not only unjust, but contrary to the
spirit of the constitution."[38]

Sir William Molesworth revealed another inconsistency
between the disabilities and the law. He argued that Baron
Rothschild was bound by law to serve in Parliament. Rothschild
was not admitted to regular sessions where failure to subscribe to the oaths constituted a disqualification for
admission, but he could serve on an election committee.
Refusal to sit on an election committee could lead to severe
penalties specified by the law. However, not having been
proclaimed M.P., Rothschild could not have been appointed
to an election committee of the House of Commons. The
situation created by the orders of two different statutes
was simply absurd: on one hand, Rothschild was bound to
obey the order of the House to attend his place in the
election committee (7 & 8 Vic. c. 103), but on the other
hand, he could not serve without being admitted to the
House (1 Geo. I, St. 2, c. 13). "It is evident therefore,
that the law is in a very anomalous state and that the
House has no power either to enable Baron Rothschild to
perform his duties as a lawfully chosen Member of the House
or to relieve him from the obligation to perform those
duties."[39] Molesworth was not sure whether the absence
from the election committee would be considered an offense.
If it was, Rothschild would be liable to penalties by the
courts. "It is certain, however, that the House has no
power to relieve Baron Rothschild from the obligation to take
the oath of abjuration; no power to relieve him from the
obligation to attend his service in the election committee;
no power to declare his election null and void; and that no
law or custom of Parliament can be cited, no precedent can
be provided, which would justify the House in compelling
him."

Another consideration was that a parliamentary seat
ought not to remain vacant with a constituency deprived
of its right to full representation in Parliament. By barring
Rothschild from occupying his seat the law injured Christian
electors. The answer to this contention was that the London
electors violated the law by voting for a person who was
not eligible for election. The inhabitants of the metropolis knew prior to the election that Rothschild would be
disqualified for admission to Parliament, so they were[40]
responsible for their own grievance.

Toward the end of the struggle, during the years 1857-
58, such inconsistencies became conspicuous and could no
longer be ignored. The House of Commons admitted the Jewish
Member to its conferences and selected him for a parliamentary
committee that dealt with the Lords' amendments to Russell's
1857 Oaths Bill. In the Upper House, Lord Granville indicated how absurd this looked from a constitutional point
of view. "To say nothing of other arguments, the anomaly
of our not being able to prevent a Jewish Member of the

other House from sitting on a committee, acting in
conferences and taking part in every parliamentary proceeding, except sitting and voting, is so great as to make
it a mere mockery for any one to stand up here and appeal
to high Christian principles for the maintenance of such a
barren restriction."

The history of the oaths also illuminated how the
exclusion of Jews from the legislature might be held
unreasonable. Prior to the imposition of the oaths there
was no legal obstacle in the way of Jewish subjects.
Theoretically, there was a precedent for Jewish participation in government and legislation. The oath of
allegiance, first containing the words 'on the true faith
of a Christian', was enacted in 1606 by 7 Jam. I, but in
1689, as part of the Act of Settlement, the need to take
this oath prior to entering office or parliament was
abolished. The disqualifying words reappeared only in the
oath of abjuration enacted after the Jacobite insurrection.
Between the Act of the Settlement and the Insurrection there
was no legal barrier to forbid Jews to engage in politics.

During the thirty years of debates, these arguments
were in the forefront. Each side tried to prove and illustrate the arguments pertaining to its own views, either
to support or repudiate the notion that the Jews were a
separate nation; that the disabilities constituted a
discrimination and a penalty for religious opinions; that
Jewish admission would unChristianize the legislature; or
that Jewish disabilities were inconsistent in themselves
and contradictory to other laws.

How important were these debates for the advancement
of the cause? Bernard Van Oven's imaginary conversation
between Judaeus and Amicus Nobilis, published in a year of
hopeful expectation (1847), may appear to the reader a bit
too optimistic, for it ended with the persuasion of the
opponent to embrace the Jewish view. Following the classical
Jewish tradition of Medieval polemics, the debate had a
happy ending, when the defeated party admitted: "I thank
you sincerely, my excellent friend, for all that you have
said. I confess myself a convert fully to your views and
opinions. I confess that the veil has been removed from
my eyes. I can now clearly see the fair and honourable path
of duty; and that path I will endeavour to pursue."[41]
For the emancipationist, information about the Jewish
grievance and public debates over the subject necessarily
lead to the desirable settlement.

In reality, the eloquence of the advocates was less
effective. Yet one ought not to underestimate the importance
of these discussions. During the thirty years of propagating

the cause, public opinion changed dramatically in favor
of the Jews. The most serious newspapers and periodicals
buttressed the defense with their own arguments and the
majorities in the House of Commons grew steadily. The
Lords capitulated, in spite of themselves, to irresistable
outside pressures. However tedious and repetitive the
debates were, they played an important role in the
promotion of Jewish emancipation.

Notes

[1] Macaulay to Russell, 6 April 1858, quoted in G. P. Gooch, The Later Correspondence Of Lord John Russell, 1840-1878 (New York, 1925), Vol. II, p. 228.

[2] Hansard, Third Series, Vol. 18, p. 50.

[3] Hansard, Third Series, Vol. 146, pp. 1220-1236.

[4] Hansard, Third Series, Vol. 57, p. 93.

[5] T. B. Macaulay, "Civil Disabilities Of The Jews", Edinburgh Review LII (1830-31), 366-67.

[6] Hansard, Third Series, Vol. 95, p. 1268.

[7] F. H. Goldsmid, The Arguments Advanced Against The Enfranchisement Of The Jews (London, 1833).

[8] Ibid. p. 18.

[9] Bernard Van Oven, Ought Baron Rothschild To Sit In Parliament? (London, 1847), p. 9.

[10] Hansard, Third Series, Vol. 96, pp. 506-7.

[11] Op. Cit., Goldsmid, p. 11.

[12] Hansard, Third Series, Vol. 146, p. 1241.

[13] Hansard, Third Series, Vol. 96, p. 5223.

[14] Hansard, Third Series, Vol. 125, p. 113.

[15] "Emancipation Of The Jews", Tatler, No. 176, March 28, 1831.

[16] Review of Hyman Hurwitz's Introductory Lecture, University of London, Westminster Review 10 (1828-29), 435-443.

[17] "Religious Disabilities", Westminster Review 19 (1833), 102-110.

[18]Hansard, Third Series, Vol. 22, p. 798.

[19]Hansard, Third Series, Vol. 18, p. 55.

[20]Hansard, Third Series, Vol. 95, pp. 1352-3.

[21]Hansard, Third Series, Vol. 57, p. 757.

[22]Ibid.

[23]Ibid.

[24]Hansard, Third Series, Vol. 96, p. 510.

[25]Op. Cit. Van Oven, pp. 25-26.

[26]Gentleman's Magazine 147 (1830), 86-114.

[27]Bernard Van Oven, An Appeal To The British Nation, p. 51; "Lord Winchelsea And The Jews", Times, April 6, 1857.

[28]Arthur Cohen, The Lords And The Jews (1853), p. 22.

[29]Hansard, Third Series, Vol. 113, pp. 398-458.

[30]Hansard, Third Series, Vol. 24, p. 798.

[31]Hansard, Third Series, Vol. 98, p. 1336.

[32]Hansard, Third Series, Vol. 98, p. 1404.

[33]Hansard, Third Series, Vol. 78, p. 525.

[34]According to J. H. Plumb, England In The Eighteenth Century (Penguin, 1950), p. 86, Jews participated in municipal activities throughout the eighteenth century.

[35]Hansard, Third Series, Vol. 78, p. 520.

[36]Op. Cit., Macaulay, pp. 366-367.

[37]F. H. Goldsmid, Remarks On The Civil Disabilities Of British Jews, p. 16.

[38] David Salomons, Alteration Of The Oaths Considered, p. 16.

[39] Hansard, Third Series, Vol. 86, p. 258.

[40] W. J. Fox said in the House of Commons on December 16, 1847: "But the question was not so much one concerning religious opinions, as one connected with civil rights. It concerned much more nearly the civil disabilities of Christians, than it concerned the Jews. The motion of the noble lord (Russell) would in effect go to remove a great Christian disability from the electoral body and the constituencies of the country. The question was really related to the partial disenfranchisement of the city of London and might be stated thus: 'have the electors a right freely to choose the person which they would entrust with the defence of their interests in the House, or have they not such right, and are they mistaken in their attempt to exercise a free choice." Henry Goulburn replied: "Parliament would neglect its duty to the state if it encouraged any constituency to return to the House of Commons a person whom the laws of the country for the time being disqualified from sitting." Hansard, Third Series, Vol. 85, pp. 1267-8.

[41] Bernard Van Oven, Ought Baron Rothschild To Sit In Parliament?, pp. 28-29.

CONCLUSION

THE HISTORICAL UNIQUENESS OF THE ANGLO-JEWISH EMANCIPATION

Jewish historians dealing with assimilation have always been impressed by the pathological rejection of traditional Judaism by assimilating Jews. During the modern era, European Jews tended to accommodate themselves to modernity not only by sheer acculturation, but also by developing a profound hatred of their ancestral tradition. The promise of removal of civil and political disabilities, heralding the termination of an anomalous Jewish existence, reinforced the desire to break away from Jewishness. There is a consensus among Jewish historians that in the anticipation of political and civic emancipation, Jews were ready to weaken their attachment to Judaism. For the most part, the emancipators stated clearly that in exchange for civil rights, they expected Jews to relax their religious observance and adjust more readily to the customs, lifestyle, culture and mentality of their Christian countrymen. In Continental Europe, pressures in this direction were enforced by law and policy making.

The most obvious illustration of an external pressure on European Jews to reform their creed is provided by the French Revolution. When the Jewish question was under discussion in the National Assembly of Revolutionary France in 1789, Clermont Tonnerre, a liberal advocate, declared: "From the Jews as a nation we must take everything, but to the Jews as individuals we must give everything. We cannot have a nation within a nation."[1] Another sympathizer with French Jewry, the revolutionary Abbe Gregoire, manifested a similar approach in a list of questions about English Jews, which he asked of the Abolitionist Thomas Clarkson in 1789. The information was apparently sought in preparation for putting to the Assembly his motion for the emancipation of French Jews.[2] Gregoire asked Clarkson, for example, whether English Jews were disposed to transfer their Sabbath and make certain adjustments that would facilitate harmony with the Christian nations among which they resided. Abbe Maury, speaking for the conservative opposition, based his arguments against the liberation of the Jews on the idea that "the name Jew denotes not a religious sect but a nation", and that a Jew faithful to his national traditions could not be a good Frenchman. The difference between the two attitudes was that the liberals believed Jews would give up part of their Jewishness, whereas the conservatives were convinced that European Jews would not act in this spirit.[3]

A similar tendency can be traced in the various German states during the nineteenth century. After 1850, for instance, when Germany swung toward an intolerant and brutal nationalism, Jews felt strong pressures to conform to the national

creed at the expense of their own heritage. And as
nationalism became increasingly illiberal, the nation state
cultivated an abhorrence of any form of deviance. German
liberal Protestants hoped that Jews would be ready to pay
for civil rights by sacrificing their ancestral tradition.
They would not tolerate Jewish separateness within the
context of modern nationalism. Fritz Stern observed that
"many Germans hoped for this surrender of Judaism not
because they disliked Jews but because they disliked
pluralism and were made uneasy by a group that still had
a great deal of internal cohesion."[4]

In view of the German and French emancipationist
experience, Jewish historians feel that for the emancipators,
the removal of civil and political disabilities had a price.
Generally, emancipation was conditional. The nation state
made its terms quite clear before emancipating the Jews.
For the most part, Jews responded to such pressures and their
integration into the non-Jewish society signified a break
with their own traditions. The pathological rejection of
Judaism was, to some extent, a consequence of the expectations
of the emancipators. In other words, European movements
of emancipation generally encouraged assimilation, acculturation and a break with the past. The anticipation of equality
generated a desire to make Judaism more acceptable within
the environment and in some cases, to renounce it altogether.

One ought to keep in mind that in Continental societies,
emancipation was a tempting offer. Jews felt the limitation
on economic and professional opportunity. They were society's
outcasts, a pariah group living marginally in a permanent
condition of deprivation. Jews were subject to arbitrary
discriminatory political decisions, were exposed to legal
and social deprivation and had few chances for advancement.
The situation was anomalous to the considerable portions
of Jewish minorities in various countries ready to join
protests by political dissidents. The mass participation
of Jewish middle class elements in the German revolution
of 1848 is a clear indication that for many Jews, the
situation seemed so grim that they no longer had much to lose
from the collapse of ancient regimes.

In Britain, the emancipationist experience was completely
different. The legal disabilities did not create a feeling
of oppression. The restrictions were irritating; even
humiliating, but their existence could hardly stir anybody
to join radical oppositions or militant revolutionary parties.
The implications of the Anglo-Jewish grievance were not as
severe as those experienced on the Continent.

External pressures to renounce Judaism were heavy, but
they were social rather than legal. The pressures put on
Jews to conform to a national idealogy were weaker than
those felt elsewhere in Europe. The Anglo-Jewish emancipation

was a product of a growing belief in the merits of liberalism, of a genuine acceptance of religious liberty and cultural pluralism. The readiness to emancipate religious minorities was implicit in a rationalist-pragmatic conviction and in such enlightened ideas as the abolition of slavery and the enlargement of the political franchise. The only unconditional Jewish emancipation in Europe was effected in the country where the forces of liberality and tolerance had triumphed.

In Britain, Jews were not asked to reform any religious practice as a prerequisite to their equalization in status. Their Jewishness was taken for granted, whether compatible with the modern concept of nationality or not. Also, their communal autonomy and separateness remained untouched. The Board of Deputies retained control over marriages, education, welfare and other domestic concerns. In 1836 it was given statutory recognition by Parliament as the marriage registrar for the Jewish community and in 1852, the chief rabbi and head of the Portuguese congregation were entrusted with the responsibility of supervising educational grants allocated from parliamentary endowments. The House of Lords consented in 1857 to exempt Jews from the provisions of the Divorce Law passed that year and leave Jewish divorces to rabbinic jurisdiction. British politicians constantly refused to intervene in internal Jewish disputes even when asked to do so by Jewish dissidents. In 1845, as we have seen, Isaac Lyon Goldsmid appealed to Sir Robert Peel against the re-solution of the Deputies to exclude his congregation from the right of solemnizing marriages, but the Premier would not get involved in an internal Jewish conflict.

The tendency to allow English Jews to retain their traditional autonomy was unique. In the various German states or in France, Jews were forced to relinquish communal independence. In Prussia, for example, Jewish congregations were subjected to the supervision of the Ministry of Interior Affairs, which interferred with even purely ritual-istic or dogmatic concerns. Abraham Geiger, for instance, was prevented by the authorities from introducing his religious reforms because of orthodox opposition. Through-out his tenure of office in Breslau, Geiger had to face restrictions imposed by the Prussian state which generally sided with his orthodox rival, Rabbi Tiktin. England was in fact the only European country where Jews continued to retain an autonomous management of their domestic affairs during a process of emancipation.

Jews were no exception in this matter. Quakers too were emancipated unconditionally, although their religious tenets were also at odds with the notion of modern citizen-ship. They presented a similar dilemma because, as with Jews, they were charged with dual loyalties. Quakers were also accused of entertaining firmer attachments to their

co-religionists overseas than to Englishmen of other
religious persuasions. They did not marry members of
other religious sects until the 1870s; they refused to take
oaths, fight or pay taxes for wars. Yet they were granted
full civil rights in three separate measures in 1833, 1837
and 1838.

In Britain, religious emancipations differed sharply
from those effected on the Continent. Emancipation did
not necessitate radical adjustment on the part of the
beneficiaries. British statesmen did not accept the
solution formulated by Napoleon for the treatment of the
Jewish question. In 1806 and 1807 Napoleon convened the
Assembly of Notables and the Sanhedrin in order to
interrogate them in public. This interrogation was to
determine whether the Jewish creed was sufficiently universalistic and whether Jews were ready to alter it whenever
it seemed anti-social. But this solution could not apply
to Victorian needs. No British statesman would consider
enforcing a single religious uniformity in the atmosphere
of the nineteenth century. The movement for religious
emancipation in fact legitimized the sharp divisions along
religious lines. Exclusion on the basis of dissent was no
longer acceptable.

Yet there was a serious endeavor to protect both the
Anglican establishment and certain historical privileges
reserved for the national church. To defend the Anglican
particularism, the polity had to acknowledge the peculiarities of other religious minorities and to tolerate them
unconditionally. The religious diversity of the nation and
the long established tradition of toleration required a
solution of pluralism, rather than uniformity. Characteris-
tically, in 1835, when Peel addressed the electors of
Tamworth in his famous manifesto, he tried to persuade them
that the extension of citizenship to Nonconformists was
not necessarily harmful to the national church.[5] As long
as the various religious sects were granted civil rights
within a pluralistic framework, there would always be a way
of securing the position of the Anglican establishment.

For reasons inherent in the nineteenth century, Anglo-
Jewish emancipation was not accompanied by heavy pressures
to break with the ancestral tradition. Jewish peculiarities
were not treated as anomalies and no external pressure was
exercised to purge them from the ritual. Jewish communal
autonomy remained immune from government interference and
the organization of Jewish congregations went unaltered.
This unparalleled experience made Anglo-Jewish emancipation
unique from a historical perspective. Quite rightly, English
Jews still regard the years of emancipation as their finest
hours and they have good reasons to dissent from the
historiographic tradition of underrating the value of
emancipation. For Anglo-Jewry, political emancipation is

not as futile and worthless as it seemed to disillusioned European Jews, to Zionist ideologists and Socialist thinkers. Anglo-Jewish freedom proved to be a safe avenue toward social integration and acceptance. Emancipation entailed the heritage of a particularistic dilemma that found its solution within a universalistic context.

Notes

[1] S. M. A. de Clermont Tonnerre, *A Speech spoken by the Count Clermont Tonnerre, Christmas eve last, on the subject of admitting non-Catholics, Comedians and Jews to all the privileges of citizens, according to the Declaration of Rights* (1790).

[2] *Jewish Museum Papers*, MSS 160, "Questions relatives aux Juifs", (1790).

[3] See Simon Dubnow, "Letter on Old and New Judaism" in K. S. Pinson, ed. *Nationalism And History* (New York, 1959), pp. 111-112.

[4] Fritz Stern, *Gold And Iron, Bismarck, Bleichroeder, And The Building Of The German State* (London, 1977), p. 462.

[5] For the Tamworth Manifesto see, Norman Gash, ed. *The Age of Peel, Documents Of Modern British History* (New York, 1968), pp. 74-79.

Benjamin Disraeli And The Emancipation Of The Jews

     On November 15, 1837 Benjamin Disraeli took his seat
in the House of Commons after winning an election that ended
five years of campaigning and successive defeats. When he
was finally admitted to Parliament, Disraeli had to face
the Jewish problem. Almost the first item of business after
the opening formalities was a vote on Jewish disabilities
following the presentation of petitions by the sheriffs of
London (one of whom was Sir Moses Montefiore). For the new
Member for Maidstone the Jewish issue constituted a serious
dilemma. He did not feel sufficiently confident to support
Jewish emancipation in public because of the hostile responses of most Tories. It is unknown whether he sympathized
at that stage with the claims of English Jews. For the
moment, it seemed prudent to Disraeli to distance himself
from Jewish emancipation by voting with the majority against
the measure.

     "Nobody looked at me," he wrote his sister Sarah after
the division, "and I was not at all uncomfortable, but voted
in the majority with the utmost sangfroid ..."[1]   However,
there are good reasons to believe that Disraeli was uneasy
when he had to confront the Jewish issue. His Jewish descent
was one of the most embarrassing objects of ridicule during
his election campaigns of 1832-1837, and the bigotry of
many M.P.s would, in all likelihood, continue to make his
Jewish background a liability. A personal recollection of
young Disraeli during that period, recorded by the mother
of a close friend, Lady Dorothy Neville, reveals his
attitude toward his Jewish birth.

     My mother well remembered 'Dizzy' in what she used
     to call the 'curly days', by which she meant the era
     of masculine ringlets, black velvet dress coats ...
     The memory of 'Dizzy' was always dear to my mother,
     and often she would recall the tremendous struggle
     of his younger years and against a sea of debts
     contracted when living with the reckless exquisites
     with whom he loved to consort, they were also against
     the prejudice aroused by his Hebrew descent.[2]

Not surprisingly, Disraeli, during the 'curly days', chose
to remain silent when Jewish issues were being debated in
public. From 1837-1847 Disraeli refrained from involvement in the disputes over Jewish emancipation, although
he witnessed the crucial debates of 1841 and 1845.

     In 1847, Benjamin Disraeli changed his mind. When
the issue was raised at the end of the session, he openly
and publicly espoused the Jewish cause and he delivered his
most famous speech in behalf of Jewish emancipation. Most
of Disraeli's biographers are captivated by this speech

and by three others he delivered on the subject during
the years 1850, 1854 and 1856. From his verbal expressions
they conclude that he was, in principle, supportive of
Jewish emancipation, even at some risk to his career.
Disraeli's authoritative and highly respected biographers
William Flavell Monypenny and George Earle Buckle ended
their analysis of the subject with the following statement:

> There was, it should be remembered, in spite of that
> inbred conservatism which Disraeli claimed as
> characteristic of the Hebrew race, no party interest
> to serve. Success could only add another vote to the
> opposite side: for Rothschild, though a personal
> friend of Disraeli's, was, like most of the Jews of
> the day, a Liberal in politics and a follower of
> Russell. When all the circumstances are considered,
> it cannot be gainsaid that in his unfaltering support
> of the Jewish claims Disraeli manifested in a very
> high degree adherence to principle, disregard of self-
> seeking, and courage. He proved in the most convincing
> manner that he was ready to act, even when strongly
> against his own interest, on the doctrine proclaimed
> throughout his writings, that 'All is race'.[3]

Monypenny and Buckle felt that Disraeli was consistent
at this point and that he genuinely advocated Jewish
emancipation. They explained his frequent silent votes and
two opposing speeches to Jewish relief bills as products of
a clash between the Jewish question and other related interests
They also accepted Disraeli's clarifications of his two
negative votes, that of 1850 and 1854, as sufficiently
warranted by political expediency. Thus, the two biographers
felt that those instances in which Disraeli objected to
Jewish emancipation could not raise doubts about his
sincerity in this matter. Lord Blake, another eminent
biographer and a recent one, also insists that Disraeli
"consistently voted according to his conscience -- the
allegations to the contrary have no substance -- and in
1858 had the satisfaction as leader of giving personal support
to the Bill which finally settled the matter by a compromise
allowing each House to make its own rules about the form
of the oath."[4]

If this is the case, one must consider Disraeli's ten
years of silence on the Jewish question. In my opinion,
Disraeli was ambivalent toward Jewish emancipation and his
declarations of endorsement were partially based on a careful calculation. The main argument advanced in this paper
is that Disraeli's treatment of the Jewish issue was
careful and astute; it was far from the carefree manifestation
of personal convictions depicted by many of his biographers.
Disraeli had good reasons to change his position in 1847;
and, considering the bombastic rhetoric he used when defending
the Jewish cause, one might have expected him to act more
favorably in practice.

Disraeli's aloofness from the Jewish question was based, to some extent, on his negative sentiments toward Judaism during the 1830s. I have already treated the subject elsewhere, so it will be sufficient to summarize the argument briefly.[5] After his 1830 visit to the Holy Land, Disraeli returned to his father's house at Bradenham and there wrote The Wondrous Tale of David Alroy. In this novel he exhibited serious reservations about Judaism. Like his father, with whom he was in daily contact, he sympathized with popular negative attitudes toward rabbinic Judaism. For them, Jewish orthodoxy represented the most decadent and debased human qualities. Orthodox Jews, as the younger Disraeli depicted them, were aesthetically and physically repulsive, ill-bred, greedy, false and hypocritical. David Alroy's first encounter with rabbinic circles in Jerusalem was drawn in this perspective. When first arriving at the city, Alroy met an old Jew whom he asked about the chief rabbi's residence. At first Zimri was suspicious and uncooperative; however, when Alroy pledged to "offer next Sabbath in the synagogue more dirhems than you would perhaps suppose", Zimri mellowed and exclaimed: "A very worshipful young man! And he speaks low and soft now! But it was lucky I was at hand."

Disraeli expressed contempt of the rabbinic tradition when he described the debates in Rabbi Maimon's Yeshivah. The study of the Talmud was but a nonsensical discourse and a futile investigation of trivia. Disraeli's cynicism when dealing with the topic is noticeable in two passages:

'These are high subjects,' continued Maimon, his clear eyes twinkling with complacency. 'Your guest, Rabbi Zimri, just read the treatise of the learned Shimei, of Damascus, on Effecting Impossibilities.'
'This is a work!' exclaimed Zimri.
'I never slept for three nights after reading that work,' said Rabbi Maimon. 'It contains twelve thousand five hundred and thirty-seven quotations from the Pentateuch, and not a single original observation.'
'These were giants in those days,' said Rabbi Zimri; 'we are children now.'
'The first chapter makes equal sense, read backward or forward,' continued Rabbi Maimon.
'Ichabod!' exclaimed Rabbi Zimri.
'And the initial letter of every section is a Cabalistical type of a King of Judah.'
'The temple will yet be built,' said Rabbi Zimri.
'Ay, ay! that is learning!' exclaimed Rabbi Maimon; 'but what is the great treatise on Effecting Impossibilities to that profound, admirable, and --[6]

'Eliezer,' said Zimri, addressing himself to a young Rabbi, 'it is written, that he took a rib from Adam

when he was asleep. Is God then a robber?'
The young Rabbi looked puzzled, and cast his eyes on
the ground. The congregation was perplexed and a little
alarmed.
'Is there no answer?' said Zimri.
'Rabbi,' said a stranger, a tall, swarthy African
pilgrim, standing in a corner, and enveloped in a red
mantle, over which a lamp threw a flickering light;
'Rabbi, some robbers broke into my house last night,
and stole an earthen pipkin, but they left a golden
vase in its stead.'
'It is well said; it is well said,' exclaimed the
congregation. The applause was loud.

This derogatory portrayal is enhanced by the location in
which the Talmudic studies were being held. Of all possible
situations, Disraeli chose to place them in a graveyard,
and the mockery is increased by the explicit announcement of
Rabbi Zimri that "we hold our meetings in an ancient cemetary."

    Such feelings can explain Disraeli's indifference to
the Jewish question during the 1830s. The appearance of
Sir Moses Montefiore and other sheriffs of London seemed
'amusing', and one can hardly ignore the irony recorded in
the portrayal of the first Jewish baronet. "It was rather
amusing the other day in the House', he wrote his sister
Sarah on December 5, 1837. "The Sheriffs of London, Sir
Bob or Tom, and Sir Moses, and no mistake, appeared at the
bar in full state to present, according to the privilege
of the city of London, some petitions, after which they took
their place under the gallery and listened to the debate,
which turned out to be the Jew question by a sidewind."[7]

    Apparently feeling little sympathy for Jewish
emancipation during his first ten years in Parliament,
Disraeli consistently ignored the subject. He said nothing
during the 1841 debate over Edward Divett's bill to enable
the admission of Jews to municipal offices. Divett, the
Member for Exeter, proposed to exempt Jews from pronouncing
the words 'on the true faith of a Christian' when making
the 1828 declaration. The Bill passed its three readings
in the House of Commons without difficulty, but was defeated
by the Lords.[8] Perhaps even more astonishing is Disraeli's
aloofness from the solution to David Salomons' grievance
through a Jewish Disabilities Removal Act that passed the
legislature in 1845 under the auspices of Peel's Conservative government. This time Disraeli was not bound by party
opposition to Jewish relief, but he still preferred to remain
silent. Salomons was elected alderman of Portsoken Ward,
London, in September 1844, but was denied admission to the
Court of Aldermen because he refused to take the oath as
prescribed by the law on conscientious grounds. Salomons

subsequently persuaded Peel that legislation was essential
to solve the problem, and the Prime Minister instructed
Lord Chancellor Lyndhurst to draft the appropriate bills.[9]
Again, Disraeli stayed out of the controversy.[10]

The first time the House of Commons heard Disraeli's
views on the subject of Jewish emancipation was during the
debate of December 16, 1847, when Lord John Russell's
Government proposed to alter the form of the oath of abjuration so as to enable Baron Lionel de Rothschild to take
his seat. Rothschild had been elected by the city of London,
but he would not take the oath on the New Testament nor
pronounce the words 'on the true faith of a Christian',
which were included in the oath. Disraeli's speech has been
analyzed by his biographers time and again, so there is no
need for a lengthy discussion. Disraeli took the opportunity
to inform the House that he advocated Jewish emancipation,
but not on the ground of religious liberty, the liberal
basis for the Jewish claims. He stressed that he was speaking
on the matter from a Christian standpoint: "Yes, it is
as a Christian that I will not take upon me the awful
responsibility of excluding from the legislature those who
are of the religion of which my Lord and Saviour was born."[11]
Disraeli stressed the point that his defense of Jewish
emancipation was based on pietistic sentiments embedded in
his genuine Christianity.

Lord Blake has pointed out that in this speech,
Disraeli managed to offend both Jews and their Liberal allies.
The Jews were irritated by the argument that emancipation
would serve the cause of their conversion to Christianity.[12]
Members of the House must have felt uncomfortable with the
Disraelian rhetoric, as Lord Blake observes:

> In Tancred Disraeli had gone so far as to argue that
> Christians should be positively grateful to the Jews
> for having prevailed on the Romans to crucify Christ.
> He did not quite repeat this claim to the House of
> Commons, but his whole approach was deeply repugnant
> to the other members, and this repugnance was enhanced
> by his curious trick -- unconscious self-revelation
> perhaps -- of referring to 'your Christianity', and what
> 'you owe to this people', as if he felt himself, in
> some sense, alien to both sides; which indeed he was.[13]

As much as he tried to distance himself from Jews and
liberals, Disraeli was anxious to express his complete
acquiescence in the opinions expressed by one speaker, Lord
Ashley, the Member for Bath. He made several references to
Ashley's speech and repeatedly asserted his agreement with
the pietistic, philo-Judaic, millennarian and visionary
statements made by Ashley.

I place the present question upon the religious grounds
on which it was based by the noble Lord the Member for
Bath; and I mix it up neither with the principle of
religious liberty, nor with those principles which
other Gentlemen have advocated, that you should not
look to faith, but admit all faiths like you. I
dismiss all those considerations, and I say it because
this is a Christian country, that the Jews ought to find
a reception among you.[14]

By thus associating himself with zealous Evangelical
arguments Disraeli displayed an original attitude to the
Jewish question which, at the same time, was based on religious
and traditional Tory principles. A letter from the Evangelical theologian J. Binney to the Earl of Shaftesbury,
dated from April 15, 1852, reflects the success he enjoyed
in these circles:

I have had read to me parts of Mr. Disraeli's life of
Lord George Bentinck, especially his chapter on the
Jews. He has some strange extravagant ideas about the
Hebrew race, which he has brought out in two or three
of his former works and which he repeats in this. Yet,
he has, it seems to me, got hold of some right thoughts,
especially about Christianity being the Jewish religion
in another form. It so happens that I have lately been
developing this idea myself and though Mr. Disraeli
will not agree with some of my views, yet there are
others so considered with his own that I should rather
like to get him to read my dissertation if I could.[15]

Shaftesbury furthered this request, forwarding Binney's
essay and letter with a covering letter of his own to Disraeli.

Why did Disraeli espouse such opinions after ten years
of complete silence? In March 1847, Tancred appeared with
similar extravagant views on the historic mission of Judaism
and its significance for Christianity, the importance of
the Jewish 'genius' for the development of Western civilization and the unique capacity for survival of the 'Hebrew'
race. And shortly after December 1847, in the Political
Biography Of Lord George Bentinck, he repeated the same
arguments.

One possible reason for his sudden intervention in the
Jewish question was the realization that the party's opposition
to emancipation was doomed to failure. After 1845, the only
remaining disability affecting British Jews was their exclusion from Parliament, and it became clear that the press,
public opinion and the House of Commons were in favor of
ending this discrimination. In view of the passage of similar
relief acts in 1828 (for the benefit of Protestant Dissenters),
1829 (Roman Catholics), 1833, 1837, 1838 (Quakers, Moravians
and Socinians), the exclusion of Jews on account of the form
of the oaths became increasingly anachronistic. British

society was in the process of establishing religious freedom and nothing now could set the clock back. Disraeli was
perfectly aware that the Tory position on the Jewish question
was unpopular, so in his 1850 speech he accentuated the
friendly reception of Jewish emancipation in public and in
the House of Commons. What was the point of adhering to a
lost cause? And if the question had to be settled sooner
or later, better to do it on one's own terms and at one's
own leisure. After all, the irksome question of municipal
disabilities had been solved by the Tory Government of Sir
Robert Peel and his Lord Chancellor, Lyndhurst.

To cover and explain the party's necessary change of
position, Disraeli was prepared to advance important new
arguments. It is important to stress that a genuine
intellectual process was occuring; Disraeli was sincerely
captivated and moved by issues he now confronted. Basing
the advocacy of Jewish civil rights on pietistic Christian
sentiments was not novel; it was often employed during the
earlier debates over Jewish emancipation by Anglican and
Dissenting sympathizers. Disraeli, however, only in the
1840s became fascinated with the strength of the religious
imperative in the history of the Jewish people, during his
Young England period. He was puzzled by the ability of faith,
racial consciousness and suffering to create a bond of such
intense unity among the members of a dispersed and despised
minority. Perhaps he even found in Jewishness certain aspects that were missing in current British patriotism, such
as racial harmony, religious unity and the capacity for
retaining a cultural uniqueness. When he became preoccupied
with the Young England ideology and experimented with the
fostering of a new form of national solidarity and social
cohesion, he experienced perhaps for the first time the appeal
for the Jewish heritage. In the ancestral tradition, which
his father despised and led him to disdain, he suddenly
observed some of the traits he prescribed as possible
remedies for the English malaise.

For Disraeli, as well as other leaders of the Young
England faction, the 1840s was a period of searching. They
were ready to try new ideas and solutions to current political problems, because right wing Conservatism then had
little to offer beyond stale Protectionism. Disraeli was
not the only one who realized the Party needed new ideas
to become a vibrant political force. Lord John Manners
observed in an August 15, 1846 letter to Disraeli that
"to belong to a party with only one idea is unsatisfactory."[16]
There was a grave shortage of ideas in the Tory ranks. Under
these circumstances, Disraeli would be inclined to articulate
new thoughts,to devise new solutions, to advance new pro-
posals which would invigorate the dull political program
of Protectionism. The position of the Party on the Jewish
question especially called for reform, as has already been

pointed out, for a serious opposition to Jewish emancipation was realistically a lost cause. To be able to harmonize a new position with Young England ideology and and Tory precedents by using Christian philo-Semitism could have led, had it been accepted by the squires, to a satisfactory settlement of the Jewish question.

In all likelihood, December 1847 was also the right time to settle Disraelis' personal problem of his own Jewish birth. Disraeli was not yet the Party leader, but he was clearly a strong competitor. He was a major manipulator of the Tory opposition to Peel's free trade policy, and Peel's defeat was, no doubt, a great personal victory. He was not popular with the squires, but both they and he knew perfectly well that the party had no other talent to place at the top. Lord George Bentinck was not sufficiently committed nor capable; Granby was a colorless nonentity. Who, besides Disraeli, could lead the Party and turn it into an influential political power? Disraeli knew his high standing in Protectionist circles was not based on popularity. If the squires needed him so badly, now was the time to state his own terms. Disraeli knew that the insults about his Jewish origins he had previously endured would be insignificant in comparison with those he would hear after rising to a position of prominence. If he was to be leader, the Party would have to accept his Jewish extraction and the sooner the better. For Disraeli, the admission of his Jewish background was not a great manifestation of courage. As Richard W. Davis has already argued convincingly; what was the alternative?[17] To ignore a fact that was widely known in public? Whether he admitted it or not, once he moved to the forefront he became more vulnerable and his Jewish ancestry became more of a problem. Trying to obscure the facts by being apologetic, as Jewish assimilationists had, was not his style and would do little good anyway. By publicly accepting his Jewishness he demonstrated he would not be intimidated by insults aimed at his religion. The results of this strategy were profitable; even his enemies admired his courageous and determined vindication of Jewish emancipation.

But the enthusiasm displayed in his rhetoric was not matched by his actions. Disraeli delivered only four speeches on the subject and in two of them (1850 and 1854) he raised objections to the proposed relief measures. His support of bills advanced in 1849, 1851, 1853, 1857 and 1858 was accompanied by silent votes. Moreover, while his expressions of concurrence were generally based on broad, abstract and ideological grounds, his disapproval of two relief measures was specific. In other words, Disraeli did little to offer or promote solutions to the Jewish problem. He preferred to wait for others to do so and then agree or dissent. His role in the parliamentary debates was passive, and the only occasion on which he initiated action was his 1858 intervention with Lord Derby to effect a compromise between the two Houses of Parliament.[18] Derby, however, resented the pressure. This intervention can earn Disraeli little credit. As Polly Pinsker has argued in an article published in Jewish Social Studies in 1952, the settlement of the Jewish grievance was achieved through an irresistable public and parliamentary pressure.[19] A solution to the problem was found only when the Liberal majority in the House of Commons threatened to pass a Resolution to seat Rothschild, regardless of the Lords. As the head of the Conservative party in the Lower House, Disraeli feared that the continuation of conflict over the question could end in a constitutional deadlock, embarrassing to him and to the party.

Furthermore, Disraeli's reaction to an 1850 parliamentary debate over Jewish emancipation is highly questionable. After the House of Lords twice rejected relief measures that had passed the House of Commons, Baron Lionel de Rothschild was again elected M.P. by the city of London. Rothschild presented himself before the Speaker on July 26, 1850 and asked to be sworn without pronouncing the objectionable words in the oath of abjuration. The question was raised late in the session, so there was no time to bring forward a new bill; however, the Attorney General, on behalf of the Whig Government, moved two resolutions to indicate the matter would neither be forgotten nor abandoned. The first resolution suggested that Rothschild was not entitled to sit and vote till he should take the oath in the legal form; the second, that the House would take the object into serious consideration at the earliest opportunity next session. Disraeli voted against both resolutions. He argued that the first was declaratory of the law and therefore unnecessary and that the second pledged the future policy of the House and was unconstitutional. He criticized the Government for postponing debate on the question till late in the session when it was unsuitable for parliamentary action. What Disraeli resented in particular was the attempt to dissent from the Lords' decisions of 1847 and 1849. Not only was the procedure selected by the Government wrong, he claimed, but it implied criticism of the peers.

At this point, however, Disraeli turned from the Whig Government to attack the leading Jewish emancipationists. They seemed to him too impatient, pushy and aggressive:

> Sir, with respect to Englishmen professing the Jewish religion, I am bound to say that it does appear to me that there is no class of religionists in this country who have less cause to complain of the spirit of the community, or the temper of the Legislature. When I remember what was the position of that class a very short period back -- hardly, indeed a quarter of a century ago -- When I contrast that position of

social degradation and political disability with the
position which they now occupy and enjoy, I own that
I am proud and gratified by the comparison. It is,
indeed, one which I am bound to say shows the possession on the part of the Jews the social footing higher
than that which any other body in the kingdom, whose
religion is not the religion of the State, could have
arrived at within so brief a space. The Roman Catholics
were for a much longer period disqualified from the
possession of many more offices and the enjoyment of
many more rights than the Jews. Every class of
Dissenters in this country have really had to undergo
a more prolonged and more severe struggle than the
Jews, in order to obtain the rights and privileges
of which they are now in possession; and I think, that
at a moment like the present, when there is a degree
of impatience evinced by the electors of the city of
London, at not immediately accomplishing the results
to which they have aspired, it is expedient for us to
take a calmer and more comprehensive view of the
circumstances of the case than we have yet done; ...
But, Sir, if the English Jews have little cause to
complain of the bigotry of the community in which they
live, and of want of toleration in the spirit of this
age, have they a fair quarrel with the conduct of the
other branch of the Legislature whose conduct has, in
the course of the discussion been subjected to some
criticism which, in my opinion, is not only harsh but
unjust?[20]

Disraeli advised Anglo-Jewry to display more caution
and to wait calmly till the Lords decided to espouse Jewish
emancipation:

The case of the House of Lords, as I have already
shown you, is clear, and free from every blemish.
They have given to a novel and important proposition
an impartial and solemn consideration; and upon two
instances though they rejected the measure, they have
never rejected it by an overwhelming or overbearing
majority, and upon the last occasion that majority
was diminished in number. As far, therefore, as the
temper of the community of the Legislature was
concerned, there was nothing very discouraging to
those who believed they were passing just claims.[21]

Jewish emancipationists were angry at these comments.
Doubtless they wondered how a man whose conversion to another
religion had certainly promoted his own career opportunities
could display so little sympathy with their own aspirations.
At any rate, as shown elsewhere, the Anglo-Jewish and American-
Jewish press reacted furiously to Disraeli's arguments.[22]
The leading Jewish emancipatioists tended to keep their
distance. David Salomons urged Peel, Russell and Gladstone

to press the cause, but the Disraeli Archives contain almost no Jewish appeal for involvement in the struggle for emancipation. Even Disraeli's close friend, Lionel de Rothschild, had serious reservations about his conduct in this matter. On July 16, 1858 Rothschild wrote to his wife that he had told Disraeli "that we were very anxious to have the royal assent to the Bill in time to enable me to take my seat this year, but you know what a humbug he is. He talked of what is customary without promising anything ... Mrs. Dizzy dined at Mayer's and told them the old story again, saying how much Dizzy had done for us and how angry he was once because we would not believe it."[23]

The onslaught on the Government seems as unfair as the attack on the Jews. By pushing the two resolutions in the House, Lord John Russell did not mean to confront or challenge the House of Lords. He only meant to show that he would not drop the issue even though it was too late to handle it through a new piece of legislation. Disraeli not only opposed the two resolutions on procedural grounds, but magnified unnecessarily the point that they constituted a disagreement with the Lords' verdict on two former measures. He stated he would not go along with any attempt to bypass the peers, although no one suggested such an attempt was being made. The Government was too weak to confront the Lords on this issue and had no intention of redressing the Jewish grievance by bypassing the Lords. It was Disraeli who made that allegation, and by playing politics he managed to obscure the real issue. By advancing the first resolution, Russell wanted to indicate he would stick to the law. Therefore Disraeli's fierce attack seems extreme and unjust. Certainly it seems out of line with the expression of sympathy for the Jewish cause, which he reaffirmed at the end of his speech, while rejecting Russell's famous accusation that he was betraying the cause.

Disraeli's private reaction to Baron Rothschild's attempt to occupy his seat was exceptionally cool. "The Rothschild business has made a great stir and delayed everything", he wrote to Frances Anne, Marchioness of Londonderry, on August 2, 1850. "The House sits every day from 12 till 1/2 past 2 in the morning, which is severe."[24] His is an indifferent, aloof, matter-of-fact tone; perhaps too distant for a man who had previously pledged himself to the cause as Disraeli had. Disraeli might have shown more flexibility on parliamentary procedures and more interest when he commented on the issue in private.

Three other statements Disraeli made on the subject in Parliament are consistent with the original position he took in 1847. In 1851, during a debate over the alteration of the oath of abjuration resulting from David Salomons' attempt to take it without pronouncing the objectionable words, Disraeli joined the majority that resisted the move. He felt, like the majority in the House of Commons, that

any change in the form of the oath depended on a new piece
of legislation and that the current effort, to alter the[25]
form of the oath without such legislation, was illegal.

On May 25, 1854 Disraeli again spoke in public on the
subject of Jewish emancipation, this time to raise objections
to Lord John Russell's Oaths Bill that proposed to amalgamate
the current parliamentary oaths into a simplified new oath
from which the objectionable words would be totally omitted.
Disraeli had two major criticisms of the new measure: First,
he wondered, "why is it necessary to effect the emancipation
of the Jews by the omission of these words?"[26] He felt
strongly that the words 'on the true faith of a Christian'
were an integral part of parliamentary oaths and ought to
remain there. The Jewish grievance could be redressed by
giving Jews a special exemption from pronouncing these
words. But far more annoying to him was the idea that the
new measure would abolish the oath especially designed for
Roman Catholics in 1829 and would place them, as well as
Protestants with Romanising convictions, on terms of equality
with Anglicans. This, in Disraeli's opinion, was a violation
of constitutional principles with which he could not concur.
The result was a devastating attack on the Government which
led to an overwhelming defeat of Russell's bill. Disraeli
ended his speech with a personal apology in which he expressed
his regret for having been compelled to resist another relief
measure. He insisted that the course he had chosen during
the session was entirely compatible with his personal
conviction:

> I trust the House will not set down to egotism these
> expressions but as there have been unfair insinuations
> of attempted influence on my conduct in respect to
> this subject at various times by those political friends
> with whom it is my happiness to act, I may be permitted
> to add, Sir, that at no time, and under no circumstances,
> has a single word ever escaped from any gentleman near
> me which would tend to control or influence my conduct
> in that respect. They knew from the first, and all
> must have known it who have condescended to inquire
> into my opinions, how profound and fervent were my
> convictions on this great question. They knew that
> at all sacrifices I should uphold that cause, and though
> I deeply regret the course which the noble Lord has
> taken -- though I believe it to be one in which he
> will not only increase the difficulty with which the
> Jews have to contend, but will create in this country
> between considerable classes of Her Majesty's subjects
> misunderstandings which at a time like the present
> should have certainly have been avoided -- still it is
> my conviction, as certain as I am now addressing you,
> Sir, that the time will come when the Jews will receive
> in this country full and complete emancipation.

This time, too, Disraeli's opposition to a Jewish relief bill seems understandable and warranted. He may have genuinely supported the cause, but could not be expected to vote for a measure that violated other constitutional principles that he and his party maintained.

Disraeli's last expression of support for Jewish emancipation was his speech on Thomas Milner Gibson's Oath of Abjuration Bill of 1856 that aimed at a complete abolition of the oath in question. Disraeli chose to espouse this measure, which, as he explained, was compatible with his other political beliefs. He was agreeable to the abolition of the abjuration that was no longer relevant to current political circumstances, as long as the Christian basis was acknowledged elsewhere in parliamentary oaths. Therefore he had reservations about Milner Gibson's suggestion to omit the objectionable words from parliamentary oaths.

During the eleven years Benjamin Disraeli chose to speak on the issue in public he had adopted an unusual attitude toward Jewish emancipation. In 1847 he defended the cause in bold and courageous terms. Responses to his speech were mixed. He did not manage to captivate the squires' hearts or to influence them to compromise on this question. On the other hand, his personal integrity seemed to shine brighter than ever. This was his great chance to demonstrate he was more than a mere opportunist. The squires allowed him a deviation from party lines, which they would not do for Lord George Bentinck, like the Lords, they had difficulties digesting his arguments. Disraeli did not renounce the cause, but his support of Jewish emancipation was theoretical, and he constantly distanced himself from the Jews and their sympathizers. In principle, he said, he wanted to see the matter settled, but the settlement had to be carried on his own terms, blocking all proposed settlements. Disraeli rebuked the Jewish activists for pushing the matter too vigorously and for lacking patience. He condemned any attempt to criticize the Lords and he rejected the endeavors to put pressure on the upper House. What must be remembered is that without the outrage and determination of the majority in the House of Commons, the solution to the Jewish grievance could have been postponed indefinitely. In 1850, Disraeli's zeal, manifested in the defense of the peers, was somewhat excessive and the reasons for opposition to the Government's resolutions, questionable. Controversial issues such as this could not possibly have reached a conclusion as Disraeli wanted, in harmony, peace and agreement. Finally, and most damaging, is his silence on the subject in private. All his expressions of sympathy with the Jewish cause were public; in private, he hardly reacted. This fact above all others leads one to suspect Disraeli's attitude was calculated.

Disraeli's ambivalence in this matter is understandable, considering the intense anti-Jewish prejudices still lingering in public and the pressures he had to endure because of his Jewish birth. That he did not react to such pressures as neurotically, defensively and apologetically as most Jewish assimilationists is to his credit. Disraeli treated the unwelcome question with perfect virtuosity. Facing the problem of his Jewishness, he refused to accept any of the conventional positions devised by both Jewish and converted assimilationists. He was too original and imaginative to embrace attitudes formed by others.

Disraeli was capable of devising a strategy optimally suited to his needs, and one must admit in perspective, that his solution was far better than the expression of uneasiness, shame and even disdain of the ancestral tradition. How many people are capable of behaving as originally as he did? The question is rhetorical. In our age, when Existentialist philosophy teaches that our existence can reflect human creativity and ingenuity, Benjamin Disraeli's attitude toward his Jewish origins is growing in relevance.

Notes

[1] Ralph Disraeli, ed. Lord Beaconsfield's Correspondence With His Sister, 1832-1852 (London, 1886), p. 77. See also Richard W. Davis, Disraeli (Boston, 1976), pp. 46-47.

[2] Ralph Neville, ed. The Life and Letters Of Lady Dorothy Neville (New York, 1919), p. 150.

[3] W. F. Monypenny & G. E. Buckle, The Life Of Benjamin Disraeli, Earl of Beaconsfield (New York, 1914), Vol. III, p. 79.

[4] Robert Blake, Disraeli (London, 1966), p. 261.

[5] See my article, "Judaism, Jewishness and Jews in Disraeli's Thought", that will be published in the near future in the Bulletin of the Weiner Library.

[6] Ibid. pp. 6-7. As for Alroy himself, see comment on pp. 14-15. "David Alroy is Disraeli's epitome of Christian Messianism. Not only is he depicted as the Messiah of the Jews, their king and God's anointed, but he is also referred to as God himself. When Esther the prophetess came to murder him, in order to prevent Alroy's capture and execution by his enemies, she whispered above his sleeping body: 'They lie, the traitors, when they call thee false to our God. Thou are thyself a god, and I could worship thee!' Alroy represents a new ethic of forgiveness, compassion and love. He spared the life of his enemies, acted generously toward those he had defeated and even lost his wife, the Princess Schirene, because of his refusal to kill his prisoners, who subsequently escaped, conspired against and finally killed him. Alroy's message to the Jewish people was sharply contrasted with the savage, revengeful, cruel and fanatical attitude of Jabaster and his followers, the representatives of Biblical Judaism. Alroy, the symbol of Christian Messianic aspirations, perhaps failed to perform the task of conquering the Holy Land and of establishing there a new Jerusalem, but neither had Christian civilization achieved universal harmony and utopian perfection. Yet the blame for this failure cannot be completely attributed to Alroy's personal weakness. History played an important role in this defeat. The Jewish people never grasped Alroy's message. They rejected the creed of generosity, compassion, love, chivalry and nobility. Instead, they were blinded by religious fanaticism and obsessive bigotries that led to Alroy's betrayal. The Jews were as responsible for Alroy's defeat as were his worldly ambitions."

[7] Ibid. Lord Beaconsfield's Correspondence with His Sister, p. 77.

[8]The parliamentary debates over Divett's Jews'
Declaration Bill are in Hansard, Third Series, Vols. 56,
57, 58.

[9]David Salomons to Peel, November 6, 1844, Peel Papers,
B. M. ADD. MSS 40533, ff. 298-300; Salomons to Peel, May 13,
1844, Peel Papers, B. M. ADD MSS 40544, f. 217; Salomons to
Peel, November 8, 1843, Peel Papers, B. M. ADD MSS, ff. 245-247;
Salomons to Peel, February 9, 1845, Peel Papers, B. M. ADD
MSS 40599, f. 233.

[10]The 1845 debates of the Jewish Disabilities Removal
Act are in Hansard, Third Series, Vols. 78, 82.

[11]Hansard, Third Series, Vol. 95, p. 1330.

[12]Ibid. pp. 1328-9. "An hon. Gentleman has said, that
if you wish to convert the Jews, it is no hard matter;
the first step is to let them become acquainted with you.
And it ought not to be a hard matter."

[13]Ibid. Blake, p. 259.

[14]Hansard, Third Series, Vol. 95, p. 1327. See another
reference to Ashley on pp. 1323-1324: "... and I, for one,
thank the noble Lord the Member for Bath, for having put the
case firmly before the House."

[15]Quoted from my article "Anglo-Jewish Attitudes Toward
Benjamin Disraeli During the Era Of Emancipation", which
will be published in 1981 in Jewish Social Studies: Reference
to Disraeli Papers, Hughenden Manor, B/XXI/S/111a.

[16]Charles Whibley, Lord John Manners And His Friends
(London, 1925), Vol. I, p. 227.

[17]Ibid. Davis, pp. 83-84. "Disraeli's biographers have
accepted his stand on Jewish relief as he portrayed it --
one of disinterested courage. That it was courageous can
hardly be doubted, but whether it was disinterested is
another matter. What was the alternative? It is usually
agreed that policy would have dictated that he should have
abstained or absented himself from the debate, thus avoiding
angering the squires on the back benches and endangering
his precarious new position as one of the leaders of a great
party. Such a strategy might have worked for Bentinck, and
it is greatly to his credit that he did not pursue it. But
would it have worked for a man whose Jewish birth was well
known, and, as we shall see, only just blatantly advertised
once again in Tancred? It seems more likely that, while

gaining him little or nothing with the squires, such a course would have laid him open to such devastating sneers from his enemies as in the end to have weakened his credit with all parties. Though politicians are often slow to grasp the fact, there are times when courage and policy are the same thing. Disraeli, as Gladstone was to testify after his death, was rarely lacking in courage, or, as Gladstone probably meant to imply, in calculation. This seems to have been one of those occasions when the two qualities were combined."

[18]Disraeli's letter to Lord Stanley and Derby's letter are quoted in Monypenny & Buckle, Ibid., Vol. III, pp. 72-73.

[19]For this point see Polly Pinsker, "English Opinion And Jewish Emancipation, 1830-1860", Jewish Social Studies XIV (1952), 51-95.

[20]Hansard, Third Series, Vol. 113, p. 789.

[21]Ibid. p. 793.

[22]See "Anglo-Jewish Attitudes Toward Benjamin Disraeli During The Era Of Emancipation", Jewish Social Studies, 1981.

[23]This letter is in the archives of N. M. Rothschild & Sons Ltd. I wish to thank Professor Richard Davis for showing me his transcript of it, and N. M. Rothschild for their kind permission to cite it.

[24]Letters From Benjamin Disraeli To Frances Anne, Marchioness Of Londonderry, 1837-1861 (London, 1938), p. 92.

[25]Hansard, Third Series, Vol. 118, p. 1320.

[26]Hansard, Third Series, Vol. 133, p. 965.

BIBLIOGRAPHY

Reference Works

Emden Paul, Jews Of Britain, A Series of Biographies (London, 1953).

Encyclopedia Judaica (Jerusalem, 1976).

Hyamson, Albert M. Anglo-Jewish Notabilities, Their Arms And Testamentory Dispositions (London, 1949).

Jacob, Joseph & Wolf, Lucien, Bibliotheca Anglo-Judaica: A Bibliographical Guide To Anglo-Jewish History (London, 1898).

Jewish Encyclopedia (New York & London, 1901).

Lehman, Ruth P. Anglo-Jewish Bibliography, 1937-1970 (London, 1973).

Lehman, Ruth P. Nova Bibliotheca Anglo-Judaica: A Bibliographical Guide To Anglo-Jewish History, 1937-1960 (London, 1961).

Matthews, W. British Autobiographies: An Annotated Bibliography Of British Biographies Published Or Written Before 1851 (Berkeley, 1955).

Matthews, W. British Diaries: An Annotated Bibliography Of Diaries Written Between 1442 and 1942 (Berkeley, 1942).

Roth, Cecil, Bibliotheca Anglo-Judaica: A Bibliographical Guide to Anglo-Jewish History (n.e. London, 1937).

Rubens, Alfred, Anglo-Jewish Portraits: A Bibliographical Catalogue Of Engraved Anglo-Jewish and Colonial Portraits From The Earliest Times To The Accession Of Queen Victoria (London, 1955).

Primary Sources

Manuscript Material

Board of Deputies of British Jews, Minute Books I-IX, 1760-1864.

Board Of Deputies Of British Jews, Letter Book, Notices And Letters to Deputies, 1856.

Brougham Papers, Watson Library, University College.

Broughton Papers, British Library.

Corporation Of London Record Office, Guildhall, Common Hall Book.

Corporation Of London Record Office, Guildhall, Proceedings Of The Court Of Aldermen.

Disraeli Papers, Hughenden Manor, Courtesy of National Trust.

Gladstone Papers, British Library.

Goldsmid, I. L. Two Letter Books, Watson Library, University College.

Jewish Museum Papers.

Mocatta Miscellaneous Papers.

Moses Montefiore-Louis Loewe Correspondence, courtesy of Mr. Raphael Loewe.

Peel Papers, British Library.

Russell Papers, Public Record Office.

Printed Sources: Parliamentary Records

Journals Of House Of Commons.

Journals Of House Of Lords.

Hansard's Parliamentary Debates, New and Third Series.

Sessional Papers: 1845, February-August, XIV (631), pp. 1-160. (May 30, 1845), First Report Of Her Majesty's Commissioners For Revising And Consolidating The Criminal Law.

1857, Session 2, 1853 IX, pp. 477-84 (August 10, 1857). Proceedings Of The Select Committee Of The House Of Commons To Examine The Oaths To Be Taken By Members.

1859, Session February-April (205), Vol. I, Book III, pp. 35-66 (April 11, 1859). Reprint from The Select Committee On The Jews' Act Together With Proceedings Of The Committee And Minutes Of Evidence.

Newspapers And Periodicals

Anglo-Jewish Magazine.

Asmonean.

Edinburgh Review.

Gentleman's Magazine.

Hebrew Observer.

Hebrew Review And Magazine Of Rabbinical Literature.

Israelite.

Jewish Chronicle & Workingman's Friend; from 1854, Jewish
     Chronicle & Hebrew Observer.

Jewish Messenger.

Kentish & Surrey Mercury.

Morning Chronicle.

Observer.

Occident & American Jewish Advocate.

Press.

Punch.

Quarterly Review.

Spectator.

Tatler.

Times.

Voice of Jacob.

Westminster Review.

Diaries, Memoirs & Pamphlets

Anonymous Writers. A Clergyman's Apology For Favouring The
     Removal Of The Jewish Disabilities As Bearing On The
     Position, Prospects And Policy Of The Church Of England
     (1847).

     A Few Words On The Proposed Admission Of Jews Into
     Parliament, By A Graduate Of Cambridge University (1845).

     A Letter To The Rev. Henry Mackenzie, A.M. Minister Of
     The Parish Of Great Yarmouth (1847).

     A New Song To A Old Tune (1841).

     Adonijah's Letter To The Editor Of The Sunday Times On
     The Emancipation Of The Jews (1830).

An Appeal To The Public In Behalf Of The Jews, With
Considerations Of The Policy Of Removing Their Disabilities. (1834)

An Appeal From A High Priest Of The Jews To The Chief
Priest Of Canterbury On The Extension Of Catholic
Emancipation To The Jews (1829?).

'Che Sara, Sara'; Or Lord John Russell And The Jews (1848).

Cosmopolite, A Letter To The Right Hon. Sir Robert Peel,
Bart. On The Civil Disabilities Of The Jews (1844).

Diagmma, The Exclusion Of Baron de Rothschild From
Parliament (1850).

D. R. An Imaginary Speech In Parliament Against The
Jewish Disabilities Bill (1850).

Emancipation Of The Jews, By A Christian (n.d.).

Euphron, Remarks On The Proposed Bill For Admitting
Jews Into Parliament Respectfully And Earnestly Addressed
To The Members Of The Legislature (1848).

Exclusion, No Intolerance. To The Right Hon. S. H.
Walpole, M.P. (1856).

Forty Reasons For Resisting The Removal Of The Jewish
Disabilities (1848).

Jewish Disabilities Bill: Protest By A Believing Jew (1854).

Jewish Emancipation. A Christian Duty. By A Country
Vicar (1853).

Jewish Emancipation, By An Israelite (1845).

Lines Written By A Jew On The Rejection Of The Bill For
The Removal Of The Jewish Civil Disabilities (n.d.).

Phoenix, Scriptural Reasons In Support Of The Jewish
Claim To Sit In The Commons House Of Parliament Addressed
To The Conscience Of The Christian People Of The British
Empire (1850).

Progress Of Jewish Emancipation Since 1829 (1848).

Quizinus, Cursory Glance At The Present Social State
Of The Jewish People Of Great Britain (1844).

Remarks On The Civil Disabilities Of The Jews By A
Conservative (1842).

Russellas, A Politcal Poem From 'The People' By One Of Themselves (1865).

Second Letter To The Right Hon. Earl Of Derby On The Jews' Bill Commonly Called The Oaths Bill (1858).

Some Arguments Against The Admission Of Jews Into Parliament By A Protectionist (1852).

Some Remarks Upon The 'Series Of Anomalies' In The Leading Article Of 'The Times' Newspaper And The Maiden Speech Of Mr. Frederick Peel, M.P. For Leominster, By An Observer (1828).

Statement Of The Civil Disabilities And Privations Affecting The Jews In England (1828).

The Case Of Mr. Salomons, Alderman Elect Of The Ward Aldgate. Letters Of Britannicus, Reprinted From The Morning Chronicle (1836).

The British Jew To His Fellow Countrymen (1853).

The Jew Question Considered In A Letter Addressed To Sir Robert H. Inglis, Bart. M.P. By Veritas (1851).

The Jews: Their Present State And Prospects (1838?)

The Jews, Our Lawgivers (1853).

Thoughts On The Oath Of Abjuration, In A Letter To The Earl Of Aberdeen By A Member Of The Late Parliament (1853).

Abrahams, Israel, Jewish Life Under Emancipation (1917).

Anchini, P. A Few Remarks On The Expediency Of Emancipating The Jews, Addressed To His Grace The Duke Of Welling-ton, K.G. (1829).

Argyll, Eighth Duke, Autogiography And Memoir Of George Douglas ed. Dowager Duchess Of Argyll. 3 Vols. (London, 1906).

Arnold, Matthew, Letters Of Matthew Arnold, 1848-1888 ed. G. E. F. Russell (London, 1901).

Baird, Robert, Religion In America (London, 1844).

Barnett, M. A Word With The Earl Of Winchelsea By 'One Of The People' (n.d.).

Benisch, Abraham, The Principal Charges Of Dr. M'Gaul's Old Paths, As Stated By Mr. Newdegate In The House Of Commons, Considered and Reviewed (1858).

Bird, Charles C. The Vicar Of Gainsborough To His Parishoners On The Question Of The Removal Of The Jewish Disabilities (1847).

Birks, T. R. A Letter To The Right Hon. Lord John Russell, M.P. On The Admission Of Jews Into Parliament (1847).

Blunt, John E. A History Of The Establishment And Residence Of The Jews In England With An Enquiry Into Their Civil Disabilities (London, 1830).

Burditt, J. An Appeal To The Humanity Of The British Nation In Behalf Of The Jews (1812).

Campbell, W. F. A Short Statement Of The Grounds Which Justify The House Of Lords In Repeating Their Decision Of Last Year Upon The Jewish Question, Being A Substance Of A Speech Delivered In H. Of Commons On May 4, 1848 (1849).

Campbell, W. F. Speech In The Town Of Jedburgh On Moving A Petition To Repeal The Oath Of Abjuration, December 2, 1857 (1858).

Cohen, Arthur, The Lords And The Jews (1853).

Cohen, Lucy, Arthur Cohen, A Memoir By His Daughter For His Descendants (London, 1917).

Coles, John, Observations On The Civil Disabilities Of British Jews (1834).

Cooksley, W. G., Thoughts On The Admission Of Jews To Parliament And On The Separation Of Church From State Suggested By The Late Election Of Representatives Of The University Of Oxford (1848).

Croly, George, The Claims Of The Jews Incompatible With The National Profession Of Christianity (1848).

David , Arthur L., Letter On The Emancipation Of The Jews (1833).

Disraeli, Benjamin, Lord George Bentinck, A Political Biography (n.e. London, 1905).

Duncombe, Thomas S., The Jews Of England. Their History And Writings (1861).

Edwards, J. C., A Jew To Sit In Parliament? Why Not? A Letter To A British Clergyman (1855).

Elkin, Benjamin, "Is The Oral Law Of Divine Origins And Therefore Binding On The Jews?" The Advocacy Of The Question Contested By A Member Of The Community (1842).

Egan, Charles, The Status Of The Jews In England (1848).

Emanuel, C. H. L., A Century And A Half Of Jewish History.
Extracts From The Minutes Of The Board Of Deputies
(London, 1920).

Faudel, Henry, A Few Words On The Jewish Disabilities Addressed
To Sir Robert Harry Inglis, Bart. M.P. (1848).

Faudel, Henry, Suggestions To The Jews For Improvements In
Reference To Their Charities, Education And General
Government (1844).

Gawler, Colonel George, The Emancipation Of The Jews Indis-
pensable For The Maintenance Of The Protestant Profession
Of The Empire, In Other Respect, Most Entitled To The
Support Of The British Nation (1847).

Gawler, Colonel George, Observations And Practical Suggestions
In Furtherance Of Jewish Colonies In Palestine (1845).

Gillmor, Clothworthy, Jewish Legislators: A Word In Season
On The General Subject Of Jewish Disabilities (1847).

Goldmid, Augustus, ed. Report Of The Case Of Miller Versus
Salomons, M.P. With A Summary Of The Parliamentary
Proceedings In The House Of Commons (1852).

Goldsmid, Francis H., Memoir Of Sir Francis Henry Goldsmid,
Bart. M.P., ed. D. Marks & A. Loewy (London, 1882).

Goldsmid, Francis H., The Appeal Of The Congregation Of The
West London Synagogue Of British Jews To Their Brother
Israelites Throughout The United Kingdom (1846).

Goldsmid, Francis H., Two Letters In Answer To The Objections
Against Mr. Grant's Bill For The Relief Of The Jews (1830).

Goldsmid, Francis H., The Arguments Advanced Against The
Enfranchisement Of The Jews, Considered In A Series Of
Letters (1833).

Goldsmid, Francis H., A Few Words Respecting The Enfranchisement Of British Jews Addressed To The New Parliament (1833).

Goldsmid, Francis H., Reply To The Arguments Advanced Against
The Removal Of The Remaining Disabilities Of The Jews (1848).

Green, Aaron Levy, Dr. Croly L.L.D. Versus Civil And Religious
Liberty (1850).

Granville, Charles F., Journals Of The Reign Of Queen Victoria
1852-1860, 2 Vols. (London, 1887).

Hart, Solomon A., Reminisences Of Solomon Alex Hart, R.A.
    ed. Alexander Brodie (London, 1882).

Hawkes, Henry, Position Of The Jews (1843).

Haynes, Matthew P., The Position Of The Jews As Indicated
    And Affected By The Return To Parliament Of Baron
    Lionel de Rothschild With Considerations Whether He
    Can Take His Seat (1847).

Herschell, Ridley, A Brief Sketch Of The Present State And
    Future Expectations Of The Jews In A Letter Addressed
    To Christian Friends (1834)

Higgison, Francis, A Free Inquiry Into The Policy Of Admitting
    The Jews Into Parliament And Full Participation Into The
    Advantages, Honours And Privileges Of British Denizens,
    Viewed As Regard Religion, Justics And Expediency (1848).

Holland House Diaries, 1831-1840. The Diary Of Henry Richard
    Vassall Fox, Third Lord Holland ed. Abraham Kreigel
    (London, 1976).

Hughes, Henry, A Few Plain Thoughts On The Christianity Of
    Excluding A Jew From Parliament, Suggested By The Recent
    Division Of The Lords (1848).

Jewish Dogmas, A Correspondence Between Dr. Raphall, M.A.
    And C. N. Newdegate, M.P. (1849).

Kennard, Robert B.,The Admission Of Jews Into Parliament.
    The Subversion Of The British Constitution. A Plea
    For The Maintenance Of Our National Christianity (1857).

Lewis, Frederick H., To My Fellow Jews, These Observations
    In Reference To The Salomons Testimonial (1856).

Lissack, M., Jewish Perseverance Or The Jew, At Home And
    Abroad. An Autobiography (1851).

Loewe, Louis, A Discourse Delivered In The Spanish & Portu-
    guese Jews Synagogue In Bevis Marks On The Day Of The
    Funeral Of H. R. H. Prince Augustus Frederick, Duke
    Of Sussex, May 4, 1843 (1843).

Lupton, James, Should Jews Be Admitted To Civil Offices
    Among Their Fellow Subjects? A Sermon Preached At
    St. Paul's Cathedral, August 31, 1856 (1857).

Mackenzie, Henry, On Petitioning In Favour Of The Removal
    Of Jewish Disabilities. A Letter To The Parishoners
    Of Great Yarmouth By Their Minister (1847).

Macaulay, The Letters Of Thomas Babington Macaulay, ed.
    Thomas Pinney, 3 Vols. (Cambridge, 1974).

Malmesbury, Third Earl, Memoirs Of An Ex-Minister. An
    Autobiography, 2 Vols.(London 1884).

Mills, John, The British Jews (London, 1853).

Montague, Basil, A Letter To The Right Hon. Lord Bishop Of
    Chichester Upon The Emancipation Of The Jews (1834).

Montefiore, Diaries Of Sir Moses And Lady Montefiore ed.
    Louis Loewe 2 Vols. (London, 1890).

O'Brian, Thomas, Two Lectures Upon Jewish Claims, Delivered
    At The Crown & Anchor Tavern On March 7 and April 9, 1841
    (1841).

Oxlee, John, Three Lectures Humbly Submitted To The Consid-
    eration Of His Grace, The Most Reverend The Lord
    Archbishop Of Canterbury, Primate Of All England And
    Metropolitan, On The Inexpediency And Futility Of An
    Attempt To Convert The Jews To The Christian Faith In
    The Way And Manner Hitherto Practised (1842).

Padley, Alfred, An Answer To Some Of The Opinions And State-
    ments Respecting The Jews Made By B. Disraeli, Esq. M.P.
    In The 24th Chapter Of His Biographical Memoirs Of Lord
    George Bentinck (1852).

Peel, Memoirs By The Right Hon. Sir Robert Peel ed. Lord
    Mahon & Edward Campbell 2 Vols. (London, 1857).

Pellatt, Apsley, Brief Memoir Of The Jews In Relation To
    Their Civil And Municipal Disabilities (1829).

Perceval, Dudley M., Maynooth And The Jew Bill: Further
    Illustrations Of The Speech Of The Right Hon. Spencer
    Perceval On The Roman Catholic Question (1845).

Pyne, Thomas, Judea Libera Or The Eligibility Of The Jews
    (The Ancient People Of God) To Parliament (1850).

Robinson, Travers J., Remarks Depreciating The Proposed
    Admission Of His Majesty's Jewish Subjects To Seats In
    The House Of Commons (1848).

Robinson, Travers J., The Macaulay Election of 1846, Con-
    taining Comments On The Macaulay Election Of 1847 (1847).

Salomons, David, Parliamentary Oaths. Observations On The Law
    And Practice With Regard To The Administration Of Oaths,
    Respectfully Submitted To The Chairman And Members Of The
    Committee Of The House Of Commons On Parliamentary Oaths
    (1850).

Salomons, David, Further Observations On Behalf Of His Majesty's Subjects Professing The Jewish Religion (1836).

Salomons, David, The Case Of David Salomons, Esq. Being His Address To The Court Of Aldermen For Admission For The Ward Of Portsoken On Tuesday, October 15, 1844. Revised By Himself (1844).

Salomons, David, A Short Statement On Behalf Of Her Majesty's Subjects Professing The Jewish Religion With An Appendix Containing The Jews' Relief Bill (1835).

Salomons, David, Alteration Of The Oaths Considered In A Letter To The Earl Of Derby (1853).

Salomons, David, Notes On The History Of The Oaths Of Allegiance, Supremacy And Abjuration (1857).

Samuel, Moses, An Address On The Position Of The Jews In Great Britain With Reference To Their Liberty, Political, Civil, And Religious Conditions (1844).

Street, Henry, A Plea For The Removal Of The Jewish Disabilities (1849).

Thornborrow, William, Advocacy Of Jewish Freedom (1848).

The Jubilee Of Political Emancipation, Report of Commemoration Dinner, November 30, 1908 Trans. J. H. S. E. Vol 6 (1912), 88-110.

Van Oven, Bernard, ed. Debates In The House Of Commons On A Resolution Preparatory To The Introduction, And In The House Of Lords On The Motion Of The Second Reading Of The Bill For Removing The Civil Disabilities Of The Jews (1835).

Van Oven, An Appeal To The British Nation On Behalf Of The Jews (1830).

Van Oven, Bernard, Emancipation Of The Jews, Copy Of A Letter From The Times Of 3 February, 1830 (1830).

Walpole, Spencer, The History Of Twenty Five Years 2 Vols. (London, 1904).

Secondary Works

Unpublished Dissertations

Endelman, Todd M., Jewish Modernity In Georgian England: Acculturation And Integration In A Liberal Setting Harvard U. 1976.

Rumney, J., The Economic And Social Development Of The Jews In England, 1730-1860 University of London, 1933.

Salbstein, Michael N.C., The Emancipation Of The Jews In England, With Particular Reference To The Debate Concerning The Admission Of Jews To Parliament, 1828-1860 University of London, 1974.

Scult, Melvin M., The Conversion Of The Jews And The Origins Of Jewish Emancipation In England, 1828-1860 Brandeis U 1968.

Articles

Abrahams, Lionel, "Sir I. L. Goldsmid And The Admission Of The Jews Of England To Parliament", Trans. J. H. S. E. Vol. IV, (1903), 116-176.

Ages, Arnold, "French Enlightenment And Rabbinical Tradition", Analecta Romanica No. 26 (Frankfurt A.M. 1970).

Altholz, Joseph, "A Note On The English Catholic Reaction To The Mortara Case", Jewish Social Studies (J.S.S.) XVIII (1961), 111-118.

Baron, Salo W., "Great Britain And Damascus Jewry In 1860-1", J.S.S. II (1940), 179-208.

Cohen, Israel, "The Civil Emancipation Of Jewry", Jewish Review Vol. 5 (1914), 3-15.

D'Avigdor Goldsmid, Sir Henry, "Lord George Bentinck And The Jews", Trans. J. H. S. E. 23 (1971), 44-52.

Finestein, Israel, "Anglo-Jewish Opinion During The Struggle For Emancipation, 1828-1858", Trans. J. H. S. E. XX (1961), 113-143.

Finestein, Israel, "Anglo-Jewry And The Law Of Divorce", Jewish Chronicle, April 19, 1957.

Finestein, Israel, "Arthur Cohen, Q. C. 1829-1914" in John Shaftesley, ed. Remember The Days (London, 1966), 279-302.

Finestein, Israel, "Matthew Arnold And The Jews", Jewish Quarterly 22 (1975-76), 10-17.

Gilam, Abraham, "The Reconsideration Of The Politics Of Assimilation", Journal Of Modern History 50 (1978), 103-111.

Henriques, Ursula, "The Jewish Emancipation Controversy In Nineteenth Century Britain", Past And Present 40 (1968), 126-146.

Hyamson, Albert M., "The Damascus Affair, 1840", Trans.
J. H. S. E. XVI (1952), 47-71.

Hyamson, Albert M., "British Projects For The Restoration
Of Jews To Palestine", Publications Of The American
Jewish Historical Society 26 (1918), 127-164.

Hyamson, Albert M., "The First Jewish Peer", Trans. J. H. S.E.
17 (1957), 287-290.

Jacob, Alex M., "Aaron Levy Green, 1821-1883", Trans.
J. H. S. E. 25 (1977), 87-106.

Liberles, Robert, "The Origins Of The Jewish Reform Movement
In England", Association Of Jewish Studies Review 1
(1976), 121-150.

Lincoln, Ashe F., "The Non-Christian Oath In The English Law",
Trans. J. H. S. E. 16 (1951), 73-76.

Lipman, Sonia, "Judith Montefiore, First Lady of Anglo-Jewry",
Trans. J. H. S. E. 21 (1968), 171-188.

Lipman, Vivian D., "A History Of Anglo-Jewry In 1851", Trans.
J. H. S. E. 17 (1957), 171-188.

Marrus, Michael R., "European Jewry And The Politics Of
Assimilation: Assessment And Reassessment", Journal of
Modern History 19 (1977), 89-109.

Pinsker, Polly, "English Opinion And Jewish Emancipation,
1830-1860", J. S. S. Xiv (1952), 51-95.

Roth, Cecil, "The Jews In The English Universities", Misc-
ellanies Of J. H. S. E. IV (1942), 102-115.

Shaftesley, John, "Dr. Abraham Benisch As Newspaper Editor",
Trans. J. H. S. E. 21 (1968), 287-303.

Sharot, Stephen, "Secularization, Judaism And Anglo-Jewry",
A Sociological Yearbook Of Religion In Britain 4 (1971),
121-140.

Susser, Bernard, "Social Acclimatization Of Jews In Eighteenth
And Nineteenth Century Devon", Industry And Society In
The South West ed. Roger Burt (Exeter, 1970), 51-69.

Books

Blake, Robert, Disraeli (London, 1966).

Brown, M. D., ed. David Salomons's House, Catalogue Of
Mementos 2 Vols. (Privately Printed, 1968).

Barnett, Arthur, The Western Synagogue Through Two Centuries, 1761-1961 (London, 1961).

Battiscombe, Georgina, Shaftesbury, The Great Reformer, 1801-1885 (Boston, 1975).

Cecil, Lord David, Melbourne (London, 1934).

Clark, Kitson G., Peel And The Conservative Party, 1832-1841 (London, 1964).

Clive, John, Macaulay, The Shaping Of The Historian (New York, 1975).

Cohen, Abraham, An Anglo-Jewish Scrapbook, 1600-1840: The Jew Through English Eyes (London, 1943).

Conacher, J. B., The Peelites And The Party System, 1845-52 (Devon, 1972).

Conacher, J. B., The Aberdeen Coalition, 1852-1855. A Study In Mid-Nineteenth Century Party Politics (Cambridge, 1968).

Dolling, Lord & Ashley, Evelyn, Life Of Lord Palmerston Vols. I-III (1874), Vols. IV-V (1876).

Davis, Richard W., Dissent In Politics, 1780-1830. The Political Life Of William Smith, M.P. (London, 1976).

Davis, Richard W., Disraeli (London, 1976).

Dorchester, Lady, ed. Recollections Of A Long Life By Lord Broughton 5 Vols (London, 1910).

Dubnow, Simon, Nationalism And History ed. K. S. Pinson (New York, 1958).

Finestein, Israel, A Short History of Anglo-Jewry (London, 1957).

Gash, Norman, Sir Robert Peel, The Life Of Sir Robert Peel After 1830 (London, 1972).

Gash, Norman, Politics In The Age Of Peel. A Study In Technique Of Party Representation, 1830-1850 (London, 1953).

Gash, Norman, ed. The Age Of Peel, Documents Of Modern History (New York, 1968).

Gillen, Mollie, Royal Duke, Augustus Frederick, Duke Of Sussex, 1773-1843 (London, 1976).

Goodman, Paul, Moses Montefiore (Philadelphia, 1925).

Henriques, H. S. Q., Jewish Marriages And The English Law (London, 1909).

Henriques, H. S. Q., The Jew And The English Law (Oxford, 1908).

Henriques, Ursula, Religious Toleration In England, 1787-1833 (London, 1961).

Hodder, Edwin, The Life And Work Of The Seventh Earl Of Shaftesbury 3 Vols. (Cassell, 1887).

Hyamson, Albert M., David Salomons (London, 1939).

Hyamson, Albert M., The Sephardim Of England. A History Of The Spanish And Portuguese Jewish Community, 1492-1951 (London, 1951).

Hyamson, Albert M., History Of The Jews In England (London, 1908).

Jennings, Louis J., The Correspondence And Diaries Of The Late Right Hon. John Croker Wilson, L.L.D. F.R.S. Secretary To The Admirality From 1809 To 1830 3 Vols (London, 1885).

Katz, Jacob, Emancipation And Assimilation: Studies In Modern Jewish History (Westmead, Farnborough, 1972).

Katz, Jacob, Out Of The Ghetto: The Social Background Of Jewish Emancipation, 1770-1870 (Cambridge, Mass. 1973).

Longford, Elizabeth, Wellington, Pillar Of State (St. Albans, Herts. 1975).

Lipman, Vivian D., Three Centuries Of Anglo-Jewish History (London, 1961).

Lipman, Vivian D., Social History Of The Jews In England, 1850-1950 (London, 1954).

Mahler, Raphael, A History Of Modern Jewry, 1780-1815 (1971).

Magnus, Sir Philip, Gladstone (New York, 1954).

Martin, T., The Life Of Lord Lyndhurst From Letters And Papers In Possession Of His Family (London, 1883).

Marsh, P. T., The Victorian Church In Decline, Archbishop Tait And The Church Of England, 1868-1882 (Pittsburgh, 1968).

Monypenny, W. F. & Buckle, G. E., Life Of Benjamin Disraeli, Earl Of Beaconsfield 6 Vols. (London, 1910-1920).

Morley, John, The Life Of William Ewart Gladstone 3 Vols. (London, 1903).

New, Chester W., The Life Of Henry Brougham To 1830 (Oxford, 1961).

Parker, C. S., Sir Robert Peel From His Private Papers
    3 Vols. (London, 1891-1899).

Parker, C. S., Life And Letters Of Sir James Graham, 1792-
    1861 (London, 1907).

Perry, Thomas W., Public Opinion, Propaganda And Politics In
    Eighteenth Century England: A Study Of The Jew Bill Of
    1753 (Cambridge, Mass. 1962).

Piccioto, James, Sketches Of Anglo-Jewish History ed. Israel
    Finestein (London, 1956).

Philipson, D., The Reform Movement In Judaism (1907).

Prest, John, Lord John Russell (London, 1972).

Ramsay, A. A. W., Sir Robert Peel (n.e. 1971).

Ridley, Jasper, Lord Palmerston (London, 1970).

Roth, Cecil, Anglo-Jewish Letters, 1158-1917 (London, 1938).

Roth, Cecil, The Rise Of Provincial Jewry: The Early History
    Of Jewish Communities In The English Countryside, 1740-
    1840 (London, 1950).

Roth, Cecil, Benjamin Disraeli, Earl Of Beaconsfield (New
    York, 1952).

Roth, Cecil, Essays And Portraits In Anglo-Jewish History
    (Philadelphia, 1962).

Roth, Cecil, History Of The Jews In England (Oxford, 1941).

Rude, George, Revolutionary Europe, 1783-1815 (London, 1964).

Russell, Agatha & MacCarthy, Desmond, eds. Lady John Russell,
    A Memoir With Selections From Her Diaries And Correspon-
    dence (London, 1910).

Stanley, A. P., The Life And Correspondence Of Thomas Arnold,
    D. D. (London, 1877).

Stewart, R., The Politics Of Protection, Lord Derby And The
    Protectionist Party, 1841-1852 (Cambridge, 1971).

Whately, E. J., Life And Correspondence Of Richard Whately,
    D. D. Late Archbishop Of Dublin 2 Vols. (London, 1886).

Whibley, Charles, Lord John Manners And His Friends 2 Vols.
    (London, 1925).

Wilberforce, R. G., Life Of The Right Reverend Samuel
     Wilberforce 3 Vols (London, 1881).

Wolf, Lucien, Sir Moses Montefiore, A Centennial Biography
     With Selections From Letters And Journals (New York, 1885).

Wolf, Lucien, Essays In Jewish History ed. Cecil Roth (n.e.
     1934).

Ziegler, Philip, Melbourne, A Biography Of William Lamb,
     Viscount Melbourne (New York, 1976).

Index

Goldsmid, Abraham   4, 10
Goldsmid, Anne   4
Goldsmid, Sir Francis Henry   3, 8, 12-14, 16, 42-44, 81, 83,
                            94, 115, 123, 135, 140, 142
Goldsmid, Sir Isaac Lyon   2-3, 9, 12, 15-16, 18, 20-21, 42-43,
                            59, 72-81, 85, 90, 94, 98, 151
Goldsmid, Jane   5
Goldsmid, Jessie   5
Goldsmith, Louis   93
Goulburn, Henry   101
Graham, Sir James   116
Granby, Marquis   98, 162
Grant, Sir Charles (Lord Gleneg)   52, 75, 77
Grant, Sir Robert   13, 59-60, 75-77, 79, 81, 83, 88
Granville, Lord   109, 143-144
Green, Aaron Levy   55
Gregoire, Abbe   149
Grey, Earl   61, 80-81
Grote, George   78, 86-87
Gurney, Samuel   19, 78

Hall, Sir Benjamin (Baron Llanvoer)   103-104
Hall, F. R.   40-41
Hall, W. W.   24
Harpour, Sir W.   9
Harris, Harry   63
Henriques, H. S. Q.   i
Henriques, J. G.   42
Henriques, Ursula   i
Herbert, Sidney   108
Hirschell, Solomon   43, 49, 55
Hobhouse, John Cam   29, 79, 81, 104
Holland, Lord   59, 61, 72-73, 75-76, 80, 82, 85, 87, 88, 90
Horseman, Edward   116
Hume, Joseph   31, 78, 101
Humphrey, John   40, 85
Hurwitz, Hyman   13
Huskisson, William   31, 74, 77

Ibsen, Henrik   32
Inglis, Sir Robert   23, 40-41, 81, 98, 134, 141

Jacobs, Bethel   89
Jonassohn, David   2
Jekyll, Sir Joseph   118
Jessel, George   14, 122
Johnson, Thomas   92
Jones, James Law   85
Joseph, Michael   9

Keeling, Henry   52, 110
Kelly, Sir Fitzroy   105
Kent, Duke   4
Keyzer, L.   80
Keyzer, Samuel Levy   60